HOMESCHOOLERS'
COLLEGE
ADMISSIONS
HANDBOOK

CAFI COHEN

Linda Dobson, Series Editor

HOMESCHOOLERS' COLLEGE ADMISSIONS HANDBOOK

PREPARING 12- TO 18-YEAR-OLDS FOR SUCCESS IN THE COLLEGE OF THEIR CHOICE

PRIMA PUBLISHING
3000 Lava Ridge Court • Roseville, California 95661
(800) 632-8676 • www.primalifestyles.com

PRIMA PUBLISHING and colophon are trademarks of Prima Communications Inc., registered with the United States Patent and Trademark Office.

Prima Home Learning Library and seal are trademarks of Prima Communications, Inc.

Cover photos © EyeWire and PhotoDisc.

Library of Congress Cataloging-in-Publication Data
Cohen, Cafi
    Homeschoolers' college admissions handbook : preparing 12- to 18-year-olds for success in the college of their choice / Cafi Cohen.
        p. cm   (Prima home learning library)
    Includes index.
    ISBN 0-7615-2754-0
    1. Home schooling—United States—Handbooks, manuals, etc. 2. Universities and colleges—United States—Admission—Handbooks, manuals, etc. 3. College choice—United States—Handbooks, manuals, etc. I. Title: Home schoolers' college admissions handbook. II. Title. III. Series.

LC40.C643 2000
378.1'61—dc21   00-046948
                                                                                        CIP

00 01 02 03 BB 10 9 8 7 6 5 4 3 2 1
Printed in the United States of America

HOW TO ORDER

Single copies may be ordered from Prima Publishing, 3000 Lava Ridge Court, Roseville, CA 95661; telephone (800) 632-8676, ext. 4444. Quantity discounts are also available. On your letterhead, include information concerning the intended use of the books and the number of books you wish to purchase.

Visit us online at www.primalifestyles.com

CONTENTS

Introduction · vii

Acknowledgments · x

PART ONE Homeschoolers and College · 1

1. College Admissions and Homeschooling · 2

2. College or Not? · 22

3. High School at Home · 42

4. Shopping for Colleges · 66

PART TWO Paper Trails · 93

5. Administrivia: Documentation Choices · 94

6. What Counts?: Creating Credit and Granting a Diploma · 116

7. Compiling a Portfolio · 138

8. Writing a Transcript · 158

9. Dazzling Application Essays · 188

10. Outside Evaluations: Recommendation Letters, College Admissions Tests, and College Classes · 208

PART THREE The Admissions Process · 229

11. Up Close and Personal: Campus Visits and
    Interviews · 230

12. Finding Money · 250

13. Timelines: Putting It All Together · 272

14. "How Do They Do?"—College Experiences of
    Homeschoolers · 292

Index · 309

INTRODUCTION

$\mathcal{L}$AST YEAR, thousands of teenagers who never attended high school and therefore lacked official diplomas entered college. Some were admitted to high-powered institutions, such as Harvard, Stanford, and the military academies. Many others won acceptance to hundreds of state and private colleges and universities. Dozens were recognized as National Merit Scholars. Most received thousands of dollars in academic scholarships, grants, ROTC awards, athletic scholarships, and other financial aid to continue their education.

All of these successful college applicants learned advanced math, biology and chemistry, history and government, and many other subjects not as high school students but instead as homeschoolers. Their families took responsibility for planning, implementing, and finally explaining high school at home to college admissions officers. Although getting into college as a homeschooler may sound difficult, any family that plans ahead can succeed.

Hence this book. To determine exactly how real home educators handle college admissions, we sought volunteers via Internet discussion boards and e-mail loops. In response to our pleas for help, thirty-two homeschooling parents and fourteen homeschool graduates generously donated their time to complete lengthy surveys. You will find throughout this book the survey respondents' hard-won expertise relating to academic preparation, record keeping, and other related topics. Although we have assigned aliases to all the survey respondents, their locations and the names of the colleges they dealt with have not been changed.

We also provide all the background information homeschooling families need for college admissions. You will find the most important information—statistics about admissions for homeschoolers—

up front. These numbers can help you decide whether high school at home makes sense for your teenager. The first chapter includes detailed descriptions of changing college admissions policies and a list of homeschool-friendly institutions.

In the following chapters, we discuss the topics you would expect to find in any book on college admissions—exploring alternatives to college, researching colleges, taking the SAT and ACT, writing application essays, visiting campuses, interviewing, and applying for financial aid—all from a homeschool perspective. In addition, we talk about subjects of special concern to home educators. These include creating narratives, transcripts, and portfolios; calculating credit and grade point averages; granting diplomas; handling unreasonable testing requirements; and conducting your own financial aid search.

Throughout this book you will find examples of real reading lists, course descriptions, transcripts, application essays, résumés, and other documents homeschooling families have developed for their children's college applications. We also include money-saving tips and resource lists to help you confidently act as your home-schooled teenager's high school counselor.

In chapter 13, we help you put everything together with a timeline for grades 7 through 12. Finally, in chapter 14, we hear again from some of our survey respondents, homeschooling parents, and graduates. They address the question "How do homeschoolers do in college?" From their experiences we learn that homeschoolers can expect a period of adjustment, just like everyone else. Do these teenagers succeed when they move from the kitchen table to the classroom? After reading the last chapter, you will only be able to answer a resounding "yes."

With college admissions policies changing so rapidly, we urge you always to obtain specific information directly from applicable sources—admissions and financial aid officers and the College Board, which administers the SAT, for example. Do not assume that because the University of Illinois does things one way, the University of Indiana will do them the same way. Also, do not assume that the University of Illinois does things the same way this year as last year.

As a homeschooling mom emeritus, I know that any children you homeschool through high school will succeed. Your teenagers may go to college, win scholarships, and graduate with four-year degrees—or not. Although Harvard on a full scholarship may have crossed your mind, please do not make that your goal. Listen to twentieth-century educational psychologist Jerome Bruner, who wrote, "I think parents should forget the genius bit—what you want is a human being, a mensch, not a genius." Few of us raise Ivy League contenders. Home education allows all of us, however, to aim for a higher goal—raising good people and productive citizens.

ACKNOWLEDGMENTS

My sincere thanks and appreciation to the survey respondent homeschooling families who took time out of their busy lives to answer my detailed questionnaire about their high school, college admission, and other post–high school experiences. In addition, approximately one dozen graduate homeschoolers completed a survey about their transition to college and the working world. Their unique insights give this book credibility.

Thanks, also, to the literary lights that helped to shaped and mold the work—Linda Dobson, who read all the drafts; my agent, Ling Lucas, who likes my writing and supports home education; the Prima editors, especially Jamie Miller, who saw the need for this title, and Andi Reese Brady, who gave the book its final readable form.

Without my family's love and support, this information would exist only as randomly scribbled notes on my desk. Thanks to John and Dolores Fischer and Bernice Cohen, my parents, and Jeffrey and Tamara, my children, for their continual support and encouragement. And a very special thanks and "I love you" to my husband, Terrell Cohen, who holds down the fort.

Finally, thanks to God, who makes all things possible.

Part One

HOMESCHOOLERS AND COLLEGE

1

COLLEGE ADMISSIONS
AND HOMESCHOOLING

In This Chapter

✦ Homeschool-friendly colleges

✦ GED dilemmas

✦ Colleges requiring homeschoolers to leap
tall buildings in a single bound

✦ The fine art of negotiation

✦ Back-door college admissions

✦ Simple starting points

✦ Resources

"We look for a clear sense of intellectual growth and a quest for knowledge in our applicants. What is their level of intellectual vitality? How have they sustained their curiosity? Homeschooled students may have a potential advantage in this aspect of the application since they have consciously chosen and pursued an independent course of study."

—From "Homeschooling and the
admission evaluation process," at the
Stanford University (CA) Web site

*I*N THE PAST ten years, the number of homeschoolers applying to college has increased from a trickle to a steady stream. With home education growing 5 to 15 percent each year and an increasing percentage of families homeschooling teenagers, this stream threatens to become a flood. Sean Callaway—homeschooling father, Pace University School of Education Director of College Placement, and member of the National Association of College Admissions Counselors (NACAC)—says that colleges and universities may see as many as 225,000 to 350,000 homeschooled applicants over the next decade.

What a change. In 1990, because they received one or two applications from homeschoolers each year, most colleges evaluated graduates of home-based programs on a case-by-case basis. Probably fewer than ten schools nationwide had written recommendations and procedures for dealing with students taught in nonaccredited programs at home. Now, according to a NACAC 1999 survey, 51 percent of the institutions responding have policies relating to homeschoolers, up from 41 percent the previous year.

> Despite problems at a few schools, it appears that homeschooling presents no significant barriers to admission to more than 95 percent of the colleges and universities in the United States.

What do these policies say? Are they favorable or unfavorable? What are the overall trends?

The most current comprehensive answer to those questions comes from the National Center for Home Education (NCHE). In February 2000, NCHE issued a report titled "1999 College Survey: College Admissions Policies Opening to Home Schoolers." The NCHE surveyed 917 colleges and universities and received responses from 513. Approximately 68 percent of the 513 colleges responding reported equal treatment of homeschooled applicants. These colleges said they evaluated homeschoolers based on family transcripts or portfolios plus the same admissions tests and essays required of all applicants. An additional

28 percent of the 513 colleges responding imposed another requirement: They requested a General Educational Development (GED) test score from homeschooled applicants who do not have a diploma from an accredited school.

Finally, the NCHE report said that approximately 3.5 percent of the colleges responding to their survey—three to four out of every hundred—had overtly discriminatory policies. These schools required additional achievement test (SAT II Subject Test) scores of students from home-based education programs. A few required higher scores on all tests taken by homeschoolers.

Although many state-funded schools give homeschoolers a fair shake and treat them just like everyone else, the NCHE report makes clear what many homeschoolers already know from reading individual accounts: State colleges and universities are more likely than private schools to have discriminatory policies. Even in the absence of outright discrimination, state schools—mired as they are in bureaucracy—can be more difficult to deal with than private colleges.

Despite problems at a few schools, it appears that homeschooling presents no significant barriers to admission to more than 95 percent of the colleges and universities in the United States. The extensive Colleges That Admit Homeschoolers Web page, at the School Is Dead, Learn In Freedom Web site, maintained by homeschool father Karl Bunday, further supports this conclusion. He lists more than one thousand colleges nationwide that have accepted homeschooled applicants.

With this background, let's examine the homeschooling admissions percentages at some colleges and universities. And let's hear

QUICK & EASY

Attend the next college fair in your area with your teenager. Visit as many of the booths as possible and ask about admissions policies and financial aid for homeschool graduates. It can't hurt to get colleges thinking about creating scholarships especially for home-schooled applicants. To find upcoming fairs in your area, call local high school counseling offices and ask about dates and locations.

more from some of the homeschooling families that we surveyed for this book.

HOMESCHOOL-FRIENDLY COLLEGES

IN FEBRUARY 2000, the *New York Times* reported that Stanford University, a highly selective private university in California, had admitted four out of fifteen homeschooled applicants the previous year—27 percent. At the same time, it offered admission to approximately 12 percent of their entire applicant pool. According to the *New York Times* report, homeschoolers won admission to Stanford at double the rate of their schooled counterparts.

We find equally encouraging results at other schools. In 2000, Grove City College, a conservative Christian school in Pennsylvania, admitted 35 out of 55 (about 64 percent) of its homeschooled applicants. The same year, it admitted about 44 percent of its regular applicant pool. Thomas Aquinas College, a small, private "great books" institution in California, welcomes homeschoolers and states on its Web site: "In the 1999–2000 academic year, 29 percent of our students had been taught at home!"

> Thomas Aquinas College, a small, private "great books" institution in California, welcomes homeschoolers and states at its Web site: "In the 1999–2000 academic year, 29 percent of our students had been taught at home!"

Some colleges throw out the welcome mat by offering scholarships earmarked for homeschooled graduates. These include Nyack College (NY) and Belhaven College (MS). Bryan College (TN) offers a thousand-dollar grant for homeschoolers in their freshman year.

Many homeschooling parents are pleasantly surprised by how easy college admission is—even in the absence of specific policies. Dan and Beth in Alabama write, "The process was relatively painless. Faulkner University (AL) did

COLLEGES RECOMMENDED BY HOME EDUCATORS

This list could easily be much longer. We focused on those institutions listed by our survey respondents. Space does not permit us to list hundreds of homeschool-friendly schools.

Abilene Christian University (Abilene, TX)

Auburn University (Auburn, AL)

Belleville University (Belleville, NE)

Bryan College (Dayton, TN)

Cedarville College (Cedarville, OH)

College of William and Mary (Williamsburg, VA)

Concordia University (Mequon, WI)

Dartmouth College (Hanover, NH)

Dordt College (Sioux Center, IA)

Faulkner University (Montgomery, AL)

Florida Gulf Coast University (Fort Myers, FL)

Goddard College (Plainfield, VT)

Gordon College (Wenham, MA)

Houghton College (Houghton, NY)

Hunter College (New York, NY)

Johnson and Wales University (Providence, RI)

Lee University (Cleveland, TN)

Mississippi College (Clinton, MS)

New College (Montpelier, VT)

Rose-Hulman Institute of Technology (Terre Haute, IN)

Samford University (Birmingham, AL)

Sheldon Jackson College (Sitka, AK)

Simon's Rock of Bard College (Great Barrington, MA)

Southern Nazarene University (Bethany, OK)

Spring Arbor College (Spring Arbor, MI)

Stanford University (Palo Alto, CA)

Thomas Aquinas College (Santa Paula, CA)

United States Air Force Academy (Colorado Springs, CO)

University of Indiana (Bloomington, IN)

University of Rochester (Rochester, NY)

University of South Alabama (Mobile, AL)

University of Tennessee (Chattanooga, TN)

University of Virginia (Charlottesville, VA)

Yale University (New Haven, CT)

HOMESCHOOL GRADS SAY

Contact someone in the admissions department and tell them about your background. One of the reasons I was so interested in the University of Rochester originally was that when I told them I was homeschooled, the admissions officer seemed really excited. The people I corresponded with throughout the admissions process were very helpful.

—JANIE, A FRESHMAN AT THE UNIVERSITY OF ROCHESTER

not have guidelines for evaluating homeschooled students. Nevertheless, they wanted to admit our two sons, based on their accomplishments and ACT scores, so they wrote an admission policy for homeschoolers."

Pam, who has been homeschooling since 1986, writes, "College admissions was surprisingly easy. However, our son had already been contacted by Florida Gulf Coast University (FGCU) in Fort Myers, Florida, and asked to apply to the honors program, based on his ACT scores. FGCU holds one-day events where prospective students can bring transcripts and ACT/SAT scores and be accepted that day. FGCU is a relatively new state university and still small—a perfect transition for homeschoolers."

Daniela, a relaxed, eclectic homeschooling mom in Wisconsin, says that her son had a positive experience with Concordia University in Wisconsin in the 1999–2000 college application year: "We were surprised at how little they required and even more surprised that they were looking for homeschooled students."

Serena's daughter, who has been homeschooling since 1992, had good luck with admissions. She applied to Ohio State (OH), University of Toledo in Toledo (OH), and Indiana University in Bloomington (IN). Serena writes, "Since we were not applying to any highly selective schools requiring essays or interviews, the process was relatively easy. I simply filled out all the guidance counselor forms, wrote a transcript, and returned the application package. I was surprised by how readily everyone accepted our package. Indiana University was actually enthusiastic!"

Most homeschoolers applying to community and junior colleges (two-year schools that grant associate of arts degrees) find open doors. Karen, a homeschooling mom in Pennsylvania, reports, "As our daughter had decided on a community college for her first few years, the whole procedure was very easy. They sent us an application and a form to be signed by her evaluator (we live in Pennsylvania, and evaluations are required). Based on the form and our transcripts, she was accepted. She then met with a counselor to discuss her plans.

HOW WE DID IT

It was a very intense time, considering the caliber of schools to which our son applied. We first found out how the schools viewed homeschoolers. Stanford has its own Web page for homeschoolers, so you get a good feel for what they look for—for example, they want a different essay from homeschoolers than from the 'schooled' students. College of William and Mary and the University of Virginia had specialists in homeschool admissions who could answer our questions. California Institute of Technology was the least flexible, although it might be that we didn't ask the right questions.

Given our son's admit rate, our experience was positive. He is ecstatic to be offered the Echols scholar program at University of Virginia and even more blown away by his admittance to Stanford! It was scary, though, not knowing what the response would be to a homeschooling student and trying to guess at what the universities wanted to see on transcripts.

—DENISE IN VIRGINIA

HOW WE DID IT

Overall, the college admissions process was positive. We started by attending a Christian college fair and getting some ideas of what questions to ask, what the different requirements were, how they felt about homeschoolers, scholarship information, and so on. Then we made campus visits. Our son narrowed his choices to three—expensive, middle-of-the-road, and cheap. The application forms, all very detailed, are time-consuming. We filed financial aid forms, got financial aid offers, and made the decision.

What surprised me was the fact that our son is now attending the most expensive school, without our going into debt. And we are a typical, middle-class homeschool family, with no college savings. Of course, our son earned the majority of the money and will have to come home this summer and work hard again to earn for next year.

—DARIA IN ALABAMA

The counselor asked her to take math and reading tests for placement. In the spring of 1999, our daughter began her first early childhood education class at age 16. I was surprised at how easy it was and equally surprised by the number of colleges calling her regularly. I now think she would have had no trouble getting into most colleges."

Homeschooling families with children applying to more-selective schools find that preparing good documentation eases the application process. Julie in Colorado, whose son was admitted to Vanderbilt University (TN), Northwestern University (IL), Indiana University (IN), and the University of Colorado, Boulder (CO), explains, "We did lots of work filling out forms. We tried to stay fairly organized during the high school homeschooling years, gathering information that would show what we had done. We were really glad to have all that assembled. Even so, it was still a lot of work. We took enormous pains to make sure everything looked perfect."

Kara in Georgia, whose four homeschooled children were admitted to competitive colleges, including Rice University (TX) and Rose-Hulman Institute of Technology (IN), sends a cautionary message about record keeping: "Overall, the college application process was easy when we had the documentation, transcripts of previous college credits, Scouting records, and other reports all in a file. With one son, who waited until the last minute, it was hectic. We found ourselves in the post office, asking for same-day postmarking and certification—not to mention making sure all the documents, essays, and other paperwork were in order. Those last twenty-four hours were a family event we would not wish to repeat."

GED DILEMMAS

AS THE National Center for Home Education report points out, just under one in three colleges nationwide requires a General Educational Development (GED) test score to admit graduates of nonaccredited schools, a category that includes most homeschoolers. They base this requirement on the perceived need for a GED score to qualify for financial aid.

Homeschooling families take two approaches to this requirement. Some simply have their children take the test and get on with college and with life. Catherine in Saudi Arabia explains, "The admission process was very straightforward. No diploma? Give us a GED and you're in. My daughter had no difficulty in passing the GED even though she only followed a curriculum through grade 8 (Calvert). Thereafter, she studied whatever interested her. She did brush up in math and science in preparation for the GED examination."

It can be as simple as that. If a school requires a GED test score, help your teenager prepare for and take the test. You will find preparation materials online and in the study guide section of any large bookstore (see Resources at the end of this chapter). Most agree that students with good eighth-grade skills can pass this high school diploma equivalency test.

Some families find the GED requirement humiliating, nonsensical, and even ridiculous. They say that the GED, often associated with high school dropouts, is not appropriate for their hardworking homeschoolers. During the college admissions process, some of these families eliminate schools that require a GED. Denise in Virginia, whose son was admitted to Stanford, writes, "We became aware that some schools would not even look at our son, because he had not taken a GED! That was one hoop that he would not consider. After all, he was a National Merit Scholarship finalist and had a very good record at the community college, taking advanced courses."

Other families challenge the GED requirement and try to get admissions personnel to change their minds. Leo and Penny, homeschoolers since 1987, explain, "After being notified that our son would not be considered for admission to University of Wyoming until he had taken the GED, we decided to take a solid stand against the policy. A few letters and phone calls later, the GED requirement was waived. Our son was immediately admitted. The admissions office called our home and apologized, saying that their policies were outdated and in need of revision."

COLLEGES REQUIRING HOMESCHOOLERS TO LEAP TALL BUILDINGS IN A SINGLE BOUND

UNFORTUNATELY, SOME COLLEGES have adopted discriminatory admissions policies. The University of North Carolina, Wilmington, for example, requires a certain number of high school credits in English, math, science, history, and foreign language and an SAT score, just as most other schools do. The school also says, "In addition to meeting the freshman admission requirements, home-schooled applicants must obtain a satisfactory score on three Subject Tests (SAT II's, formerly called Achievement Tests), one each in English, mathematics, and science."

Ironically and illogically, this policy comes from a college that admits students with high school grade point averages as low as 2.0 on a 4.0 scale (as low as a C average). Probably a significant percentage of its freshman could not produce acceptable scores on three SAT II subject achievement tests.

MONEY SAVER

Find free GED study guides in the reference section of most public libraries.

Other schools currently requiring SAT II Subject Test scores from homeschoolers—but not from graduates of accredited high schools—include the University of Notre Dame (IN), Georgia State University (GA), Portland State College (OR), Purdue University (IN), Rhodes College (TN), Rice University (TX). Depressing? Yes. But keep in mind that colleges sometimes change their policies. Indeed, some of the schools named in this paragraph may have rethought their positions by the time you read this. Southern Methodist University (TX) used to require additional SAT II scores from homeschoolers. They no longer do.

How can you deal with discriminatory policies? You have at least four choices.

1. Vote with your feet. There are approximately 3,200 two-year and four-year colleges in the United States. Take your business elsewhere, to colleges that treat homeschoolers fairly.

2. Try to change their minds. You may find that what appears to be a hard-and-fast policy (for example, scores on four SAT II Subject Tests from homeschoolers) may be waived or reduced in certain

circumstances. If your homeschooler has won a Reserve Officer Training Corps (ROTC) or National Merit Scholarship or is a stand-out athlete or even has simply completed one semester of community college classes with straight A's, the admissions office may discover a loophole that allows them to waive the requirement.

3. Prepare for the additional testing, and plan ahead to satisfy the college's requirements. Julie in Colorado reports success with this tactic: "Indiana University asked for more than just the usual SAT I and three SAT II Subject Tests. From homeschoolers they wanted four subject tests, including history. We did it, and they admitted our son to their honors program."

4. Send your child to school for his senior year. Serena in Ohio explains, "Our homeschooled oldest daughter approached Purdue University. They were very negative, requiring special SAT II tests from homeschoolers. She ended up enrolling in public high school in her senior year and applied to Purdue with a public school transcript. They accepted her in a matter of weeks, with no additional tests required."

THE FINE ART OF NEGOTIATION

IF A COLLEGE or university's stated requirements for homeschoolers seem unfair, do write to the admissions department and discuss the matter with them.

Admissions officers are often unfamiliar with homeschooling. They don't understand that homeschoolers may have transcripts, college credits, and unusual, impressive accomplishments, such as running a business or publishing a book. Explaining home education can go a long way.

Judy in Virginia writes, "While at first it appeared that they might not be very easy to deal with, our daughter negotiated with Virginia Polytechnic Institute and State University to change what they required from her. She had a long back-and-forth e-mail conversation with the dean of admissions that eventually resolved all of their concerns in her favor."

It is also important to fully understand the policies at a given college and to talk to the right people. "The right people" usually does not include the first person who answers the phone in admissions. Kate explains, "At South Dakota State University, the secretaries questioned the records we provided. I had to point that their published admissions policy was not a misprint but that any person—homeschooled or not—could be admitted on the basis of their ACT scores alone. Further up the line, the admissions officers themselves had no problem."

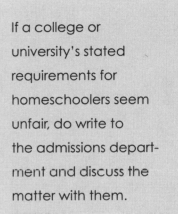

If a college or university's stated requirements for homeschoolers seem unfair, do write to the admissions department and discuss the matter with them.

Policies may be vague or nonexistent, but don't let that deter you. Daria in Alabama writes, "Auburn University had a sentence in their catalog, 'Applicants from nonaccredited high schools will be considered on an individual basis by the Admissions Committee.' Our homeschool was definitely nonaccredited. But our son received acceptance within three weeks after mailing his application! He had a pretty good (not great) ACT score and a fairly normal-looking transcript, and I think that's what helped."

If you live in California, the California State College and University system can present special problems.

Jeanette describes her family's unfortunate situation: "Our two homeschooled children both attended Barstow Junior College as part of their high school homeschooling. One son applied to California State University, San Marcos, three classes short of an AA degree. They told us that he would not be accepted without a high school diploma, because he had not completed his AA degree. However, had he applied as a homeschooled student with no junior college classes, he would have probably been accepted with his SAT scores and a portfolio. The process was ridiculous. I sent my children to

QUESTIONS FOR COLLEGE ADMISSIONS OFFICERS

Begin with this list and add other questions specific to your situation.

✦ How many homeschoolers applied for freshman undergraduate spaces at your school last year?

✦ How many of those homeschoolers did you admit?

✦ How does this compare with your overall admittance rate?

✦ Do you have special policies for dealing with applicants who home-schooled through high school? (This could be in the form of an internal memo, Web information pages, special application and information packets you send to homeschoolers, and so on.) If yes, what are those policies?

✦ How do you evaluate homeschooled applicants? Do you require any-thing different from them than from applicants who attend public schools, for example? (Assume here that homeschoolers submit standardized test scores, transcripts, and all other paperwork, just like everyone else.)

✦ What are your concerns with homeschoolers?

✦ If you require additional documentation from homeschoolers, how does this compare with documentation you require of applicants from small, private, unaccredited schools?

junior college during their high school homeschooling years to fill gaps in their education and also to let them pursue their interests. However, this backfired when my son applied to the California State system."

The obvious lesson here is to ask questions ahead of time (see sidebar, above). And talk to the right people—people in a position to make a decision. Many schools now assign all homeschooled applicants to one or two admissions counselors. If the school has not designated a homeschooling specialist, ask to speak to the head admissions officer to be certain you get the right answers.

NCHE makes two excellent recommendations. Be prepared. And be persistent. Do not wait until your homeschooler's senior year to learn about admissions policies. Start your research in grades 8 and 9 or even earlier. Back preparation with persistence. Don't give up—especially in the face of difficulties. As NCHE points out in its online article titled "Preparing for College," "'No' does not always mean there is no way." We encountered problems when our son applied to the United States Air Force Academy. We questioned every obstacle and answered every objection until no more remained and our son was admitted. He graduated from the academy in 1997 and now lives his dream, flying jet aircraft.

> To get around the traditional admissions process, your homeschooler enrolls in courses at a college of interest as a non-degree-seeking student.

BACK-DOOR COLLEGE ADMISSIONS

FINALLY, SOME HOMESCHOOLERS—just like many students who graduated from public school—now go around the college admissions process. They never take standardized tests like the SAT and ACT, and they never submit transcripts and application essays. Instead, they win admissions to degree-granting programs through the back door.

To get around the traditional admissions process, your homeschooler could enroll in courses at a college of interest as a non-degree-seeking student. Most colleges allow students to take classes if they can pay the fees and meet the prerequisites. After taking one to three semesters of classes part-time, students then apply for admission to a degree program. For documentation, they use the college transcript generated by the classes taken.

This option works well for students who are unsure of their direction and perhaps want to work and attend college part-time before making any decisions about a degree program. The downside? It is almost impossible to get financial aid when you take classes outside a degree program. Nevertheless, back-door college admission is ideal for some homeschoolers. Always check with the college in advance to determine if classes taken in nondegree status can be used later to satisfy degree requirements.

College admission for homeschoolers is easier at some institutions, more difficult at others. Some colleges go out of their way to welcome graduates of home-based programs. A few, with discriminatory admissions policies, actively discourage homeschooled applicants.

Just as you will eliminate some colleges from consideration because of their educational philosophies, the majors offered, location, or cost, you will cross some schools off of your list because their administrators cannot see the value of home education. Learn about the policies at different schools. Establish working relationships with those who welcome homeschoolers and offer what you want.

SIMPLE STARTING POINTS

INVOLVE YOUR homeschooled teen in all research and decision making about college—including trying each of the following suggestions:

+ Gather data from homeschoolers in your community. Ask members of your local support groups about their experiences with college admissions.

+ If your homeschooler has not yet decided which colleges interest him, do a small research project. You and your teenager can call a local community college, a nearby four-year state college or university, and one or two private colleges. Ask questions suggested earlier in this chapter regarding their history of accepting homeschoolers and their current policies regarding homeschooled applicants.

✦ Get specific information on admissions from any schools you know your teen will apply to. If any policy seems unreasonable, ask why the policy exists and begin a discussion of your situation with the admissions office.

✦ Visit Web sites suggested below in the Resources for the most up-to-date information about colleges that accept homeschoolers.

RESOURCES

Books

Cohen, Cafi. *And What About College? How Homeschooling Leads to Admissions to the Best Colleges and Universities, Second Edition.* Holt Associates, 2000.

Colfax, David and Micki. *Homeschooling for Excellence.* Warner Books, 1988. Also, *Hard Times in Paradise.* Warner Books, 1992.

Herzog, David Alan. *GED Mathematics Workbook.* IDG Books, 1998.

Hogan, Katherine. *Barron's GED Writing Workbook.* Barron's, 1998.

McKee, Alison. *From Homeschool to College and Work New Revised Edition.* Bittersweet House, P.O. Box 5211, Madison, Wisconsin 53705, 1999.

Martz, Geoff, and Laurice Pearson. *Cracking the GED 2000.* Princeton Review, 1999.

Web Sites

1999 NCHE College Survey: http://www.hslda.org

College and University Reviews—Homeschool Admission Policies at Eclectic Homeschool Online Web Site: http://eho.org/collrev. htm

College Admission Policies: Good News, Bad News Colleges at Homeschool-Teens-College: http://www.homeschoolteenscollege .net

Colleges That Admit Homeschoolers at Karl Bunday's School Is Dead, Learn In Freedom Web Site: http://learninfreedom.org /colleges_4_hmsc.html

GED Preparation Page: http://www.petersons.com/testprep/ged.html

GED Testing Service: http://www.acenet.edu/calec/ged/home.html

Homeschool-Friendly Colleges and Universities: http://rsts.net /colleges/

Homeschooling Today College Resource Section: http://www .homeschooltoday.com

2

COLLEGE OR NOT?

In This Chapter

✦ The alternatives

✦ College now?

✦ Simple starting points

✦ Resources

"If you know what kind of work you want to do, move toward it in the most direct way possible."

—John Holt in *Teach Your Own*

COMPUTER SOFTWARE DEVELOPER Bill Gates, newsman Walter Cronkite, and architect Frank Lloyd Wright all followed John Holt's advice on the previous page. Each began working in the field that most interested him, and all eventually achieved worldwide recognition—without college degrees.

College has been the default button on our child-raising menu for too long. It is almost a mantra in our society: "Go to college, make money, have a good life." Too often this mantra leads to "You will only have a good life if you earn a four-year degree." We have reached the point where most families automatically push their children to attend college regardless of their sons' and daughters' interests, talents, and occupational goals.

Homeschooling families—all families—should question conventional college-to-rewarding-career wisdom. Most students will have to raise anywhere from $10,000 to more than $100,000 to finance four years of study. That's if they finish. A study by the National Center for Education Statistics says that more than 30 percent of students who begin college do not return for their sophomore year. And an appalling 75 percent of students who enter college have no degree five years later.

> We all know college graduates who man cash registers, drive taxis, or are otherwise "underemployed"— or should we say "overeducated"?

Students who stick it out will devote four to six years of their lives to obtaining a degree, a degree that may or may not lead to a rewarding work. We all know college graduates who man cash registers, drive taxis, or are otherwise "underemployed"—or should we say "overeducated"? This occurs because more than 70 percent of jobs in the United States require only alternative education or on-the-job training. With the demand for Web page designers and other self-taught computer experts, that percentage may rise even higher in the first decade of the new millennium.

To choose between college and the alternatives, it helps to have more information. What are other homeschool graduates doing? How do their parents feel about their choosing an alternative to college?

Emma's daughter, who graduated as a homeschooler in 1999, has chosen to study violin privately and pursue other interests rather than attend college. Emma writes, "We have always said that college

OCCUPATIONAL OUTLOOK

The jobs listed below are those projected to have the greatest percentage increase in growth from 1990 to 2005 (note that only two [*] require college):

Home health aide	Radiological technologist
*Computer systems analyst	Medical secretary
Personal and home care aide	*Psychologist
Medical assistant	Travel agent
Human service worker	Correction officer

These jobs are projected to experience the largest increase in overall numbers from 1990 to 2005 (note that none of these require a four-year college degree):

Salesperson, retail	Manager and executive
Registered nurse	Janitor, maid, and cleaner
Cashier	Nursing aide, orderly
Office clerk	Food counter worker
Truck driver	Food service

—FROM THE JOB SEEKING SKILLS WEB SITE,
WWW.BCIT.TEC.NJ.US/JOBSEEKING/CHOSCAREER.HTM

HOMESCHOOL GRADS SAY

Few people know what they want to do from the get-go. I graduated as a homeschooler and have been in and out of four colleges and several jobs. Even without a degree, I am happily employed in a full-time job for which I am well compensated. My advice? Try to decide what you want to do before spending a heap of money on college.

If you cannot decide what you want to do and have limited funds, don't go to college. Find an entry-level job in a business or organization, doing work that looks interesting to you. Your first job may be boring and low paying, but you never know where it will lead. Hard work always draws attention. Comparing college and full-time-work environments, I know that working teaches you much that college cannot. Nothing compares with being out in the real world.

—TARA IN CALIFORNIA

was something to do if it got you where you wanted to go. We advise skipping it if it does not serve your needs. College for the sake of college, we feel, is too expensive and time-consuming. Attending college just because one wants to go, of course, is fine. We reject the notion that everyone should go and therefore must go. Fortunately, homeschoolers are less inclined than most people to be corralled by such thinking."

Of course, certain occupations demand college preparation. Examples include medicine, veterinary medicine, architecture, engineering, college teaching and research, and teaching in public schools. Entry to other fields—law, nursing, business management, and science research—is often smoother with a college degree.

Some look beyond the immediate career benefits associated with a bachelor's degree. They say that four years on campus provides an opportunity to grow personally, intellectually, spiritually, and so-cially—all at a time of life when most people have no conflicting demands of family or earning a living.

That said, homeschoolers, more than most teens who attend school, are in excellent positions to delay college and explore alternatives. As homeschooling parents and teenagers, you already think outside the box. You homeschooled through high school, usually without the assistance of credentialed teachers—often in the face of doubting friends, relatives, and neighbors. You succeeded, probably in part because you know how to network for opportunities. I have interviewed hundreds of homeschoolers who—at ages 13 to 18—got occupational head starts by trying home-based businesses, internships, apprenticeships, and paying jobs during their high school

ALTERNATIVES TO COLLEGE

Other ways to spend four to six years and tens of thousands of dollars:

Traveling (including working
  your way around the world)
Internships
Working for community-service
  organizations (AmeriCorps,
  for example)
On-the-job training
Apprenticeships
Culinary careers
Alternative-medicine careers
  (naturopathy, massage
  therapy, for example)

Training for a trade
  (electrician, cosmetologist,
  for example)
Outdoor jobs
Artistic endeavors
  (screenwriting, acting,
  for example)
Military enlistment
Self-taught computing
Starting a business

years. By the time they graduated, they were more than ready to put these skills to use to find meaningful employment.

Grace Llewellyn, author of *The Teenage Liberation Handbook,* points out another reason to delay college. She looks forward to the day when homeschoolers and self-directed learners—without college degrees—successfully apply for graduate study in M.A. and Ph.D. programs, MBA programs, and medical and dental school. She envisions adults copying high school homeschoolers—documenting real-world learning—to win graduate school admission without a college transcript.

> Interestingly, most college admissions officers look favorably on delayed college entry—especially if the applicant did something interesting in the interim.

Alternatives to college are more plentiful and varied than you might expect. Even if your teenager plans to go to college, you may want to explore these options as a means to earn money before and during college. Some teens, instead of opting out of college, prefer to delay it a year or two. Interestingly, most college admissions officers look favorably on delayed college entry—especially if the applicant did something interesting in the interim. Let's examine some of the most commonly pursued alternatives and then discuss how to evaluate if college will best serve your homeschooler now.

THE ALTERNATIVES

"UNCOLLEGE" INCLUDES paid work, starting a business, self-directed learning, volunteering, homemaking, enlisting in the military, and enrolling in internships and apprenticeships.

Work

Since our daughter graduated as a homeschooler, she has alternated college attendance with full-time employment. Trying on different hats, she has found herself waiting tables, hosting in a restaurant, working at a health and tennis club, managing a health-food store, and, currently, selling advertising for a countywide newspaper—a job that pays well and offers excellent benefits. On the side, she is building a catering business. She sees her work as excellent preparation for becoming an event planner—either working for someone else or herself.

Our daughter often remarks on the many degreed individuals in the college town where she lives who barely support themselves bagging groceries. She has two things most of them do not: a debt-free life and a work résumé listing jobs with gradually increasing responsibility.

Other homeschoolers have had similar experiences. Shelley, who has taught five children at home since 1987, writes, "After one-and-one-half years at Iowa Western Community College, our son dropped out to work and get some finances in order. His college classes had been in the culinary arts, but his current route to a successful career might work out better. He is now employed in a restaurant, where he could receive his chef certification."

Working for others provides immediate feedback about various career options. Your teens learn the ins and outs and ups and downs of working in any field—something four years of college does not begin to address. Is your son or daughter interested in medicine? How about training as an emergency medical technician or an orderly or a nursing aide to see if he likes health-care settings? Not only will he get an inside view of the field, but also he will have skills that will support him should he decide to go to college later.

Entrepreneurship provides the same real-world feedback as employment. Homeschoolers start their own businesses the same way everyone else does: They see a need and try to fill it. Some of the more popular businesses with new homeschooling graduates include Web page design, teaching music, and landscape design and maintenance.

Of course, college and entrepreneurship are not mutually exclusive. Kate, homeschooling primarily for academic reasons, describes

HOW WE DID IT

My son chose work for which college does not provide training. Now 19, he graduated from our homeschool high school last year. He is a talented piano player. He loves the instrument, including how it works. With his strong mechanical inclinations, he enjoys diagnosing problems and making repairs. He started his own piano tuning and repair business over a year ago. He got initial instruction from a book that a piano tuner recommended. Then he and a friend, with basic tools and using the information in this book on piano tuning and repairing, partially refurbished the action and keys of a hundred-year-old piano.

After that, he got a job doing in-store tunings and minor repairs at a piano store. After half a year, they gave him in-home tunings. His business has taken off from there. Last fall he started a correspondence course from the Randy Potter School of Piano Technology. This course has helped him improve his tuning ability and expanded the capabilities of types of repairs he can do. He is working the equivalent of part-time while he studies the course but so far enjoys the work very much. The amount of tuning and repair work he can do in a week will determine his income potential for the future.

—MOLLY IN CONNECTICUT

her 19-year-old son's activities: "He attends college but also started his own business—a greenhouse and commercial vegetable garden—while in high school. He still has this business and plans to continue with it after college graduation."

Self-Directed Learning

Some homeschoolers decide to spend their post–high school years pursuing whatever interests them. Often parents agree to provide support while their young adult children develop talents and explore. In many cases this approach differs little from sending a child to college with an undeclared major, except that you will not incur a whopping debt.

Emma describes her daughter's situation: "As a violinist, she wants to take private music lessons, work, and continue studying other topics—Russian and creative writing—on her own. She would not have time to do all this if she were a full-time college student. She studies with a University of Illinois violin professor. She works part-time, practices, goes to violin lessons, practices, tangos, practices, and goes to the coffee shops to write and study."

Another variation on the theme of post–high school personal development is donating one's time to a worthy cause. Volunteering for one to three years after completing high school provides homeschool graduates with job skills, experience, contacts, and hands-on career exploration. A homeschooled teen living near us works as a volunteer firefighter. That has sparked her interest in emergency medical technician and paramedic training, which she will pursue in the near future.

Some homeschoolers see preparation for homemaking as their highest calling. Dan and Beth in Alabama report that their daughter did not want to go to college. Instead, she preferred to fine-tune her homemaking skills to be ready to start her own family. Seth and Karen, parents of six homeschoolers, describe a similar course for their daughter: "She attended summer classes after graduating as a homeschooler and then married the following fall. She is now a homemaker. While going to college, she worked doing child care and later at a herbal health store."

Military

Danielle Wood, author of *The Uncollege Alternative,* describes the United States military as a learning free-for-all. For those who can tolerate the minuses—living where Uncle Sam dictates and a

MONEY SAVER

Get an instant job in what Danielle Wood, author of *The Uncollege Alternative,* calls "the unarmed forces"— government organizations dedicated to improving everyday life in the United States. These programs include AmeriCorps, VISTA (Volunteers In Service To America), and the NCCC (National Civilian Community Corps). All provide living expenses and a small salary in return for training and placement in community and state do-good programs.

three-to-six-year work commitment—the army, navy, marines, air force, and Coast Guard offer pay while training for specific jobs. Additional free learning programs and opportunities to earn cash toward college up the ante further.

Military occupations go far beyond soldiering or piloting aircraft. The armed services train in thousands of fields—everything from dental technicians to aircraft mechanics. Military jobs include animal-care specialist, cartographer (map-maker), cook, and firefighter, as well as multi-media illustrator, X-ray technologist, and many other occupations highly sought after in the civilian sector.

The military—desperate for personnel in a booming economy—is doing what it can to recruit homeschoolers. Previously it placed students without diplomas from accredited high schools on a lower enlistment tier that lacked access to some of the most exciting and interesting occupations. Most branches have now rectified this situation and allow the enlistment of homeschoolers on a par with enlistees with diplomas from accredited schools.

Internships and Apprenticeships

An intern or apprentice exchanges a young adult's time and effort for the opportunity to learn about a certain kind of work. Sometimes there is a monetary exchange. Either interns and apprentices pay for training, or employers pay a minimum wage for the labor. More often, no money changes hands.

While the terms "intern" and "apprentice" are often used interchangeably, interns usually do more menial, support-type tasks (such as data entry or answering the phone), while apprentices learn specific skills in a craft or trade, such as plumbing, construction, midwifery, or interior decorating.

Internships exist in a wide range of fields, including business and technology, communications, creative and performing fine arts, public affairs, human services, and nature and recreation. While the actual work may be boring, an internship offers the opportunity to see a career field from the inside and make valuable contacts at the same time.

Alice Culbreath's and Sandra K. Neal's excellent reference, *Testing the Waters: A Teen's Guide to Career Exploration,* contains an extensive list of government and private concerns offering internships. Among them are the Drama League, in New York City, which promotes the growth of artists and audiences; the Boston YMCA; Elizabeth Glaser Pediatric AIDS Foundation, in Santa Monica, California; and the Calvin Crest Christian Camp Retreat and Conference Center, in Fremont, Nebraska. There's something for everyone in this book.

Many apprenticeships offer and deliver on the "college promise"—training in an interesting and in-demand occupation leading to job security. Apprenticeships also hold out the eventual opportunity to work for yourself. Sharon, a lifelong homeschooling mom, writes, "Our son is in his third year of an apprenticeship program with the Plumbers and Pipe Fitters Local Union 114. They meet for classes every Tuesday and Thursday evening throughout the school year, classes accredited through the local community college. In essence, he is a part-time college student while working in a five-year apprenticeship program."

> Internships exist in a wide range of fields, including business and technology, communications, creative and performing fine arts, public affairs, human services, and nature and recreation.

Many apprenticeships offer and deliver on the "college promise"—training in an interesting and in-demand occupation leading to job security.

QUICK & EASY

Visit the library reference section with your teenage homeschooler and peruse *America's Top Internships, Peterson's Internships,* and *Student Advantage Guide: The Internship Bible.* Note and discuss interesting possibilities.

Another homeschooling mom on an online bulletin board says, "Apprenticeships through local union halls are a fabulous way to develop a career. My husband went through a five-year apprenticeship with the International Brotherhood of Electrical Workers. If he were single and not needing to have time to be a husband and parent, he could make well over $100,000 a year. One of his friends is making $15,000 a month right now, working lots of overtime. I have one son that I will encourage to go that route. Language arts are not his strong suit (like father, like son). There is a lot of book work to becoming an electrician, but it all applies to the job. There are no courses in health, psychology, history, English, and so on, just lots of math and hands-on learning. Also, in the apprenticeship, you learn while you earn."

Grace Llewellyn, at her Web site on homeschoolers, reports that homeschoolers are "reinventing apprenticeships for their own purposes." She's talking about creating your own apprenticeship situation where none exists right now—simply by finding people who do work you want to do and asking them about how you could exchange labor for learning. Llewellyn points out that this works for both academic and nonacademic subjects. Homeschoolers have apprenticed themselves for weeks or years to chemists and other scientists, woodworkers, museum curators, windmill repair people, and even poets.

One homeschool graduate I know—let's call him Cory—created his own apprenticeship. As a teenager fascinated by the historical battlefields nearby, he joined a local group that recreated

Civil War scenes. Hundreds of them assembled on weekends in period clothing. Using authentic weaponry, they reenacted important battles.

By chance, Cory's group was hired as extras for the movie *Glory.* During the filming, this young man spent as much time as possible with the production crew, asking questions or just watching. Impressed with his interest, that crew remembered him. They recommended hiring him for gofer jobs on a second movie at another location. About a year later, at age 18, Cory moved to Hollywood. Using his contacts, he found immediate employment in film production. By age 22, he had worked his way up the ladder. He was earning an excellent salary in a job any new film-school graduate would envy.

COLLEGE NOW?

BEFORE YOU IMMERSE yourself and your teenager in the college application process, you should first research whether or not college now will provide the best road to a satisfying occupation and a rewarding life.

Homeschoolers like Cory above find themselves in an ideal position to begin this research at ages 12 to 17. While regular high school students have part-time and volunteer jobs, participate in internships, and develop home-based businesses, homeschoolers have an advantage. They have more time than teenagers who attend school—in most cases an additional six to ten discretionary hours each day. They can spend part of this time in career exploration with additional volunteer and paid jobs.

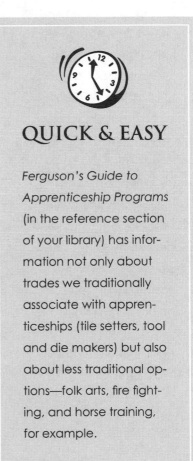

QUICK & EASY

Ferguson's Guide to Apprenticeship Programs (in the reference section of your library) has information not only about trades we traditionally associate with apprenticeships (tile setters, tool and die makers) but also about less traditional options—folk arts, fire fighting, and horse training, for example.

MONEY SAVER

Through local school districts, adult-education programs, community colleges, and in the yellow pages, develop a list of local career-counseling programs and employment offices. Many offer free or almost free services, including personal development classes, interest and skills inventories (tests), help in writing résumés and preparing for interviews, time- and financial-management strategies, and job referral and placement.

While many 16-to-18 year-old homeschoolers know exactly what they want to do and how they want to do it, some teens say they feel lost. Either everything looks interesting—or nothing does. As someone who attended college only because I could not imagine what else to do, I know how they feel.

In my workshops I recommend several outstanding aids to help parents and their teens explore interests, talents, and occupational goals. Top of the list is Herbert Kohl's book *The Question Is College.* Kohl, sensitive to the concerns of both parents and teenagers, includes many questionnaires and inventories to help teens narrow down their choices. The book emphasizes helping teenagers identify meaningful work, with or without college.

Richard Bolles annually updates *What Color Is Your Parachute? A Practical Manual for Job Hunters and Career-Changers* to reflect changes in the job market. Intended for all ages, *Parachute* helps individuals articulate interests and discover vocations. For those who bypass or defer college, Bolles's book also helps immensely with the job search.

Danielle Wood provides similar, more abbreviated personality and talent inventories in her book *The Uncollege Alternative.* Most of it includes extensive descriptions of the alternatives and how to explore them. If you want to know about internships for nature lovers, free money to attend cosmetology school, jobs involving travel, or the advantages of the air force over the army, she covers these topics, plus hundreds of others. The end-of-chapter Resources here includes other helpful titles.

Teenagers will find their niches. Or not. Some will move from job to job throughout their lives. Either way, most parents find that things work out. And sometimes they work out best if parents back off and get out of the way. I used to feel bad about my own frequent occupational changes until I read what Donn Reed wrote in *The Homeschool Source Book.* He says, "There is nothing undesirable in having a variety of work, either concurrently or consecutively. A peripatetic career can be as remunerative and often more satisfying than the single-minded pursuit of only one kind of work. . . . Choosing a career should be done only if one *wants* a career."

SIMPLE STARTING POINTS

+ Peruse your local help-wanted ads over several months with your son or daughter. Use this as a starting point to discuss the advantages and disadvantages of different kinds of work.

+ With your teen, talk to people working in fields that she finds interesting. Ask them if college has figured in their success.

+ Help your homeschooled teenager find one or more volunteer jobs in your community. Don't restrict yourself to places that have volunteer programs. Ask interesting businesses, government agencies, and community-service organizations about exchanging labor for the chance to observe and learn.

+ If your teenager has a paid job, help her list the advantages and disadvantages of the kind of work in which she is currently involved.

+ Using the questionnaires and inventories in Herbert Kohl's *The Question Is College* and Danielle Wood's *The Uncollege Alternative,* help your teenager determine if college will best serve him now.

RESOURCES

Books

Bolles, Richard. *What Color Is Your Parachute? A Practical Manual for Job Hunters and Career-Changers.* Ten Speed Press, updated annually. Also, *What Color Is Your Parachute Workbook: How to Create a Picture of Your Ideal Next Job or Next Career.* Ten Speed Press, 1998.

Culbreath, Alice N., and Saundra K. Neal. *Testing the Waters: A Teen's Guide to Career Exploration.* JRC Consulting, 1999.

Duffy, Matt. *HotHouse Transplants: Moving from Homeschool into the Real World.* Home Run Enterprises, 1997.

Eikleberry, Carol. *Career Guide for Creative and Unconventional People.* Ten Speed Press, 1999.

Ellis, Lee, and Larry Burkett. *Finding the Career That Fits You: The Companion Workbook to Your Career in Changing Times.* Moody Press, 1998.

Gurvis, Sandra. *The Off-the-Beaten-Path Job Book: You CAN Make a Living AND Have a Life!* Citadel Press, 1995. Also, *Careers for Nonconformists: A Practical Guide to Finding and Developing a Career outside the Mainstream.*

Fireside, Byrna J. *Choices for the High School Graduate: A Survival Guide for the Information Age.* Ferguson Publishing, 1999.

Hailey, Kendall. *The Day I Became an Autodidact.* Out of print, but worth searching out in libraries and used-book stores.

Kohl, Herbert. *The Question Is College: On Finding and Doing Work You Love.* Heinemann, 1998.

Latimer, Jon. *Peterson's Vocational and Technical Schools and Programs.* Peterson's Guides, 1997.

Lee, Linda. *Success without College.* Doubleday, 2000.

Llewellyn, Grace. *The Teenage Liberation Handbook.* Lowry House, 1998.

Montross, David H. *Real People, Real Jobs: Reflecting Your Interests in the World of Work.* Consulting Psychologist Press, 1995.

Murphy, John. *Success without a College Degree: The Secrets of How to Get Ahead and Show Them All.* Achievement Dynamics, 1997.

Oakes, Elizabeth. *Ferguson's Guide to Apprenticeship Programs.* Ferguson Publishing, 1998. Also, *Career Exploration on the Internet: A Student's Guide to More Than Three Hundred Web Sites!* Ferguson Publishing, 1998.

Tieger, Paul, and Barbara Barron-Tieger. *Do What You Are—Discovering the Perfect Career for You through the Secrets of Personality Type.* Little, Brown, 1995.

Treat, Casey. *Fulfilling Your God-Given Destiny.* Thomas Nelson, 1995.

Unger, Harlow. *But What If I Don't Want to Go to College: A Guide to Success through Alternative Education.* Checkmark Books, 1998.

Wood, Danielle. *The Uncollege Alternative: Your Guide to Incredible Careers and Amazing Adventures outside of College.* Regan Books, 2000.

Web Sites

America's Job Bank: http://www.ajb.dni.us/seeker

AmeriCorps: http://www.americorps.org

Army National Guard: http://www.1800goguard.com

Business Owner's Toolkit: http://www.toolkit.cch.com

Career Mosaic (job search site): http://www.careermosaic.com/cm/jobs.html

Career Zone (career exploration and descriptions): http://www.explore.cornell.edu/newcareerzone

FlipDog (job search site): http://www.flipdog.com/home.html

Job Seeking Skills Website (contains interest inventory): http://www.bcit.tec.nj.us/JobSeeking

Peace Corps Volunteers: http://www.peacecorps.gov/home.html

United States Air Force: http://www.airforce.com

United States Army: http://www.goarmy.com

United States Coast Guard: http://www.uscg.mil/jobs/

United States Navy: http://www.navyjobs.com

Yahoo Careers!: http://careers.yahoo.com/employment/

Courses

Gordon, Beverly Adams. *Home School, High School, and Beyond* (nine-week, half-credit course): Castlemoyle Books, 15436 42nd Avenue South, Seattle, WA 98188. Phone: 206-787-2714. Fax: 206-787-0631. E-mail: orders@castlemoyle.com.

Apprenticeship PLUS (Patterning Learning Upon Scripture): Education PLUS (864-281-9316), P.O. Box 1029, Mauldin, SC 29662: http://www.edplus.com/Index.html.

3

HIGH SCHOOL AT HOME

In This Chapter

✦ Independent-study programs

✦ Do it yourself

✦ Off-the-record, but essential

✦ Simple starting points

✦ Resources

"If the home-educated teen understands that college is primarily a place where one goes to acquire credentials and not likely to be a place where learning is taken as seriously as it was in the home, he or she will probably not have a hard time understanding that a certain amount of instrumental goal-oriented behavior will be necessary to meet the admission requirements of most schools."

—David Colfax, author of *Homeschooling for Excellence*

*D*AVID COLFAX SHOULD know. In the early 1980s—at a time when most people stared blankly if you mentioned home education—three of Colfax's homeschooled sons were admitted to Harvard. With the phrase "instrumental goal-oriented behavior," he makes an important point about homeschooling high school. Your teens may never have studied school textbooks. You may never have given grades. However, to make your children competitive for slots at selective colleges or for big scholarship awards from any school, you will need to play the game—at least a little.

Instrumental goal-oriented behavior comes automatically to some families. These traditional-approach home educators carefully plan high school studies around recommendations of colleges. Some go so far as to use only courses from accredited independent-study schools.

HOMESCHOOL TERMS

Although thousands of variants on How to Homeschool exist, you will hear certain terms over and over.

✦ *Traditional approach* homeschoolers say that children learn best with texts, schedules, and grades.

✦ *Unit study* advocates says that children learn best with real-world, hands-on, in-depth projects.

✦ *Unschoolers* say that children learn best when their interests direct the learning.

✦ *Eclectic home educators* say that there is no one way that all children learn best all the time. They combine traditional materials, unit studies, and unschooling time to put together the best program.

Families at the other end of the homeschool spectrum—unschoolers who refuse to separate learning from living—will also have to think in "schoolish" terms during the application process. They need to prove that their teenagers have accomplished something comparable, if not identical, to other applicants.

For example, one of the Colfax boys developed a dairy goat breeding business and wrote articles for dairy goat journals. To succeed with this enterprise, he taught himself an incredible amount about goats and animal husbandry. Nevertheless, come college application time, he also worked through a biology textbook to prepare for the biology achievement test (now an SAT II Subject Test). He probably learned more life science working with his goats. Nevertheless, he had to prove standard textbook learning to win admission to Harvard.

Any homeschooling approach will work for college admissions—so long as you create solid documentation, as described in later chapters. Even with that reassurance, many new home educators *and* some experienced homeschoolers feel tentative about high school. That uncertainty leads some to investigate independent-study programs (ISPs). For that reason, the next section provides information on evaluating these rapidly proliferating organizations.

Even with the growth of the ISP business, a majority of families homeschooling their teenagers proceed without them and operate independently. Following the ISP section, we describe how our survey respondents and others have designed and implemented their own high school programs. Read on to learn how academics, projects, working in groups, classroom learning, and leadership experiences contribute to high school at home.

QUICK & EASY

Visit the Homeschool-Teens-College Web site, www.homeschoolteens college.net/articles.htm, to read dozens of articles by and about home-schooling teenagers.

INDEPENDENT-STUDY PROGRAMS

INDEPENDENT STUDY PROGRAMS (ISPs) and umbrella schools (schools that help homeschoolers homeschool) come in more flavors than Baskin-Robbins ice cream. Although most are private, hundreds of public schools enter the ISP business every year. Historically, many umbrella schools and ISPs have been Christian. Now an increasing number specify no religious affiliation. Some ISPs and umbrella programs are highly structured. Others allow complete flexibility with respect to what your teenager learns, how he learns, and when he learns.

Although ISPs are not for everyone, families homeschooling teenagers use ISPs and umbrella schools for many different reasons. The following list of services ISPs provide can help you determine whether an ISP or an umbrella school makes sense for your teenager.

✦ *No government intrusion into your homeschooling program.* In some states, enrolling in a private ISP or umbrella school means that you no longer have to comply with the reporting and testing requirements of a state homeschooling statute. Of course, the requirements of some ISPs can be even more stringent, so you'll have to shop carefully.

✦ *Diploma from an accredited school.* In most cases your teenager will not need a diploma from an accredited school (see chapter 6 for more discussion of this point). There are exceptions, however, such as the University of California, Los Angeles, which requires that all high school courses be accredited. If you think your teenager may apply to a college or university that requires a diploma from an accredited school, some ISPs, such as American School in Illinois, can supply that.

✦ *Independent evaluations.* Some teens seek external assessment and validation. For academic subjects especially, they prefer to bypass their parents and deal directly with adults outside the home.

HOW WE DID IT

My homeschooler attended government school for ninth grade after having been homeschooled for grades 4 through 8. That was when we realized how ridiculous the high school scene had gotten. We pulled him out for grades 10 through 12. We used Bob Jones University Video School for biology, chemistry, algebra 2, and Spanish 1 and 2. We did other subjects on our own. He also took some refresher English and math courses at the community college.

For our son, it worked better to concentrate on only a few subjects at a time. He did biology, Spanish, and math for a quarter, then chemistry, Spanish, and history for a quarter. I was not certain my son would finish college, so I wanted him to have a diploma from an accredited high school. We used Cambridge Academy, an accredited correspondence program, for his last year of high school.

—VIOLA, WHOSE HOMESCHOOLED CHILDREN

WENT ON TO JUNIOR COLLEGE

✦ *Group activities and resources.* Many local umbrella schools provide activities that rival anything local schools offer—choirs, orchestra, science, foreign language, and even competitive sports, such as basketball. Umbrella schools also may maintain resource rooms with microscopes, laboratory equipment, foreign-language videos, and educational games.

✦ *Money.* In a few locations—most notably Alaska, but also in some California school districts—public school ISPs provide texts and other learning materials and also reimburse homeschoolers' educational expenses. Unfortunately, many public ISPs require that you use public school curricula and submit to periodic teacher visits and standardized testing. Still, some families welcome the free books and appreciate the teacher support.

✦ *Testing the waters.* Some homeschooling families choose independent-study programs to give their teens a taste of traditional academics prior to college.

SHOP SMART: QUESTIONS FOR UMBRELLA SCHOOLS AND ISP'S

✦ What is your program's educational philosophy?

✦ How long have you been in business?

✦ Will you mediate with local school officials if they have objections to our teenager's enrollment in your school? (Not a question for public school ISPs.)

✦ What are the backgrounds of your school's operators and staff?

✦ How do you deliver formal coursework? Strictly by mail? Modem and computer? Video and audiocassettes?

✦ How do enrollees get help? 800 number? E-mail?

✦ What are your fees? Does this include all books, study guides, and extra materials like laboratory equipment and foreign-language tapes? Do fees include the diploma?

✦ How many students are enrolled?

✦ How many students do you graduate each year? What are some of your alumni doing now? What colleges were they admitted to?

✦ How many mentors and support teachers do you have? How many students are assigned to each instructor?

✦ How long do students wait to receive back-graded and evaluated work?

✦ What records do we need to keep?

✦ How do you assign grades?

✦ *Records.* Umbrella and independent-study schools will create records and transcripts for you. Of course, you can do that yourself, as discussed here in chapters 6 through 8. Some parents feel that an

✦ Does your school or program offer foreign language? Which languages and how many years?

✦ How do you cover laboratory science? Which science courses include a lab?

✦ To complete grades 9 through 12 in four years, approximately how many hours each day do enrollees use your materials?

✦ Can students test out or challenge required courses?

✦ What is your money-back-guarantee time period for review of initial materials?

✦ How do you assign credit for previously completed high school work?

✦ Can enrollees work on materials at their own pace? What is the minimum enrollment period to earn a diploma?

✦ If your school has a fixed course of study, can we make reasonable substitutions (for example, world literature for English literature or bookkeeping for consumer math)?

✦ If you offer "computer" courses, what exactly does that mean? E-mail with instructors? With other students? Synchronous, on-line classes? Self-paced on-line classes? Integration of the World Wide Web into instruction?

✦ What do your transcripts include?

✦ Do you give credit for volunteering and sports and music?

✦ What additional services do you offer? On-line classes, graduation ceremonies, resource rooms, activities, conferences?

HOMESCHOOL GRADS SAY

I studied a lot of interesting things in high school, although generally in a rather unorganized fashion. My freshman year, our family's first year of homeschooling, we used a prepackaged curriculum. I enjoyed the materials very much (particularly history, literature, and philosophy), but I did not have the discipline to finish everything each day. We were perpetually behind. We did finish the courses several months after the end of the school year. In the meantime my mom found a different arrangement for my sophomore year.

A small parent-run school just a two-hour drive from our home was interested in helping homeschoolers. We received some coursework through them and attended occasional classes. Overall I read a lot of good stuff, because I was interested in it, and learned Latin well, because it was a class with scheduled assignments (a priest from the local Catholic high school taught a small group of homeschoolers every week). I also perceived lots of gaps that didn't turn out to be problems and wasted an awful lot of time in between.

Homeschooling benefited me most in two areas. First, I spent a lot of time with my older siblings and their families. Second, I had diverse, extensive extracurricular activities, volunteer work, and so on that would not have been possible in a traditional school setting—karate, three choirs, work at a book publishing company, coaching a children's soccer team, and so on.

A lot of homeschool parents seem to be concerned about transcripts and curriculum. I believe that study skills and self-discipline are not always considered as seriously as they should be. Read the book *The Seven Habits of Highly Effective People,* by Steven Covey, and apply some of the author's ideas to your life before you get into college. It really helps to figure out what matters in your life and how to develop the motivation and self-discipline necessary to attain these goals. Practice setting goals and completing them within a certain time period. Learn to follow a schedule, even if your homeschooling is very unstructured, and try to develop good habits of self-discipline.

—ALEXA, WHO GRADUATED FROM THOMAS AQUINAS COLLEGE IN 1992

external transcript—not a homeschool transcript—has more credibility. Many others have succeeded with home-brewed records.

✦ *Covering it all.* Some homeschooling parents feel that using an independent-study program ensures that their teenagers receive a "well-rounded education."

✦ *Expertise for difficult subjects.* Independent-study schools use time-tested self-instructional materials to cover difficult subjects, like chemistry or French or trigonometry.

DO IT YOURSELF

MORE THAN 80 percent of our survey respondents operate independently and put together their own programs. Many have homeschooled since their children were preschoolers. They confidently choose resources and take advantage of the many learning opportunities that present themselves in everyday life. Others, although newer to home education, still do not want the restrictions imposed by ISPs and umbrella schools. Unsure of a direction, they rely more heavily on curriculum, scope and sequences (lists of who learns what when), and college entrance requirements to assemble a credible program.

Julie, whose son was admitted to Vanderbilt University (TN), Northwestern University (IL), Indiana University, and the University of Colorado, describes their high school homeschooling as academic but with plenty of room to explore interests: "We put together our own program, a combination of semistructured homeschooling activities and some classes in school," she explains. "In ninth grade this was still fairly relaxed, with lots of group activities such as putting on plays, hosting a medieval banquet, and participating in other wonderful, imaginative events. Gradually, our son's course of study became more serious, until in the second semester of eleventh

More than 80 percent of our survey respondents operate independently and put together their own programs.

HOW WE DID IT

Our days varied too much for any to be described as typical. Each year in late summer, we would brainstorm together about where her interests were leading her so I could help her find materials and resources. In addition, she would add activities as they arose during the year.

As an unschooler, I didn't assign daily schoolwork. While our daughter might go for months with little formal math instruction, for example, she still continually learned and deepened her math background through participation in a math club. Then suddenly she would intensively study a math text for weeks or months on end.

There was one brief period that was different. We reacted to fear generated by a homeschool mom who was also a certified teacher. She talked about the difficulty our daughter might have getting into college. I was unable to adequately counter this. So, at the beginning of high school, our daughter asked for a rigorous college prep course of study, which I duly drew together from lots of sources. It left her little time for her writing, reading, and other activities. She dropped it by late winter, and we went back to our eclectic, unschooling approach. Because she liked them, she kept her Saxon math books and the literature books.

Our daughter did a lot of activities we called clubs—math club (seven years), book discussion club (four years), geography club (four years), creative writing club (seven years), science-by-mail club (three years), young astronauts (two years). Her preparation for and participation in these activities made up the bulk of her curriculum.

Two subjects she did that looked fairly schoollike were math and English, using textbooks. I got her the teacher's editions with all the answers and the conversations that the teachers were supposed to have with the student so she could have some familiarity with those kinds of discussions. Other than briefly during the beginning of ninth grade, we never tested.

—JUDY, WHOSE DAUGHTER WAS ADMITTED TO VIRGINIA POLYTECHNIC'S HONORS PROGRAM AND THE UNIVERSITY OF ROCHESTER (NY)

grade, he was working very hard, actively preparing for college entrance tests."

Denise's son was admitted to Stanford University (CA) in spring 2000. Here she briefly describes his preparation: "Our son decided early that he wanted to study science. We did not use a

HOMESCHOOL GRADS SAY

A typical day began with Bible study and Mom reading aloud to my younger brother and sister and me. The reading aloud was often a chapter from a classic or a historical novel from the time period we happened to be studying. During most of my high school years, we also studied history together. We generally kept up timelines, read books from the library, and did projects together.

We combined English with history to some extent with the writing projects assigned, and I also used various grammar, writing, and literature textbooks.

Although I always loved reading, I had a procrastination problem with writing projects, something I worried about when leaving for college. I worked on science, Spanish, and math on my own, doing the lessons and then correcting my own work. I very seldom had trouble with this method of teaching myself, only once or twice having to ask for some help from a church friend with my chemistry lesson. My outside activities included piano lessons, ballet class, and physical education with the local homeschool group.

I advise homeschooled teens to take leadership positions. It is not necessary to know before you get to college exactly what you want to study, but do develop your own personal strengths and abilities. Homeschooling gives you a unique opportunity to do this. Work hard at school, but don't worry too much. Homeschooling will prepare you for college. Don't think you won't know enough. Just make the most of your time.

—KAREN, A SOPHOMORE AT HILLSDALE COLLEGE IN MICHIGAN

correspondence course. We planned our curriculum ourselves. We used various sources—textbooks and writing, math, and book discussion clubs. Our son started taking classes at the community college in his sophomore year. One of the most important things he did was to take an advanced-level physics course there. His physics instructor, serving as his mentor, helped him get summer internships. The same instructor also wrote many of our son's college recommendation letters."

> Commitment and depth of study impress most college admissions officers more than crossing all the T's and dotting all the I's.

Curriculum suppliers and many published works can help you plan high school at home. Some families begin with a published curriculum or homeschooling supplies catalog. Others rely heavily on scope and sequences, lists of who learns what when (see end-of-chapter Resources). Still others read published guides and reviews, such as Cathy Duffy's book *The Christian Home Educator's Curriculum Manual.* (Going into depth about planning high school is beyond the scope of this book. For help in this area, do read my book *Homeschooling: The Teen Years,* plus additional titles listed in the Resources section of this chapter.)

In general, be aware of typical high school diploma requirements and use them as rough guidelines—nothing more. The sidebar on page 55 lists basic, solid, and strong college preparatory programs. Remember that colleges recommend preparation based on typical high school courses. Certainly, if your teenager displays talents in a specific area, consider branching out and making substitutions. An astronomy research project could take the place of physics. Extensive reading and study of one author—say, Shakespeare—could translate into an English or drama class. Commitment and depth of study impress most college admissions officers more than crossing all the T's and dotting all the I's.

Certainly, in planning specifics you will want to research the recommended preparation of colleges in which your teen expresses interest. Just don't feel constrained by these lists.

COLLEGE PREPARATORY PROGRAMS

BASIC PROGRAM

Math: three years (through geometry)

Science: two years (physical science and biology)

English: four years

Social studies: three years (world history, U.S. history, government)

Foreign language: two years

Electives: four years

SOLID PROGRAM

Math: four years (algebra through precalculus)

Science: four years (including biology, chemistry, physics)

Social studies: three years (as above)

English: four years

Foreign language: two years

Electives: four years

STRONG PROGRAM

Math: four years (geometry through calculus)

Science: four years (biology, chemistry, physics, and one Advanced Placement science class)

Social studies: four years (as above plus sociology, psychology, or political science)

English: four years

Foreign language: four years

Electives: four years

We asked our survey respondents how much attention they paid to college academic recommendations in planning their home-schooling. Some followed recommendations exactly. Others branched out. And a few ignored them completely.

Helen in Arizona says she and her teenager paid close attention to what colleges said they wanted: "Our state universities increased their requirements beginning in fall of 1998. We were aware of this in junior high, and our curriculum took that into account. We met the requirements and then some."

Judy in Virginia took a different tack: "We were aware of the general sort of background colleges wanted. Our daughter had wide interests. When we documented the things she did over the years, most requirements were covered—with some differences. In the sciences she had a horticulture credit rather than the typical biology credit. Her chemistry credit did not include a lab, but she had a rigorous calculus-based physics course with lab and an ecology lab credit, both courses taken at community college."

Judy continues: "Our daughter followed her interests rather than specifically prepared for any college requirements. She participated for five summers in intensive Shakespearean theater workshops because she loved it. This (along with reading numerous plays and seeing numerous productions, both amateur and professional) translated into a Shakespearean literature credit for English."

Liz and Nathan, whose son now attends Hunter College in New York City, say that they paid absolutely no attention to college preparatory recommendations. According to these two former schoolteachers, "We did not ever separate learning from living, so words like 'high school,' 'study program,' 'learning materials,' and 'courses' are irrelevant. We were not preparing for college—we were all living our lives the way we thought best."

Living interesting, productive lives usually creates outstanding learning outcomes. And focusing on the quality of life—rather than checking off courses recommended by colleges—often leads to supe-

MONEY SAVER

Most community organizations—service clubs, churches, political action groups, and orchestras and choirs and drama groups—offer free or inexpensive classes, talks, and activities. Find announcements for activities in your local newspaper and at the library. Investigate activities that sound interesting. You can call most of them "school."

rior academic preparation. Leo and Penny, whose son was admitted to the University of Wyoming in 2000, comment on courses of study: "While college recommendations are always in the back of our minds, they are not the focus of our curriculum design. We pursue the highest standards for our children, which often far surpassed college academic requirements."

Great advice. Be aware of standards. But don't let them limit you.

OFF-THE-RECORD, BUT ESSENTIAL

ALTHOUGH ACADEMICS ARE most probably your initial concern, don't stop there. Most college admissions officers know about homeschoolers, but many still know little about home education. With no hands-on experience with homeschooling, the typical questions arise in their minds.

- ✦ What about socialization?
- ✦ What experience does this applicant have as a team player and working in groups?
- ✦ Can this applicant handle a classroom environment?
- ✦ What leadership skills has the applicant displayed?

Ruth, whose daughter was admitted to Calvin College and Hillsdale College (MI), explains, "Although our daughter is very bright, her scholarship applications were limited by her lack of extracurricular activities. She applied for many noncollege scholarships. Nevertheless, she received only one such award. Almost all her activities were church-related, which does not seem to impress the decision-making scholarship people."

Ruth continues, "In addition, our daughter is not sports-oriented. And she had little true leadership experience to list, although she does possess leadership qualities. Unfortunately, during her high school years, we lived on the Michigan Upper Peninsula, where opportunities were limited. We now live in a town forty-five minutes from Pittsburgh. Life here is much more varied for my younger two children. They will have a lot more activities to list on college and scholarship applications."

If you live in a remote area, you will have to be creative and help your teenager actively seek group learning and leadership experiences. Volunteering fills the gap for many. Consider libraries, hospitals, retirement homes, radio and television stations, government agencies, charitable organizations, and churches.

Whether you live in a large city, suburb, small town, or rural remote area, our survey respondents provide interesting suggestions as they recount their teenagers' activities.

> If you live in a remote area, you will have to be creative and help your teenager actively seek group learning and leadership experiences.

"Our daughter took classes at the community college (three years of French, calculus, physics, ecology lab)," writes Judy. "She participated in a number of programs through the local center for the arts (Shakespearean theater and creative writing). She was on a gymnastics team and served in a variety of leadership positions, from team captain to a fund-raising one that involved coordinating the parents."

Judy's daughter's other activities include the following:

- ✦ planning and organizing activities for homeschooled teens
- ✦ coaching a younger MathCounts team
- ✦ participating in 4-H and a number of clubs that involved working in groups, including a creative writing club in which the students wrote, published, and sold a choose-your-own-adventure-style book

Liz and Nathan, unschoolers who live in Connecticut, describe their son's class, group, and leadership activities: "He took a few classes at museums, arts-and-crafts centers, and origami conventions. He apprenticed and then taught at the Eli Whitney Museum, which offers workshops, classes, and summer camps relating to science and technology. He also took classes through our town's adult education program—calligraphy, conversational French, and photography."

Denise lists her son's homeschool experiences:

+ About 40 credits at the community college

+ Membership in many homeschooling clubs

+ Internship at the Naval Observatory

+ Job as an explainer at the Smithsonian's Air and Space Museum

+ Organization of a homeschool basketball team

+ Coediting a homeschooling yearbook

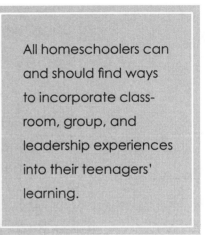

All homeschoolers can and should find ways to incorporate classroom, group, and leadership experiences into their teenagers' learning.

These examples present just a few ideas. All homeschoolers can and should find ways to incorporate classroom, group, and leadership experiences into their teenagers' learning. The activities, together with exposure to appropriate academic materials, will create a wonderful database from which you can create impressive documentation for college applications.

SIMPLE STARTING POINTS

+ If independent-study programs interest you, visit their Web sites and call them to obtain descriptive brochures.

+ Brainstorm! Talk to your teenagers about their interests and goals and plan related educational activities. Discuss with your teenager creative ways to fill "holes."

+ Help your teens choose activities that demonstrate leadership ability. Often homeschoolers need to begin an activity at midschool level to rise to a leadership position by ages 15 to 18.

✦ List possible classroom experiences for your teenager in your community. These need not be at a high school or college. Many private agencies and community education programs offer interesting classes.

RESOURCES

High School Scope and Sequence Resources

A Beka Books Scope and Sequence Nursery through Grade Twelve: 800-874-BEKA: http://www.abeka.com/ABB/Resources/98-9ScpSeq.pdf

Science Scope and *Guides to History* by Kathryn Stout, Design-A-Study, 408 Victoria Ave., Wilmington, DE 19804: http://www.designastudy.com

Standard US Homeschool Curriculum: http://www.euschool.com/curric1.html

Trivium Suggested Course of Study: http://www.muscanet.com/~trivium/ttt/tttsuggested.html

Utah State Core Curriculum: http://www.uen.org/cgi-bin/websql/utahlink/CoreHome.hts

"World Book Encyclopedia Typical Course of Study Kindergarten through Grade 12" by William H. Nault, 800-621-8202: http://www.worldbook.com/EduGuide/vjs/curr.html (under "Educational Resource and Curriculum Suppliers")

Educational Resources and Curriculum Suppliers

Elijah Company, 888-2-ELIJAH: http://www.elijahco.com

Fun Books, 888-FUN-7020: http://www.fun-books.com

Heart of Wisdom Publishing, 800-BOOKLOG: http://www.heartofwisdom.com

John Holt's Book and Music Store, 617-864-3100: http://www
.holtgws.com

Lifetime Books and Gifts, 800-377-0390: http://www.lifetimeonline
.com

Books on Planning High School at Home

Cohen, Cafi. *Homeschooling: the Teen Years: Your Complete Guide to Successfully Homeschooling the 13- to 18-Year-Old.* Prima Publishing, 2000.

Duffy, Cathy. *The Christian Home Educators' Curriculum Manual.* Grove Publishing, 2000.

Llewellyn, Grace. *The Teenage Liberation Handbook: How to Quit School and Get a Real Life and Education.* Lowry House, 1998.

McAlister, Diana, and Candice Oneschak. *Homeschooling the High Schooler,* Volumes 1 and 2. Family Academy Publications, 146 SW 153rd #289, Seattle, WA 98166.

Pride, Mary. *The Big Book of Home Learning,* Volume 3, Junior High through College. Alpha Omega Publication, 1999.

Shelton, Barbara. *Senior High: A Home-Designed Form+U+la.* Homeschool Seminars and Publications, 182 N. Columbia Heights Rd., Longview, WA 98632.

Independent Study Programs

Abbington Hills School, 732-892-4475: http://www.abbingtonhills
.com

Academy of Home Education, 864-242-5100, ext. 2047: http:
//www.bju.edu/ministries/acad_home_ed/index/html

Alger Learning Center, Independence High School, 800-595-2630: http://www.independent-learning.com

Alpha-Omega Academy, 800-682-7396: http://www.homeschooling
.com/Academy.htm

Alpha-Omega Academy Online, 877-688-2652: http://www
.switched-onschoolhouse.com/aoao/index/html

American School, 708-418-2800 or 800-531-9268: http://www.itt
.edu/~american

Branford Grove School, 818-890-0350: http://www.branfordgrove
.com

Brigham Young University Independent Study High School, 801-
378-2868: http://coned.byu.edu/is

Cambridge Academy, 800-252-3777: http://www.home-school.com
/Mall/Cambridge/CambridgeAcad.html

Christa McAuliffe Academy, 509-575-4989: http://www
.cmacademy.org

Christian Liberty Academy Satellite Schools, 800-348-0899: http:
//www.homeschools.org

Chrysalis School, Inc., 425-481-2228: http://www.chrysalis-school
.com

Citizens' High School, 904-276-1700: http://www.citizenschool
.com

Clonlara Home Based Education Program and Clonlara Compu-
High, 313-769-4515: http://www.clonlara.org

Crossroads Christian School, 850-423-1291: http://www
.crossroadschristianschool.com

Dennison Online Internet School, 323-662-3226: http://www
.dennisononline.com

Eagle Christian School, 888-EAGLE4U: http://www.eaglechristian
.org

Harcourt High School, 800-275-4409: http://www.Harcourt-
learning.com/programs/diploma

HCL Boston School, 909-585-7188: http://www.bostonschool.org

Hewitt Homeschooling Resources, 800-348-1750: http://www
.homeeducation.org

Home Study International, 800-782-4769: http://www.hsi.edu

ICS Newport/Pacific High School, 800-238-9525, ext. 7496: http:
//www.icslearn.com/ICS/courses.htm

Indiana University High School, 800-334-1011: http://www.scs.
Indiana.edu

Institute for the Study of the Liberal Arts and Sciences (includes Scholars' Online Academy and Regina Coeli Academy), 520-751-1942: http://www.islas.org

Internet Academy, 253-945-2004: http://www.iacademy.org

Keystone National High School, 800-255-4937: http://www.keystonehighschool.com

Kolbe Academy, 707-255-6499: http://www.community.net/~kolbe

Laurel Springs High School, 800-377-5890: http://www.laurelsprings.com

Malibu Cove Private School, 805-446-1917: http://www.seascapecenter.com

North Atlantic Regional High School, 800-882-2828, ext. 16, or 207-777-1700, ext. 16: http://homeschoolassociates.com/NARS

North Dakota Division of Independent Study: http://www.dis.dpi.state.nd.us

NorthStar Academy, 888-464-6280: http://www.northstar-academy.org

Oak Meadow School, 802-387-2021: http://www.oakmeadow.com

Phoenix Academies, 602-674-5555 or 800-426-4952: http://www.phoenixacademis.org

Royal Academy, 207-657-2800: http://www.homeeducator.com/HEFS/royalacademy.htm

School of Tomorrow, 800-925-7777: http://www.schooloftomorrow.com

Seton Home Study School, 540-636-9990: http://www.setonhome.org

St. Thomas Aquinas Academy, 209-599-0665: http://www.staa-homeschool.com

Summit Christian Academy, 800-362-9180 or 972-602-8050: http://www.scahomeschool.com

Sycamore Tree, 949-650-4466: http://www.sycamoretree.com

Texas Tech University Division of Continuing Education, 800-692-6877, ext. 320: http://www.dce.ttu.edu

University of Missouri–Columbia High School, 573-884-2620: http://cdis.missouri.edu/MUHighSchool/HSHome.htm

University of Nebraska, Lincoln Independent Study High School, 402-472-4321: http://www.dcs.unl.edu/disted

University of Texas at Austin High School Diploma Program, 512-232-1872: http://www.utexas.edu/cee/dec/diploma

Westbridge Academy, 773-743-3312: http://www.flash.net/~wx3o/westbridge

Willoway Academy, 610-678-0214: http://www.willoway.com

4

SHOPPING FOR COLLEGES

In This Chapter

✦ Matching college to your student

✦ Homeschooling college

✦ The lay of the land

✦ Colleges of special interest to homeschoolers

✦ Simple starting points

✦ Resources

© EyeWire

"[Homeschoolers] face a dilemma when choosing a college or university for further study. Will the college continue to foster the same love of learning? Will the curriculum challenge [their] thinking in new and exciting ways?"

—Barbara Henry, in "Helping Homeschoolers Go to College," *Home Education Magazine,* May–June 1999

*I*T'S A JUNGLE out there. Big and small colleges. Liberal and conservative campuses. Specialty and general-purpose schools. Public and private universities. Religious and secular institutions. Competitive and open-admissions schools. Campuses nearby and thousands of miles away. College at home. Choices are overwhelming and intimidating. You, like most homeschooling families, justifiably wonder how to sort them out.

College-placement firms, admissions counselors, and parents and students who have negotiated college admissions all agree. "Don't look for the best college," they advise. "Instead, find a college that offers the best fit." Does your homeschooler want to study piano performance? Locate fine arts schools and liberal arts colleges with good music programs. Are finances a major concern? Check first with community colleges and several free-tuition institutions. Is your homeschooler planning a military career? Put schools with ROTC programs at the top of your list.

In this chapter we will review important considerations for choosing colleges. You'll read, from the trenches, descriptions from our survey respondents of how their teenagers decided where to apply. We also include a discussion of homeschooling college—online or via correspondence—should you wish to continue homeschooling after high school.

MATCHING COLLEGE TO YOUR STUDENT

SEAN CALLAWAY—author of articles on homeschoolers and college admissions for the National Association of College Admissions Counselors—says that college admission is a two-step process. Step one is getting in. Step two is finding money. Finding a good college fit for your student helps with both steps. Your homeschooler has the best chance of admission when you make good matches.

TYPES OF COLLEGES

✦ Community and junior college (two-year schools that grant associates of arts degrees)

✦ Liberal arts colleges (four-year schools that grant bachelor's degrees; "liberal arts" means academic disciplines—such as languages, literature, philosophy, mathematics, and science—that provide information of general cultural concern)

✦ Universities (usually teaching and research facilities that award bachelor's, master's, and doctoral degrees—sometimes it's tough to tell colleges from universities)

✦ Agricultural and technical colleges

✦ Art and music colleges

✦ Bible colleges

✦ Business colleges

✦ Colleges of health science

✦ Engineering colleges

✦ Military colleges

✦ Seminary and rabbinical colleges

✦ Teachers' colleges

Similarly, best-fit schools will offer your teenager the most attractive financial aid packages.

To match your homeschooler with appropriate colleges, you will want to consider each of the following checklist items:

✦ Accessibility—that is, openness to accepting homeschoolers

✦ Size

✦ Distance from home

- ✦ Setting
- ✦ Educational philosophy
- ✦ Majors offered
- ✦ Cost
- ✦ Special programs (sports, ROTC, on-campus religious clubs, internships)
- ✦ Special needs (dietary, climate, accommodations for learning and physical disabilities)

Finding the best fit means first deciding what items matter most. How important to you and your teen are location, educational philosophy, majors, size, and other factors? Below, we discuss each of these items and the impact they will have on your homeschooler's college experience. Do not interpret the order of presentation as a suggested order of importance; you set that. To emphasize the point, take a minute right now to rearrange the above list in order of most to least important.

Accessibility to Homeschoolers

Don't think handicapped access here (that is further down). Instead, consider colleges' accessibility, their homeschool-friendliness quotient, their warmth and enthusiasm when you approach them. How welcoming are they?

> Consider colleges' accessibility, their homeschool-friendliness quotient, their warmth and enthusiasm when you approach them.

Sean Sullivan, homeschooled through high school, graduated from Amherst College (MA), having completed three majors: astronomy, computer science, and a self-designed interdisciplinary major. As described on his Web site, he used one question to sort out colleges: "How should I apply?" Not surprisingly, he got a variety of responses. On the "friendly" side, the University of California at Berkeley (CA) asked him to ignore the application pages that asked about high school. Cornell University (NY) said, "Why did you call us about this? Please just send the application." On the "unfriendly" side, the University of Wisconsin requested copies of the tables of contents of every book he had read. Asking for the tables of contents of every one of the hundreds (thousands?) of books this unschooler had read was—at the least—an unreasonable request.

"The way colleges handled homeschooling served as a test for me," Sullivan explains. Every homeschooler should consider ruling colleges in or out based on their admissions policies. Remember that the vast majority of colleges treat homeschoolers equitably (see chapter 1). As Sullivan points out, the few colleges that present serious roadblocks will probably end up being a poor fit anyway.

> Every homeschooler should consider ruling colleges in or out based on their admissions policies.

Judy says that homeschool friendliness was a primary consideration for her daughter, who won admission to the Virginia Polytechnics honors program. She explains, "Our daughter did not apply to several very fine schools, because they could not or would not agree that forty credits at the community college demonstrated her ability. She completely opposed taking the GED or SAT II Subject Tests."

Size

While it may not seem important on paper, the size of a college or university can make a big difference. Smaller schools, those with fewer than two thousand students, usually offer more individual attention and better student–faculty ratios. Some homeschoolers prefer the accountability and family-like atmosphere most often found on small campuses. No one blends into the crowd. Teachers notice every absence.

Sara, who describes her homeschooling approach as "curriculum-centered," says size was a major factor in college selection. She writes, "The main requirement for our daughters' colleges were that they be private Christian colleges. After that, we preferred small colleges." Her daughters applied to Samford University (AL), 2,800 undergraduates; University of Mobile (AL), 1,700 undergraduates; and Mississippi College (MS), 2,400 undergraduates.

At larger schools (two thousand to seven thousand students) and mega-schools (more than seven thousand students), teachers may never notice absences. Students on these city-sized campuses say they have to take more responsibility and act more aggressively to get what they want. At many large state universities, the best piece of advice for freshmen is "Find a club or other social niche, or you will be lost."

> Attending a geographically distant school can add $1,000 each year to your college bills.

On the plus side, larger schools offer more majors, sports, extracurricular activities, accommodations for learning disabilities, and special programs, such as internships and ROTC. Those students beginning college without definite plans will see this as an advantage. And those with special circumstances, such as handicapping conditions and learning disabilities, may find large schools can better meet their needs.

Distance from Home

Homeschooling families usually think carefully about location. First there are economic considerations. Any college away from home will incur room and board charges that will add from $3,000 to $8,000 per year to college costs. To that, append travel charges. Your homeschooler may attend college two hundred miles away—a half-day's drive. Some students move more than five hundred miles away, in which case airfares increase monetary outlay. Two or more trips home per year will impact any family budget. Attending a geographically distant school can add $1,000 each year to your college bills.

To increase their range of experience, some homeschoolers prefer distant schools regardless of costs. Southerners want to live where it snows, and Californians want to see how East Coasters live. These homeschoolers see colleges in other areas in much the same way they would view a trip to Europe— as an educational bonus.

Setting

College campuses are everywhere—in big cities, suburban areas, small towns, and out in the countryside. Setting definitely affects students and quality of life on campus. Some people love the life in large cities and point out that metropolitan areas provide opportunities unavailable in rural areas. Colleges in big towns may have an easier time placing students in internships and paying jobs.

MONEY SAVER

Include campus visits on family vacations beginning when your homeschooler is age 13 or 14. This may eliminate expensive special trips to tour campuses the summer after your teenager's junior year.

Others students like the quieter pace found in small college towns, like Yellow Springs, home of Antioch College in Ohio. Back-to-nature and hiking enthusiasts will prefer campuses in forested, mountainous areas, like Humboldt State University on the northern California coast.

Certain environments may beckon your teenager. Tara, a homeschool graduate, says, "Agnes Scott College (GA) is a place of such beauty. When I first saw the campus, everything about it spoke to me. The school nests among huge magnolia trees in Atlanta. With its large East Coast brick buildings, it resembles a mini-Harvard."

Climate considerations may also enter into preferences. Certain students will not do well in very warm or very cold regions. Depression-prone personalities should avoid areas where the sun never seems to shine.

> Always, prospective students should ask not only "Is this the right school?" but also "Is this the right place? Do I want to live *here* for four years?"

Always, prospective students should ask not only "Is this the right school?" but also "Is this the right place? Do I want to live *here* for four years?"

Educational Philosophy

Colleges and universities communicate educational philosophy in their view book, a promotional brochure designed to sell you on the school. In a view book, you will see gorgeous photos of the campus taken on the prettiest day of the year. You will also read the school's mission statement, which usually describes educational approaches, goals, and target student population. Similar information appears at most college and university Web sites.

The phrasing you see in view books and on Web sites can help you determine whether a school is a good match from an educational perspective. Check out these excerpts from the Web sites of several colleges around the country:

Rhodes College (TN)
+ "small, friendly college with talented, accessible professors"
+ "highly competitive liberal arts"
+ "metropolitan location provides a wide range of internship and job opportunities"

Colorado College (CO)
+ "students are independent and individualistic"
+ "ranks 4th among small colleges in current Peace Corps volunteers"
+ "we require all students to live on campus for three years"

Wheaton College (IL)
+ "private, interdenominational Christian school"
+ "promote the development of whole and effective Christians"

✦ "the curriculum is informed with solid, well-articulated
   values"

University of Virginia (VA)
✦ "students and faculty who take seriously their commitment
   to their community and their world"
✦ "public school, highly selective"
✦ "a rich collection of traditions"

Of course, three statements cannot begin to adequately represent any college. Nevertheless, applying these statements to your situation, you can see how easy it is to rule schools in or out with just a little knowledge of their goals and practices. Kara in Georgia, who

HOW WE DID IT

We researched schools at the library, wrote for catalogs to preview majors and programs, attended local "college nights," visited a number of campuses for tours, and wrote to deans of admissions and heads of various departments. We looked for good liberal arts programs as well as strong engineering and technical programs to accommodate our daughter's disparate interests.

We visited a variety of schools over the years—large and small, rural and urban, and so on. Our first visits were informal and not associated with the admissions process (as part of gymnastics competitions and as part of travel with her father when he attended conferences). On a more serious basis, we visited about a dozen campuses during our daughter's junior year and the summer prior to her senior year.

As the parents, we merely were looking for a good match for the emotional and educational needs of our daughter.

—JUDY IN VIRGINIA

HOMESCHOOL GRADS SAY

All of the colleges I finally applied to were small and within driving distance of home. After visiting several colleges, I was impressed by the atmosphere of academic excellence and the strong liberal arts core at Hillsdale (MI). Hillsdale emphasizes the classical Western tradition, a foundation I thought would be helpful.

Hillsdale's art department and fine arts building are outstanding for a college of its size. Hillsdale teaches classical techniques in traditional media rather than the expression of one's feelings or creativity—exactly what I wanted. Finally, I liked that there are so many Christian professors at Hillsdale and that the Christian student groups are so alive and active. This especially stood out in comparison with some of the Christian colleges I visited, where faith seemed to be taken for granted, without much enthusiasm.

—KARENA, A SOPHOMORE AT HILLSDALE COLLEGE,
HOMESCHOOLED FROM GRADES 2 THROUGH 12

has been homeschooling her four children since the 1980s, comments, "The brochure from Rose-Hulman Institute of Technology (IN) was especially captivating, as it advertised the engineering school 'for those who take their tinker toys seriously.' Now, that really got our attention."

Kara continues: "We sought small, academic colleges, respected in their fields and teaching according to the interests of our children. Our son had won the Illinois Westinghouse Science Talent Search Competition. Very creative, he needed a project-based school full of students like him. Some schools, very theory-oriented and teaching by sequential methods, would have been mismatches."

Competitiveness

Want to hear a well-kept secret? A majority of applicants get into most colleges and universities.

Sure, places such as MIT (MA), Harvard University (MA), Rice University (TX), Stanford (CA), and West Point (NY) take only one out of every six to ten applicants. Amazingly, though—and all advertising to the contrary—only about a hundred schools nationwide admit under 50 percent of their applicants.

The remainder—more than three thousand colleges and universities in the United States—admit more than half of all those who apply. Some colleges—Wilmington College (DE), Emporia State University (KS), and Bluefield State College (WV), for example— admit everybody. In addition, almost all two-year community colleges practice open admissions.

HOW WE DID IT

We were fortunate in that both of our children had a good idea of what they wanted to study, and that made the selection process easier. Our son wanted a good business program at a school with a good Chinese program. Both of our children wanted to stay in the Midwest. We looked at all sizes of colleges.

Initially our son thought he would prefer a small college, but my husband and I encouraged him to consider a large college that would offer greater options for experiencing the variety the world has to offer.

We started our search with standard college guides such as Peterson's. We also used the Web, attended college fairs, and talked a lot to people who had recently graduated from various colleges.

—SERENA IN OHIO

HOMESCHOOL GRADS SAY

I looked into several Catholic schools with a classical emphasis. When I visited Thomas Aquinas College (CA), I got excited about the whole package. The tutors and students were genuinely interested in what they were studying. There was a certain camaraderie, because everyone knew each other and studied the same materials. The college's Catholicity did not prevent open and intellectually honest discussions of everything.

—ALEXA, WHO GRADUATED FROM THOMAS AQUINAS COLLEGE (CA)

For most homeschoolers, college selectivity will not be an issue. If your teenager will be applying to a competitive school, however, you will want to make a good match between his standardized test scores (SAT I or ACT) and the average SAT scores of those admitted the previous year. Find standardized-test-score information in college view books and catalogs and on their Web sites. Many report a twenty-fifth to seventy-fifth percentile range for the SAT. Generally, to match your homeschooler's abilities to the challenges at any given school, you will want to assure that her scores fall in that range.

Majors and Programs of Study

Some homeschoolers know exactly what they want to study at college. Others have no idea; they figure they will start and eventually pursue whatever catches their interest.

If your teen finds himself in the first camp, you will, of course, identify colleges that offer programs in his field. Future physicians and engineers will look for good science programs. Those who want to learn to fly will compete for spaces at the United States Air Force and Naval Academies. Some homeschoolers will want the logical-thinking and writing skills imparted by colleges that offer great books programs—schools like Reed College (OR) and St. John's College (NM).

Finding colleges with appropriate majors is not as difficult as you might think. Visit your library's college reference section, and check out Barron's *Profiles of American Colleges* and similar reference books. In the front or back index, they will list colleges by major. For popular majors, such as nursing, you will find hundreds of listings. For something less common, such as oceanography, there may be only ten to twenty schools nationwide. Several Web sites offer a match-to-college-major feature. Also, check out the end-of-chapter Resources.

Homeschoolers who cannot choose a major field of study will want to focus more on educational philosophy than on particular programs of study. They should find a school with a comfortable approach that offers a reasonable selection of degree fields and avoid specialized engineering, business, or arts schools.

Students who cannot decide on a major are among those most likely *not* to return for their sophomore year. Parents of these undecided students should note the factors that *U.S. News and World Report's* "America's Best Colleges" issue says increase the percentage

HOMESCHOOL GRADS SAY

I chose my college because it was small, it was near Boston, it had a well-known design school, and, frankly, the Web site was of adequate construction. Just as a writer wouldn't go to a school that couldn't spell, a designer wouldn't go to a school that couldn't keep up with modern design on its Web site.

—DANIEL, WHO NOW ATTENDS MOUNT IDA COLLEGE (MA)

of freshmen who return for their sophomore year. Retention rates are best at the following:

+ smaller colleges
+ schools with a large percentage of full-time freshmen
+ schools where most freshmen live on campus
+ more-selective schools

Special Programs

Increasingly, colleges offer programs that few people fifty years ago would have ever conceived. Examples are accommodations for learning-disabled students, internships, credit for work experience, three-year baccalaureate degrees, pass/fail options, student-designed and general-studies majors, block scheduling (one course at a time), foreign exchanges, exotic sports like fencing, and military programs such as Reserve Officer Training Corps (ROTC).

Certainly, as you preview colleges, you will want to ask about special programs. In some cases the presence or absence of a special program will help you rule a college in or out.

Cost

Most of our survey respondents say that cost matters. Interestingly, none—even those on tight budgets—say that it has to be the first consideration for choosing colleges. They subscribe to the maxim "Make a good match and the money will follow."

Leo and Penny, who have homeschooled three children since 1987, write, "Our son chose his college mostly for its excellent music department and its nearness to home. The following factors were important to all of us: major and instructors, scholarship opportunity, cost, and location."

Cost is important, but it need not be a determining factor. Many private colleges whose tuition costs would seem to put them out of

GREAT DEALS

These colleges offer either free tuition or all expenses paid—usually in connection with a student work or service obligation:

✦ Berea College
Berea, KY
800-326-5948
www.berea.edu

✦ College of the Ozarks
Point Lookout, MO
800-222-0525
www.cofo.edu

✦ Cooper Union for the
Advancement of Science
and Art
New York, NY
212-353-4120
www.cooper.edu

✦ Deep Springs College
Dyer, CA
760-872-2000
www.deepsprings.edu

✦ United States Air Force
Academy
USAF Academy, CO
800-443-9266
www.usafa.af.mil

✦ United States Coast
Guard Academy
New London, CT
800-883-8724
www.cga.edu

✦ United States Merchant
Marine Academy
Kings Point, NY
516-773-5391
www.usmma.edu

✦ United States Military
Academy
West Point, NY
914-938-4041
www.usma.edu

✦ United States Naval
Academy
Annapolis, MD
410-293-4361
www.nadn.navy.mil

reach offer generous aid packages. Some families—after examining financial aid awards—find that private-college costs do not exceed those at public colleges and universities.

Marina in Wyoming, whose daughter won substantial scholarships to Franciscan University (OH) and University of Dallas (TX), relates, "We all agreed that religious affiliation was the most important factor. Since we live in a somewhat isolated area, we knew our daughter would have to leave for college. In the end, after comparing the costs and scholarship awards, they all cost about the same."

Encouragingly, Kate in South Dakota, whose son left home to attend Dordt College in Iowa, writes, "Our son did a good job selecting his school. Although we certainly do not have a lot of money, I never let money be a factor. Between my part-time salary and what my son earns, we have been able to pay for everything as it is due—no debts for him or us."

No one should overlook the fabulous opportunities available through local two-year community colleges. Homeschooling mom Viola explains, "On one income, with six children, we have to carefully consider all college costs. My personal history has made me a firm believer in the community college system. As a bright high school student who did extremely poorly on the SAT, I was told I would not succeed in college. I then decided to go to Long Beach City College, in California, which had great instructors who cared about me. Ultimately, I went on to other universities and obtained my master's degree at age 22. Since then I have earned eight teaching credentials and about a hundred postgraduate credits toward a doctorate. It was all due to the community college I attended."

Chapter 12 contains further discussion on minimizing expenses and applying for financial aid.

> Many private colleges whose tuition costs would seem to put them out of reach offer generous aid packages.

Special Needs

Location, setting, educational philosophy, majors, cost, and more—it seems like a lot to consider. In addition, some parents also have to think about special needs.

Daniela, an eclectic homeschooling mom in Wisconsin, writes, "Most important to us were educational philosophy and major offered, since our son wants a pre-seminary degree. Size and location were next. We also had to consider needs related to chronic illness (severe asthma and allergy) and associated environmental and dietary restrictions."

Some families inquire first about facilities and programs for learning-disabled and physically challenged students. Often college view books and other promotional materials do not address how wheelchair-bound students get around or whether the college makes special provisions for dyslexic students. Plan to inquire first about those concerns that apply to your situation.

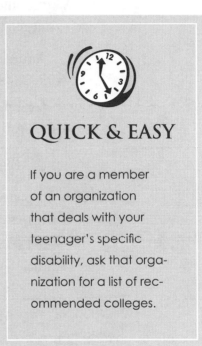

QUICK & EASY

If you are a member of an organization that deals with your teenager's specific disability, ask that organization for a list of recommended colleges.

HOMESCHOOLING COLLEGE

ALTHOUGH MOST HOMESCHOOLERS still attend traditional two- and four-year colleges, some have begun to investigate homeschooling college—either via correspondence or on-line. Cynthia in Saudi Arabia tells us that she did not initially consider homeschooling higher education for her daughter. "Now," she writes, "my daughter is looking into distance learning for a bachelor's degree in early childhood education or child psychology. Possibilities are the University of Pennsylvania and the University of Maryland."

Daniela says that they considered homeschooling college for the first year, completing basic core requirements with subsequent transfer to a residential college. She explains, "We would have used University of Wisconsin Extension and earned credits through the College Level Examination Program (CLEP)." Instead, Daniela's daughter decided she wanted an on-campus experience. She now attends Concordia College (WI).

Why should families consider homeschooling all or part of college? College-at-homers list the following reasons:

✦   Natural extension of home education. As one mother put it, "It's worked well to this point. Why quit?"

✦   Flexibility. Class and study time fit around activities, travel plans, and work schedules.

✦   Techno-advantages. Distance education offers a computer-mediated interface that some students find attractive. If you have a teen who prefers working via computer, he may want to consider one of the many college on-line programs.

✦   Reducing college costs. Although not free, college-at-home can be much less expensive than traditional college.

> Although most homeschoolers still attend traditional two- and four-year colleges, some have begun to investigate homeschooling college—either via correspondence or on-line.

William A. Draves, president of the Learning Resources Network, writes, "In the twenty-first century, on-line learning will constitute 50 percent of all learning and education." Never think that anyone will see college-at-home as second-rate. Instead, distance learning and on-line education are the wave of the future.

To investigate college-at-home possibilities, begin right outside your front door. Query nearby public and private colleges about their independent-study and distance-learning options. To find programs nationwide, check out the books and Web sites recommended in the Resources.

THE LAY OF THE LAND

NOW THAT YOU have some idea what to look for in colleges, you need to know where to look. Fortunately, most information is free—right at your fingertips, in fact, if you have a computer. (If you don't have a computer at home, use the one at your library.)

Begin by visiting college-search Web sites. These allow you to search by major, location, size, and a number of other parameters. If you prefer books, visit your library and begin with the large college handbooks on the reference shelves.

Once you have a list of interesting colleges, your homeschooler should e-mail, call, or write to them for informational brochures, application, and financial aid materials. Review these materials carefully together and discuss what you read. Create a folder for each college of interest and begin a list of questions for admissions personnel.

Eventually homeschoolers should narrow their choices to something in the neighborhood of three to six colleges to which they will formally apply. Although you can research and rule out colleges in a week's time right before your teenager completes his applications, many admissions officers recommend starting early—the ninth-grade year, if possible.

COLLEGES OF SPECIAL INTEREST TO HOMESCHOOLERS

THE COLLEGES that follow are those that have proven themselves—in one way or another—to be worth a look.

✦ Antioch College (OH and CA)
  Yellow Springs, OH
  937-767-7331; 800-543-9436

Santa Barbara, CA
805-962-8179
http://college.antioch.edu

Co-op program. All students spend half their time on campus, half their time working in the real world.

✦ Bard College
Annandale-on-Hudson, NY
914-758-7472
http://www.bard.edu

Highly individualized programs. SAT optional.

✦ Colorado College
Colorado Springs, CO
719-389-6344; 800-542-7214
http://www.cc.colorado.edu

Block plan scheduling. Students take one class at a time for three to four weeks and move on to the next class.

✦ DigiPen Institute of Technology
Redmond, WA, and Vancouver, BC
425-558-0299
http://www.digipen.edu

New college offering associate's and bachelor's degrees for video game programmers and 3-D computer animators.

✦ Drury College
Springfield, MO
417-865-8731; 800-922-2274
http://www.drury.edu

Church-affiliated school. Three-year baccalaureate degree for some majors; traditional academics; reasonably priced.

✦ Evergreen State College
Olympia, WA

360-866-6000

http://www.evergreen.edu

Seminars, original works, no textbooks. No grades. Evaluation with portfolio assessments.

✦ George Wythe College
Cedar City, UT
435-586-6570
http://www.gwc.edu

New college specifically designed to train statesmen and leaders for the twenty-first century. Bachelor's, master's, and doctoral degrees.

✦ Goddard College
Plainfield, VT
802-454-8311;
800-468-4888
http://www.goddard.edu

No SAT or ACT required. No grades or exams. Classes are small discussion groups. Appeals to creative, independent students.

✦ Grove City College
Grove City, PA
724-458-2100
http://www.gcc.edu

Competitive, spiritual, academic school. Reasonably priced.

✦ Hampshire College
Amherst, MA
413-559-5471
http://www.hampshire.edu

No tests, grades, credits, or majors. Instead papers, self- and teacher-evaluations, and concentrations. SAT not required.

✦ Kettering University
(was GMI Engineering and Management Institute)
Flint, MI
800-955-4464
http://www.gmi.edu

Students alternate academic and on-the-job semesters at this conservative business/engineering school.

✦ Landmark College
Putney, VT
802-387-6718
http://www.landmarkcollege.org

Two-year college. Programs designed specifically to meet the needs of learning-disabled students and those with ADHD.

✦ New College of the University of South Florida
Sarasota, FL
941-359-4269
http://www.newcollege.usf.edu

Intense academics. Students design their own courses of study. Written evaluations, no grades. Inexpensive.

✦ Oglethorpe University
Atlanta, GA
800-428-4484, ext. 8443
http://www.oglethorpe.edu

Small liberal arts college in big city. Good balance of small class sizes and top-quality professors.

✦ Patrick Henry College
Purcellville, VA
540-338-1776
http://www.phu.edu

Accepted first students in 2000. Bible-centered, academically rigorous education and related apprenticeships.

✦ Rose-Hulman Institute of Technology
Terre Haute, IN
812-877-1511; 800-878-7448
http://www.rose-hulman.edu

Engineering and science school. Integrated curriculum first two years combining all subjects into a single course.

✦ St. John's College (MD and NM)
Annapolis, MD
410-263-2371; 800-727-9238
Santa Fe, NM
505-984-6000; 800-331-5232
http://www.sjca.edu

One college, two campuses. Classical, structured curriculum based on the great books of Western civilization; discussion-oriented classes.

✦ Simon's Rock College
Great Barrington, MA
413-528-7317; 800-235-7186
http://www.simons-rock.edu

Four-year college wholly devoted to early admission. Most students enroll after completing tenth or eleventh grade.

✦ Thomas Aquinas College
Santa Paula, CA
800-634-9797
http://www.thomasaquinas.edu

Great books curriculum, no lectures, no tests. All material taught in small tutorials.

✦ Thomas Edison State College
Trenton, NJ
609-984-1150
http://www.tesc.edu

Grants credit via portfolio review, CLEP, and classes taken elsewhere. Leader in distance learning. Offers video and on-line courses

SIMPLE STARTING POINTS

✦   Note how your homeschooled teenager spends his free time. Many leisure interests and extracurricular activities translate into college majors.

✦   Call your local colleges—even if they are not of particular interest to your homeschooler—and see if he can take a tour and visit classes. This experience will inform his investigations of more distant colleges.

✦   Ask neighbors, friends, relatives, and other homeschoolers for college recommendations.

✦   Attend college fairs in your area. Locate these by calling the counseling offices of nearby high schools. They should be able to give you times and locations. At these fairs, collect view books and talk to admissions personnel about entrance requirements. Note "sales pitch" phrases to help you rule colleges in or out.

RESOURCES

Books for Researching Colleges

Profiles of American Colleges. Barron's Educational Series, 2000.

Custard, Edward T. *The Best 311 Colleges: 2000 Edition.* Princeton Review, 1999.

Fiske, Edward. *The Fiske Guide to Colleges 2000.* Times Books, 1999.

"Your Best College Buys Now," issued annually in the fall by *Money Magazine*; check for it on newsstands.

Web Sites for Researching Colleges

College and University Homepages: http://www.mit.edu:8001/people/cdemello/univ.html

College Choice Website: http://www.gseis.ucla.edu/mm/cc/home.html

Colleges for Homeschoolers: http://www.learninfreedom.org/colleges_4_hmsc.html

Review.com: http://www.review.com

Books on Homeschooling College and Distance Learning

Bear, John, and Mariah Bear. *Bear's Guide to Earning College Degrees Nontraditionally,* 13th edition. Ten Speed Press, 1999.

Bear, John. *College Degrees by Mail and Modem 2000.* Ten Speed Press, 1999.

Criscito, Pat. *Barron's Guide to Distance Learning.* Barron's Educational Series, 1999.

Duffy, James P. *College On-Line: How to Take College Courses without Leaving Home.* John Wiley, 1999.

The Independent-Study Catalog, 7th edition. Peterson's Guides, 1998.

Peterson's Guide to Distance Learning Programs, 2000. Peterson's Guides, 1999: http://www.petersons.com

Web Sites on Homeschooling College and Distance Learning

About.com Distance Learning College Degree Directory: http://distancelearn.about.com

Distance Learning on the Net: Colleges and Universities by Glen Hoyle: http://www.hoyle.com/distance.htm

Part Two

PAPER TRAILS

5

ADMINISTRIVIA:

DOCUMENTATION CHOICES

In This Chapter

✦ Narratives

✦ Reading lists

✦ Table of contents

✦ Logbooks

✦ Résumés

✦ Portfolios

✦ Transcripts

✦ High school profile

✦ Course descriptions

✦ Which documentation?

✦ Simple starting points

✦ Resources

"There's no need to stress too much about the absence of an official high school transcript."

—College Board Web site, http://www.collegeboard.org.

*A*s a homeschool parent, you play many roles. In addition to normal parental roles—breadwinner, caretaker, moral instructor, and role model—you also function as curriculum planner, teacher, resource person, facilitator, and record keeper. When your teenager applies to college, you assume yet another persona. You will become a registrar, somebody who submits reports of high school homeschooling to admissions and financial aid offices and scholarship committees.

Regular high school students find sending transcripts to colleges no more than a minor annoyance. They complete a form, hand it to someone in "the office," and that's it. The high school handles everything, including compiling a summary of the student's academic record and mailing it.

Home educators face a more complex task, beginning with deciding whether or not to write a transcript. Although many homeschoolers apply to college with home-brew transcripts, others—most notably those attending two-year junior colleges—find that test scores or completed application forms suffice. Still others shun transcripts, preferring narratives, portfolios, reading lists, and résumés.

> In the same way that you have customized home education to fit your teenagers, you will be able to choose documentation to show off your homeschoolers to their best advantage.

A lot of work? Yes, it can be, although we will tell you about shortcuts that make the job almost as easy as if your teenager attended school. Is this paperwork hassle a huge disadvantage to homeschooling high school? Amazingly, just the opposite is true.

In the same way that you have customized home education to fit your teenagers, you will be able to choose documentation to show off your homeschoolers to their best advantage. Unlike most schooled students, your teens have not had one-size-fits-all educations. Consequently, one-size-fits-all documentation—transcripts—may not be your best choice. A

HOMESCHOOL GRADS SAY

Many homeschoolers are the type of student colleges seek—bright and self-motivated. The trick is to convince them of this, and a lot of that is in the presentation.

—STEVE, A HOMESCHOOL GRADUATE WHO NOW ATTENDS
MACALESTER COLLEGE IN ST. PAUL, MINNESOTA

narrative or logbook or portfolio may better represent their accomplishments. Even if you choose to do a transcript, you—as the principal and administrator of your own little private school—can decide what to include and how to include it.

Homeschooling parents often discover—to their surprise—that they can competently advise their teenagers and produce impressive documentation. Remember that with respect to college admissions, you have only one or two students to monitor at a time. You know your students, your teenagers, much better than any school counselor could. Your day-to-day intimate involvement with your children's education has superbly outfitted you to guide them and present them in the best light possible. Do not fear this responsibility. Embrace it.

Ruth, a homeschooling mother of three, encourages parents to stay on top of all aspects of the college application process. She writes, "Seventeen- and eighteen- year-olds are too young and inexperienced to negotiate admissions without some adult assistance. Many families we know—homeschooling and public schooling— leave everything up to the child. This is not a good idea. Parents mistakenly trust the process

> Your day-to-day intimate involvement with your children's education has superbly outfitted you to guide them and present them in the best light possible.

HOMESCHOOL GRADS SAY

Homeschoolers need to portray their background in a way that shows admissions officers the outstanding students and good leaders they can be. By spring of your senior year, it's too late to plan new activities. Think ahead while you are still in high school.

—KARENA, SOPHOMORE AT HILLSDALE COLLEGE (MI)

and their child's motivation and understanding. Homeschooling parents are the guidance office and need to function that way."

Documentation is one area where homeschooling parents need to be fully involved. To create adequate documentation, you should have some familiarity with various reports. Read on for overviews of the following formats:

- ✦ Narratives
- ✦ Reading lists
- ✦ Tables of contents of books and textbooks
- ✦ Logbooks
- ✦ Résumés
- ✦ Portfolios
- ✦ Transcripts
- ✦ High school profile
- ✦ Course descriptions

As you learn about the different formats, keep in mind that the lines between them may blur. Some homeschoolers' résumés resemble portfolios. Some portfolios look like transcripts. And some transcripts read more like narratives.

Several sources—including homeschooling mother Alison McKee, author of *From Homeschool to College and Work*—recommend that no matter which format you use, you call your product a transcript. McKee, a lifelong unschooling mom who compiled a portfolio for her son, explains: "[He] was applying for admission to college, [so] we decided that it would be wise to adopt . . . familiar educational terminology; therefore we titled our [portfolio] a 'Narrative Transcript.'"

One of our survey respondents, a homeschooling mother in South Dakota who often advises college applicants, says the same thing: "Whatever you use has to say 'transcript' so the secretary recognizes what it is. After that, it need not resemble a public school transcript." In short, play the game, at least as it relates to naming the document in which you report academic accomplishments.

Also, keep in mind that some families use combinations of documents that best highlight their students' interests, talents, and accomplishments. Julie's son was admitted to Vanderbilt University's Blair School of Music with an honors scholarship in 1998. She writes: "We made a three-tiered transcript:

1. Summary sheet of classes taken each year with grades for the classes he took in school (official transcripts also included in the application)

2. Curriculum page for each year: list of books used and read for all subjects and a brief description of activities

3. Narrative for each year, about one to one-and-a-half pages per year."

Julie continues, "We thought this would be thorough yet allow evaluators to look at a summary first. The curriculum page gave the details, and the narrative personalized our approach and brought the plan to life. It also gave another writing sample. Our son wrote the grades 10 through 12 narratives. I did the ninth grade."

PARENT NARRATIVE

These brief excerpts come from an eleven-page homeschool narrative that covers four years:

"I have guided [my daughter's] studies for over a decade, so my assessment of her academic achievement is about as unbiased as Pygmalion's opinion of Galatea.

"She has done much of the job herself. I'll take credit for providing a rich environment, unflagging support, and the occasional prod, but the bulk of the effort has been her own. . . ."

[High school freshman year – partial excerpt]

"General biology, marine science, cellular biology, botany. I had two strategies for engaging [my daughter] in secondary-level biological studies. One was to have her read from a traditional biology text, *Man and the Natural World*. The other was to assign works by popular authors, including Rachel Carson *(The Sea around Us)* and Lewis Thomas *(The Lives of a Cell)*. Articles on related topics in *National Geographic*, *Natural History*, and *Smithsonian* filled in the gaps. She also participated in a 4-H horticulture project I was leading at the time, in which I stressed basic botanical terminology and concepts. . . .

"Algebra. [My daughter] began her study of algebra eagerly but soon grew frustrated with the prescribed algorithms. 'Why do I have to do all these steps,' she complained, 'when I already know the answer?' We bounced from one textbook to another, hoping to find a congenial spirit in at least one. In the end, we resorted to Cliffs *Math Review for Standardized Tests* with the idea of hitting all the high points in a brief time period.

"All in all, it wasn't a bad stopgap solution. She made rapid progress, grasped the concepts, and felt she was finally getting somewhere. I also bought an algebra computer program, to which she diligently applied herself until quadratic equations had lost their mystery. But it's my opinion that her best grounding in algebraic concepts came disguised in the form of logic puzzles and brainteasers, which she loved. A subscription to *Games* [magazine] kept her well supplied throughout the year."

As you can see, this family's documentation includes a narrative, a reading list, a transcript, and activities list (résumé). Most applicants will not need to generate this much paperwork. One or two documents will suffice. Those applying to high-powered schools and for big scholarship money anywhere should carefully evaluate all the possibilities, though.

NARRATIVES

MY DICTIONARY DEFINES a narrative as "a story or an account, true or fictitious." In reporting home education, your narrative will be a true story, of course.

Narratives can be written either by homeschooled teenagers themselves or by their parents. The accompanying Parent Narrative and Homeschooler Narrative contain excerpts taken from much longer documents, one by a homeschooling mother of three, the second by a senior-high homeschooler, recounting part of his eleventh-grade year.

From our examples, you can see that narratives take time and effort. That is the downside. On the upside, narratives do show both the homeschooling approach and academic details in a seamless manner that may best reflect what you actually did in your home-based program. In addition, certain circumstances—such as applications to highly selective colleges—may dictate writing a short or long narrative to submit together with more standard documentation, like a transcript. We included a short narrative, in the form of a parental cover letter, with our son's college applications.

Do not expect most large state colleges and universities to wade through narratives. These schools make most admissions decisions based on formulas incorporating standardized test scores and grade point averages calculated from transcripts. The narrative format will probably be best received at small, private, competitive liberal arts and specialized colleges, especially those that emphasize writing.

HOMESCHOOLER NARRATIVE

This excerpt comes from "Eleventh Grade Narrative," by a homeschooler admitted to Vanderbilt on a music scholarship.

"This has been my most productive year ever. In music especially I have worked very hard, and the benefits have been enormous. But although music demanded much of my time, I did not neglect my academics.

"In math, I finished the advanced-math book from the Saxon series. This covered elementary functions, trigonometry, advanced algebra, and precalculus. I also enjoyed Math Club with my longtime Math Club friends. During Math Club, we puzzled over ten to fifteen problems and discussed various solutions.

"Science consisted mostly of a study of physics using the PSSC Physics book, *Conceptual Physics,* and *The Chicken from Minsk,* a math and physics puzzle book. My favorite aspect of physics was that it offered new ways to look at the

Examples would be Amherst College (MA), Hampshire College (MA), and St. John's College (MD and NM).

READING LISTS

SAM AND KAY, whose son won a full scholarship to Hope College (MI), cite the following documentation requests they received from college admissions officers:

✦ SAT scores
✦ Reading list
✦ GED

world and explanations of many mind-boggling phenomena. I also continued my volunteer research project at USGS. This entailed testing pH, dissolved oxygen, bacteria, and algae numbers and identifying bacteria, algae, protozoa, and other 'bests' from a local reservoir. Throughout the project, my mentor . . . assisted me with procedures and materials. I also enjoyed weekly Science Club discussions with . . . a microbiologist, computer scientist, and inventor. The discussion group covered potlatches and other anthropological wonders, the development of computers and computers today, genetic engineering (cloning, DNA analysis), and general anatomy.

"United States history was the subject of my historical studies this year. I used a variety of resources and studied the history of our country in detail. I also served as a "fiddling" living history interpreter at Walker Ranch again. I also studied geography of the far side of the planet, namely Asia. I learned how to draw a free-hand map of Asia and southeast Asia."

Easy. Much easier than writing a transcript. Their son took two standardized tests, the SAT and GED. And they submitted his reading list, just authors and titles of books covered. No portfolio. No transcript. Slam dunk.

Many selective schools request reading lists—in addition to transcripts, essays, and test scores. At the same time many non-selective, open-admissions colleges accept reading lists in lieu of transcripts.

Obviously, you can reconstruct reading lists during the college admissions process. We found it far easier, though, to keep a running list. Our two teens just maintained a three-column list on our computer, one column for author, one for title, and a third with a one-to-ten ranking. We never did report the ranking information,

> Even if you keep no other records, consider having your teenagers maintain a reading list.

but our son and daughter liked commenting on books and magazines this way.

Even if you keep no other records, consider having your teenagers maintain a reading list. Include everything—academic and nonacademic reading, fiction and nonfiction, books and newspapers and magazines. You can always edit the list later, omitting unneeded items.

TABLE OF CONTENTS

WHEN YOU ASK some colleges about the documentation they require from homeschoolers, you may hear, "Just send us copies of the tables of contents of all your books." Like making a reading list, photocopying tables of contents does not sound difficult—if your homeschooler confined himself to, say, five to ten textbooks per year.

For school-at-homers and traditional approach home educators, the table of contents approach to documentation may work well. It is easier than doing a transcript or portfolio, and it does give admissions officers some idea of what you have covered. On the downside, the information is not as easy to evaluate as that presented by transcript. If a particular admissions officer requests a reading list, go ahead and comply—especially if your son or daughter is applying to a relatively noncompetitive college, one that admits more than 75 percent of applicants.

Eclectic home educators (who assemble their own programs) and unschoolers (who focus on real-life, student-directed learning) will want to avoid submitting copies of tables of contents of hundreds of books. If you encounter a college admissions officer who suggests sending tables of contents, substitute one or more of the alternative reporting documents—a narrative, reading list, portfolio, transcript, and résumé. He or she will be glad you did.

LOGBOOKS

MOST HOMESCHOOLERS SPEND large portions of their day not with their noses in textbooks but working on hands-on and community-based projects. In *Homeschooling: The Teen Years,* parents list dozens of activities in which their teenagers participate, including running a business, working at paying jobs, playing sports, caring for younger children, participating in youth groups like 4-H, teaching at church, editing newsletters, attending cultural events, playing in community musical groups, and traveling. All these activities are educational. For college applications, all should be documented.

A logbook is one of the easiest "activities" documents to create and perhaps one of the most important, even if admissions officers never see the original log. The College Board Web site explains, "[With a logbook] college admissions officers can see the applicant's learning experiences and the time spent on these activities. This is one area [where] a homeschooler can really stand out from traditional applicants. . . . For example, maybe [he] has volunteered in an animal shelter or visited a number of Impressionist art exhibits. The logbook can show the time and commitment the applicant has devoted to these activities."

> A logbook is one of the easiest "activities" documents to create and perhaps one of the most important, even if admissions officers never see the original log.

What to include in a logbook? The College Board suggests museum visits, field trips, volunteer work, internships, hours logged onto the Internet for educational purposes, and any time spent in any learning experience.

Typically, you would not submit four years of logbook pages with your college applications. A sample week—a productive week—from each year could be useful to admissions officers. If you do not want to include a résumé or more formal activities documentation with your application, representative pages from the logbook should work nicely.

QUICK & EASY

Get a calendar with big boxes for each day. Every morning, have your teenagers log all activities of the previous day.

RESUMES

MOST COLLEGE APPLICATIONS do not ask for a résumé, but homeschoolers should consider sending one anyway—particularly if your student will apply to competitive institutions and colleges that give admissions points for leadership experience.

Application packets from selective colleges often come with an "activities" form. The form will ask how long your homeschooler held a student government office, worked on the yearbook, sang in the choir, and played varsity team sports. Most homeschoolers have to leave these forms almost blank, which creates a poor impression.

As an alternative, you can offer a résumé. Just write "See résumé" in big red letters across the activities form. Remember that most college application activities forms are just that—forms, not requirements. These forms have been created to make things easy for most applicants. They contain check-off boxes for the typical applicant, a student who attends high school.

Homeschoolers have different activities. Different does not mean better or worse, just different. Résumés enable homeschoolers to report information that will not fit on an activities form or a transcript. You can organize a résumé in any way that best highlights your children's accomplishments. In our son's case, these are the résumé sections:

+ Education (total of completed credits in major subject areas) plus in-progress courses and grade point average;

+ Activities (civil air patrol, amateur radio, athletics, volunteering, and miscellaneous, with further listings and brief descriptions in each category);

+ Awards (civil air patrol, scholarships, and miscellaneous).

Your homeschooled teen can write a résumé as a narrative, an outline, or even just a simple list. The actual format does not matter as much as highlighting group learning experiences, leadership activities, and community service.

> Résumés enable homeschoolers to report information that will not fit on an activities form or a transcript.

PORTFOLIOS

ALTHOUGH YOU HEAR lots of talk among homeschoolers about portfolios, probably fewer than five percent of home educators submit this type of documentation with their college applications.

Yes, portfolios are rarely used. Nevertheless, as with résumés, more home educators should consider them. Where other types of documentation "tell," portfolios "show."

Instead of describing research papers in a course description as part of a transcript, you include one of the research papers as part of your portfolio. Rather than tell about your teen's fifty hours of flight time in a single-engine aircraft, you include a copy of the flight log and photos of him completing a preflight check. The impact can be impressive. Portfolios sometimes earn homeschoolers admission to colleges that would not have considered them based only on transcripts, résumés, and reading lists.

> Where other types of documentation "tell," portfolios "show."

Recommended contents of portfolios vary according to what you read. Cambridge Academy, an independent-study high school in Florida, lists the following for possible inclusion in a high school portfolio:

- ✦ writing samples (research papers, essays)
- ✦ computer printouts
- ✦ timelines
- ✦ maps

HOMESCHOOL RESUME

Here are an Alabama homeschooler's leadership activities, a list that she submitted with her transcript with her college applications.

[Name]

[Address]

✦   Children's choir worker [church, city, state]

I worked assisting the choir director in children's music (ages 6 to 12) for three years. I also played the piano for the choir.

✦   Vacation bible school worker

I worked in the church nursery for three years during vacation bible school.

✦   Assistant Sunday school teacher

I assist in teaching the junior high girls' class at my church.

✦   Participation in the music program of the church

I participate in the handbell choir, the youth choir, and the drama team for the youth group, and I play the guitar for the Youth Ensemble.

✦   Church leadership positions

In 1997, I served on the search committee for our church for an associate pastor. I have served on the Youth Council for two years. I am currently serving as the music leader of _____ Church.

✦   Camp counselor

I worked during the summer of 1997 at an all-girls camp as a counselor. I taught archery and worked on a ropes course. I supervised girls ages 6 to 16.

✦   Hospital volunteer work

I am currently working in the physical therapy department at _____ Hospital.

✦   Girls' softball

I participated in the girls' softball program through the _____ Recreation Department for seven years. The positions I played were pitcher, shortstop, and first base. The last four years I was named MVP for the team, and I was selected for the all-stars team each year.

✦   Job

I am currently employed at a physician's office. I transcribe medical records daily, using a medical records computer system. I have worked there for two years and will continue to work through my senior year.

✦   Medical mission to Jamaica

In November of 1996 and 1997 and February of 1998, I participated in a two-week medical mission to St. Elizabeth, Jamaica. I worked as a general helper in the clinics, assisting with crowd control, pharmacy supply distribution, and integrated health, which involved patient education and ministry.

✦   Mission to St. Petersburg, Florida

I participated in a one-week missions trip with my church youth group. We worked in a deaf community, doing landscape repair, building maintenance, and ministry activities for the residents. We also worked repairing the gardens at a group home for boys.

✦   Trip to Bulgaria

In 1994, my family adopted a child from an orphanage in Bulgaria. I traveled with my father in July of 1994 to bring him home. I spent ten days in the country helping complete his paperwork and begin his transition to life with our family. I had the opportunity to experience life in a post-communist country, witness the needs of the people, and see the condition of the orphanage.

- ✦ artwork
- ✦ brochures (for a student-run business, perhaps)
- ✦ formal letters
- ✦ photographs
- ✦ journal entries
- ✦ book reviews
- ✦ songs

I would add to this list programs, training logs, letters of recommendation, and awards.

In general, those who write about creating educational portfolios say, "Think scrapbook." If you would put it in a scrapbook, it is probably something you should save for a future portfolio. We will discuss portfolios in more detail in chapter 7.

TRANSCRIPTS

THE MAJORITY OF our survey respondents whose homeschooled teenagers applied to college submitted transcripts. At first, writing a transcript sounds intimidating. Questions abound. What do they want? What format should I use? What if I don't do it exactly right?

HOW WE DID IT

We used a simple transcript. Our [umbrella] school purchases the forms from Bob Jones University Press. We just fill in the blanks. I do have an official embossed seal that I can use on the transcript—makes it look "official."

—DARIA, WHOSE SON WAS ADMITTED TO BRYAN COLLEGE (TN),
AUBURN UNIVERSITY (AL), AND PENSACOLA CHRISTIAN COLLEGE (FL)

Fortunately, there is no One Right Way to write a homeschool transcript—or any transcript, for that matter. Examine transcripts from your relatives, friends, and family to see what I mean. From small private schools to large public schools to charter schools to homeschools, transcripts assume an incredible variety of forms. They use different grading systems—or no grading system. They report academics by semesters or, more simply, by completion date. Some look professional. Others—including some from large, well-known high schools—use a bare-bones format.

> From small private schools to large public schools to charter schools to homeschools, transcripts assume an incredible variety of forms.

Our survey respondents described their transcripts. Viola kept it simple for her son's admission to a local junior college. She says, "I found a transcript from a local high school and copied the format exactly, up to and including the use of a lowly typewriter-style font."

Kara, whose four homeschooled children ended up at institutions like Texas A&M and the Rose-Hulman Institute of Technology (IN) says, "I wrote transcripts based upon others I had seen. I did adapt them to our children's needs, however. For example, I did not put down the year in which they took the courses or did the work, because they did not work within semester or year time frames. The work was the important part, not the time period. I also granted credit for courses completed in junior high. If it was high school level, I counted it, regardless of the timing. This includes their projects (such as building a room addition), jobs they did, and 'adult' classes they took (like the tax-preparation and home-business classes from the Small Business Administration). I chose this method based upon what I knew of the process and information I knew colleges needed. Also, my children did not apply to small liberal arts schools that might actually look through a portfolio."

There are so many ways to compile a transcript that we have devoted a whole chapter to the subject. Chapter 8 discusses content and formats. It also includes copies of several successful efforts.

HIGH SCHOOL PROFILE

IN ADDITION TO transcripts, for admissions to selective schools, you may want to consider writing a high school profile. Denise, whose son was admitted to Stanford (CA), Harvey Mudd College (CA), and College of William and Mary (VA), explains: "We, the parents acting as the school counselors, supplied two things: a transcript and a school profile. While looking at Stanford's process for homeschoolers, we learned that the school profile gives the university insight into your homeschooling methods and styles. We included our school profile, explaining our homeschool method in detail, with every 'counselor's report.'"

While the information conveyed in a high school profile can also be included in a cover letter or a narrative, you might want to create a separate document.

MONEY SAVER

To view and download a free blank high school transcript form, visit Quail Haven's High School Homeschool Links, www.quailhaven.com /academy/hslinks.htm.

COURSE DESCRIPTIONS

A FINAL TYPE OF documentation you may need to generate: course descriptions. Depending on college requirements, you may submit these as part of a transcript or as your only documentation of academics. Chapter 8 contains detailed instructions for writing your own course descriptions.

WHICH DOCUMENTATION?

IF ANY OF US had to create all of the above paperwork, our homeschoolers would probably never go to college. To narrow your focus, answer two questions before you begin:

1. What do the colleges where my homeschooler will apply prefer to see?

2. What best shows off my teenager's interests and accomplishments?

Above all, don't do more than you have to do. Home education is about living and learning in a warm, supportive environment, not about creating the most dazzling records or the highest mound of paper.

Don't attempt to "snow" colleges. Be honest and complete, and make documentation choices that show you are considerate of the admissions officers' time.

SIMPLE STARTING POINTS

✦   Write a one- to two-page narrative of your teenager's homeschooling this year—or just part of his homeschooling. Read the narrative to several friends and ask them for their reactions.

✦   Start that reading list with titles your teenager has read in the past three months.

✦   With your teenager, compile a résumé of activities, projects, and volunteer and paid work to date. Discuss how college admissions officers might view the results.

✦   Do a rough transcript of your teenager's academic accomplishments to date. Don't worry about granting credits, making up grades, listing courses by semesters, or making it just like any other transcripts you have seen. Just create an outline with school name and address, student name, and a list of courses. Ask yourself, "Does this format show off my student's interests and talents?"

> Home education is about living and learning in a warm, supportive environment, not about creating the most dazzling records or the highest mound of paper.

✦   Look at the list of items in this chapter that can be included in a portfolio. With your teenager, brainstorm to make this list longer and applicable to his homeschooling.

RESOURCES

Books

Cohen, Cafi. *"And What About College?" How Homeschooling Leads to Admissions to the Best Colleges and Universities,* 2d edition. Holt Associates, 2000.

Heuer, Loretta. *The Homeschooler's Guide to Portfolios and Transcripts.* IDG Books, 2000.

McKee, Alison. *From Homeschool to College and Work: Turning Your Homeschool Experiences into College and Job Portfolios.* Bittersweet House, 1997.

Shelton, Barbara Edtl. *Senior High: A Home-Designed Formula.* Barb Shelton, 182 N. Columbia Heights Rd., Longview, WA 98632.

Web Sites

College Board Online. The Path from Homeschool to College: http://www.collegeboard.org/features/home/html/intro.html

Preparing a Homeschool Curricular Template at Eclectic Homeschool Online: http://eho.org/transcript.htm

Sample Home School High School Academic Transcript: http://ultimate1.8m.com/transcript.html

6

WHAT COUNTS?
CREATING CREDIT AND
GRANTING A DIPLOMA

In This Chapter

✦ Speaking educationese and granting credit

✦ Record keeping

✦ Diploma dilemmas

✦ Granting a diploma

✦ Testing for a diploma

✦ Simple starting points

✦ Resources

"I do not have a state-recognized diploma."

—David, homeschool graduate who now has a
master's of business administration (MBA)
degree from Auburn University

Go to college without a high school diploma? "Impossible," says the man on the street. Experienced home educators know better. Armed with home-brew transcripts, handmade diplomas, and other unofficial documents, their children have been admitted to more than one thousand colleges in the United States.

Of course, our family had none of this information when our homeschooled son applied to college in the early 1990s. Instead, we fumbled around and did the best we could, basing our actions on reports occasionally published in national homeschooling magazines and statewide newsletters.

Our experience with college admissions began one snowy November day in Colorado in 1992. We sat around our kitchen table, staring at a large accordion-style folder labeled "Jeff." Awards, photos, work samples, programs, training logs, contest entries, calendars, projects, letters of recommendation, external transcripts, test scores—you name it. Although we had not kept any formal records, we had saved almost everything—academic and nonacademic—connected with our son's years as a high school homeschooler.

Like many home educators contemplating college admissions, we had three questions:

- ✦ How do we organize this?
- ✦ What counts as credit?
- ✦ What about a diploma?

The answers we found to these questions contradict the common wisdom. We learned we could grant our own credit. Just as surprisingly, we could grant credit for subjects and educational experiences not offered at any high school. As it turns out, almost everything we do in life "counts."

In this chapter, we discuss awarding homeschool credit, keeping records, and granting diplomas. As you will see, some families make this last task—granting a diploma—an optional exercise. Our survey respondents provide helpful suggestions and practical solutions. Pick and choose from among them to fit your situation.

SPEAKING EDUCATIONESE AND GRANTING CREDIT

DANIELA, MOTHER OF THREE, began homeschooling in 1992 because of socialization problems at her oldest child's parochial school. She describes what she counted for high school credit as follows: "Reading and project lists, all participation in informal study (Bible studies, lectures attended, plays and concerts), volunteer and other activities, texts and 'courses' completed. We put these together into 'subjects' for a transcript."

Daniela gives fine arts credit for attending community drama productions, visiting museums, and playing guitar. Her son earned American literature credit for reading library books. Titles included *Cannery Row* (Steinbeck), *The Yearling* (Rawlings), and *The Red Badge of Courage* (Crane).

What Counts

Learning to speak educationese can help you generate more than enough credit for convincing and impressive documents. When we say "speaking educationese," we do not mean bureaucratic double-talk—phrases like "collaborative learning" instead of "group work," or "open dialogue, feedback, and sharing" rather than the simpler "discussion."

Instead, homeschoolers speak educationese to translate daily activities into the language of the educational establishment, specifically into high school subjects. Watching a PBS documentary on World War II fits into world history. A 4-H entomology project is science. Travel can be geography and physical education. The sidebar on pages 120–121 contains additional examples.

SPEAKING EDUCATIONESE

All activities are learning opportunities. Translate everyday life into school subjects, and everything counts!

GAMES

+ Chess = critical thinking
+ Monopoly = math, language arts, economics
+ Paintball = physical education
+ Sim-City = social studies, math, critical thinking

TELEVISION AND ENTERTAINMENT VIDEOS

+ Describing a movie or video = language arts
+ Movies such as *Gettysburg* = history
+ Nature films = science and social studies

TRAVEL

+ Hiking = physical education and science
+ Visiting museums = history, science, and fine arts

HOUSEHOLD TASKS

+ Appliance repair = science
+ Automobile maintenance = science
+ Child care = psychology, art, and independent living skills
+ Cleaning = independent living skills
+ Gardening = science and physical education
+ House renovation projects = math, science, woodworking
+ Meal preparation = math, language arts, science
+ Shopping = consumer math, mental math, critical thinking

STUDENT-SELECTED READING

+ Catalogs = consumer math
+ Fiction = American or English or contemporary literature

+ Newspapers = current events and social studies
+ Nonfiction = science, history, language arts

HOBBIES

+ Collecting stamps = history and geography
+ Model rocketry = science and physics
+ Photography and videography = science and fine arts

MUSIC

+ Attending concerts = fine arts
+ Lessons and practice = fine arts
+ Performances = fine arts

ACTIVITIES

+ Church youth groups = language arts, religion, social studies
+ 4-H and Scouts = social studies, science, language arts, math

RECREATION

+ Hiking/walking = physical education
+ Little League, martial arts = physical education

VOLUNTEER AND PAYING JOBS

+ Child care = psychology, art, independent living skills
+ Library work = language arts, social studies, math, and science

STUDENT-SELECTED WRITING

+ Contest entries = language arts
+ Journals = language arts
+ Pen pals and e-mail pals = language arts

What can you count? Just about everything. You are limited by only your imagination and your tolerance for record keeping. Most home educators find that when they compile information for transcripts and portfolios, they have so much that including everything would make their documents unbelievably long. Through trial and error, you can make decisions about what to keep and what to omit.

> Homeschoolers speak educationese to translate daily activities into the language of the educational establishment, specifically into high school subjects.

How to Count It

Not only can you count almost everything, you can also choose how to count it. Daria, a curriculum-centered homeschooling mother, reports, "Since I mostly used Christian textbooks, I considered a subject complete when our son finished a book. I will truthfully admit that we didn't do everything in the text. For some subjects, he simply read the book and completed a test or summary on each chapter in order to fulfill a graduation requirement."

Unless you report to an evaluator or an independent-study school, you—as the principal and administrator of your own little private school—will decide how to count credits. Yes, that's right. You decide. At first many parents find that scary. In a panic they try to copy local public and private high schools. If the local schools require four English and three math credits, they follow that example. Don't be limited by that standard, though.

You can do much better working one-on-one and observing your teenager closely. You can grant credit using many different criteria. These include the following:

+ seat time

+ subject or project completion

+ test-outs

+ mastery and other subjective measures

Let's discuss seat time first. The idea of seat time comes to us courtesy of public schools. They grant one credit based on anywhere from 90 to 210 hours of seat time in one class. Students may complete the work in 50 hours, but they do not get credit until they sit through the entire course.

You can apply this seat time criterion to your homeschooling. Daniela keeps subject logs that allow her to add up time for American literature or science or fine arts. On her son's fine arts log, they have a long list of plays seen and other associated activities, together with the titles and hours. From this log Daniela awards one credit when her son's totals reach 120 hours or 150 hours or whatever criterion she sets.

Some refer to this as the Carnegie credit granting system. While most authors define one Carnegie credit as representing a one-year class, they disagree on how many hours to allocate to one credit. We have read numbers as low as 90 and as high as 210. Most common are 120 and 180 hours for one Carnegie credit. If you choose to keep track of credit this way, it does not matter how many hours you assign to each credit. Just be honest and consistent.

That said, you can ignore the seat time criterion, and good reasons exist for doing so. Seat time gives no indication of how much students learn, only that they were present. Seat time credit does not encourage students to pursue excellence for its own sake.

As an alternative, you can award credits based on students' completing a textbook or a project. Our son earned the Mitchell Award after approximately a year in the Civil Air Patrol Cadet Program. We counted this as one credit of "aviation and aerospace." He probably spent in excess of 200 hours on this project, but

QUICK & EASY

If you bog down doing every activity and test with your science or history curriculum, have your teen read the material and discuss it with you. Discussion is just as valid an assessment as fill-in-the-blank work sheets, research papers, and tests.

we did not count hours. Instead, we decided that his earning this award corresponded roughly to a high school course. Other home-schoolers give a year's worth of biology credit when their teenager completes the text, whether it takes two months or two years.

Sometimes homeschoolers learn subjects on their own. Their parents then give credit when their teenagers prove that they know a subject through discussion, testing, or writing. This might work especially well for subjects like English, American literature, astronomy, and history.

Finally, you can award credit and even grades (see chapter 8) based on your subjective assessment that your teenager has mastered a certain subject. Carleen, whose son was admitted to the United States Air Force Academy, explains, "We gave one or even two credits—depending on the effort expended—when our son demonstrated that he had mastered a given subject. He might demonstrate this mastery by completing a project, taking a test, discussing an area of interest, volunteering in the community, writing an article, and so forth."

HOW WE DID IT

I compiled our daughter's activities and studies into a transcriptlike list that included 28 'credits.' I could have included more, but I ran out of room. For some subjects, completing the book completed the course. For others she had community college credits. I was also aware of various time-on-task methods to award credits and took this into consideration. The scope and depth of her accomplishments more than equaled the background necessary for a local public school diploma.

—JUDY IN VIRGINIA

You may be so uncomfortable with the idea of awarding your own credit or having your children graduate from your unaccredited homeschool that you consider sending your children back to school once they reach high school age. No need. Many of the independent-study, diploma-granting programs listed in chapter 2 have the accreditation you seek. Put yourself under their "umbrellas," use their credit-granting and graduation criteria, and continue homeschooling.

RECORD KEEPING

IF YOU DO NOT use umbrella or independent-study schools, you will grant credit based on records you devise. In addition, you may have to satisfy state record-keeping requirements such as attendance sheets, test scores, and portfolios.

> Your efforts may range from keeping absolutely no records to carefully cataloging every part of your homeschool day.

Your efforts may range from keeping absolutely no records to carefully cataloging every part of your homeschool day. Let's hear how some of our survey respondents handle the paperwork.

Rhonda, whose daughter was admitted to Lourdes College (OH) and Hocking College (OH) says that they simply keep a general log of hours spent on all subjects. Viola, a curriculum-centered homeschool mom, focuses record keeping mostly on academics. She writes, "We kept all study work, tests, quizzes, and other related materials. I did not keep a lot, though that would be advisable, because people tend to forget what they did."

Pam, whose son began his freshman year at Florida Gulf Coast University in 2000, kept both academic and other records. She explains, "I kept the daily log Florida requires, listing books used, work completed, and so on. I have one large three-ring binder with a short course description of each credit our son has earned, along with photographs, certificates, and other documents."

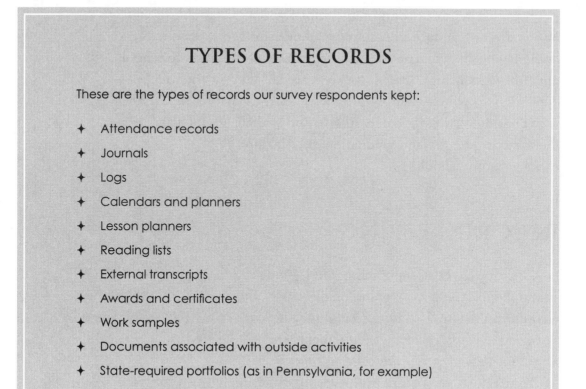

TYPES OF RECORDS

These are the types of records our survey respondents kept:

- ✦ Attendance records
- ✦ Journals
- ✦ Logs
- ✦ Calendars and planners
- ✦ Lesson planners
- ✦ Reading lists
- ✦ External transcripts
- ✦ Awards and certificates
- ✦ Work samples
- ✦ Documents associated with outside activities
- ✦ State-required portfolios (as in Pennsylvania, for example)

Maria, whose children were admitted to Oberlin Conservatory (OH) and the University of Oklahoma, reports that she keeps daily attendance, check-marked daily planners, and academic work samples. Interestingly, she adds, "No college has ever asked to see these."

Serena homeschools her five children using an academic, semi-structured approach. Her records reflect a variety of credit granting methods. "We kept representative work from various subjects; the students kept a lesson planner and recorded hours for some subjects. If we worked through the math book, I did not require an hourly log. Finishing the book resulted in a credit. For activities like watching PBS history videos and reading historical novels, we did keep an hourly log. I also kept any certificates or awards our students received."

Seth and Karen, eclectic homeschoolers, say that they log hours and activities for each course. Karen explains, "For example, a page from the log for medical career options would have the following:

3/3/98: Interviewed Dr. Chambers and added it to my notebook; 1 hour/69 hours cumulative

3/4/98: Volunteered 5 hours at the hospital, added it to notebook; 5 hours/74 hours cumulative

Regardless of the type of records you keep, experienced home educators emphasize two points:

✦   Start early.

✦   Even a modest effort pays off.

HOW WE DID IT

Our teenagers each kept a 'book' book, a spiral notebook in which they wrote down all books read. This was really handy for writing up the end-of-the-year narrative, which we did every summer for the previous year. We kept samples of work, although no one ever asked to see anything.

We kept in a file folder the plans we brainstormed periodically during the year. We also kept plans for group activities, items made, and photos, which were all handy for writing the narratives.

Every so often I would take my son's academic pulse and interview him about what his current interests were on a scale of 1–10, including his comments. This helped us think about where we were going, what we might want to work on, how to get unstuck if there were any difficulties.

—JULIE, WHO BEGAN HOMESCHOOLING IN 1989 WHEN HER EIGHT-YEAR-OLD SON SAID, "SCHOOL IS WASTING MY LIFE"

> Even a modest effort
> . . . will prevent hand-
> wringing all-nighters the
> week before your chil-
> dren's college applica-
> tions are due.

Ruth, mother of three, describes the reason for the "start early" advice. "The summer of my daughter's senior year, we began to get serious about records. I would suggest that people start sooner. As she was our first child, we learned a lot in the process. We are much more intentional and prepared with our second child, now a high school junior. I did prepare a transcript for our eldest, but not until her senior year. Backtracking took some time."

Backtracking not only takes time, it may mean that you do not create the fullest transcript or portfolio that you might have, had you kept records all along. Even a modest effort—say, a daily log in a calendar and several folders in which you keep important documents—will prevent hand-wringing all-nighters the week before your children's college applications are due.

Once you have established your record-keeping system, your teenagers can implement it with minimal supervision. Our daughter spent three to five minutes each morning logging the previous day. It didn't take much time, and we had plenty of data for college applications.

DIPLOMA DILEMMAS

APPROXIMATELY ONE QUARTER of our survey respondents say that their homeschool graduates do not have diplomas. These families did not grant them, and they did not worry about the consequences. The remainder saw that their children had diplomas. Some made them at home, using computer software. Others have diplomas from independent study programs.

Liz and Nathan kept no records and refused to classify their son's life and learning into school subject categories. No educationese for these unschooling parents. Still everything turned out well. They explain, "A high school diploma means that you sat still and did what you were told for twelve years. Who needs it?" Their son did get an "almost perfect" GED score and a 1390 on the SAT for his admission to Hunter College in New York.

"Diplomas are irrelevant. A decent college entrance test score carries much more weight than any diploma or piece of paper," according to Rhonda, whose homeschooled daughter now attends college in Ohio.

Julie agrees, commenting, "We made a slightly tongue-in-cheek diploma for our son's 'graduation.' We saw no need for a 'real' diploma. By that time he had already been accepted to college, and no one was asking for one."

Maria makes an interesting point when she adds, "Once a student has completed a year of college, he can mark 'some college' on any application asking about his education level. High school completion is assumed."

"I always instruct my children to answer 'yes' on any forms asking if they have graduated from high school or have a diploma," reports Serena, homeschooling mother of five.

This works. Think about all the job applications and even college applications you have completed. They simply ask, "Do you

HOMESCHOOL GRADS SAY

I applied to college as a homeschooler, but I also had a diploma from Kolbe Academy (CA), an independent-study school. I am certain that I would have been admitted to the college even without a diploma, as it was never an issue in my admissions process.

—ALEXA, WHO GRADUATED FROM THOMAS AQUINAS COLLEGE IN 1992

have a diploma?" Hardly ever do they say, "Do you have a diploma from an accredited school?" And rarely does anyone ask to see the actual document. Probably at least half the adult population would have trouble finding their diplomas.

Nothing prevents families from issuing their own diplomas. They simply give their homeschool a name and either complete a form or make one up, using word processing or other computer software. Some families do this to signify high school graduation, create a memento, or simply to document a transition.

Steve, homeschooled since age 9 through high school, reports, "My 'graduation' was in the backyard with a diploma that my mom and dad printed on the computer. I was the valedictorian of the class and gave a speech. We had speeches by friends and mentors as well."

Daniel, now at Mount Ida College (MA), has similar warm memories. He writes, "I do have a homemade diploma from our graduation ceremony. The ceremony was wonderful. The diploma is a keepsake. That's what I care most about."

On the other side of the coin, Viola says that having a diploma from an accredited school matters for her son. She writes, "He wants to be a hockey player, and we did not know if he would finish college." Their son enrolled in Cambridge Academy, an independent-study institution in Florida, for his last year of high school.

If circumstances dictate that your homeschoolers earn a diploma from an accredited high school, you can always enroll them in one of the many independent-study programs listed in chapter 3.

Do check on the type of accreditation independent-study schools have. You will find regional accreditation, comparable to college accreditation; state accreditation of private schools; and accreditation by special agencies. Although most home educators regard accreditation as a moot point, you should know that schools that have campus programs in addition to their independent-study programs are likely to have the most solid accreditation.

GRANTING A DIPLOMA

THOSE FAMILIES WHO grant diplomas use different criteria to decide when their homeschoolers have completed high school. Helen, whose daughters now attend Glendale Community College (AZ), says that she considers her children graduated when they complete all of the requirements needed to enter the state universities with a grade of C or better.

"We used the same diploma criteria the state of Alabama uses for an advanced diploma and then added credits in Bible," report Dan and Beth, whose two sons attended Faulkner University.

Emma, whose daughter opted out of college, took a sensible approach. She reports that their graduation requirements include completing a math program, achieving a certain level of literacy, and having a marketable skill.

Mary, whose son chose specialized training in piano technology rather than college, writes that they issued a family-granted diploma. "It was based on the typical requirements for college. When he fulfilled them, we granted the diploma."

These are some of the criteria that homeschool families use to issue their own diplomas:

- ✦ completing local high school diploma requirements (usually 20 to 25 credits)
- ✦ meeting college preparation recommendations
- ✦ admission to college
- ✦ average standardized test (SAT I or ACT) scores
- ✦ time spent or seat time
- ✦ age of the homeschooler
- ✦ ability to support oneself financially
- ✦ teenager's evaluation of his readiness to move on

Should you wish to set graduation and diploma goals, one or more of these should work for your family. Keep in mind that you need not set any goals, that you can simply graduate your home-schooler when the time seems right.

TESTING FOR A DIPLOMA

TWO TYPES OF diploma tests exist, the GED and—in a few states—special state diploma tests, like the California High School Proficiency Examination (CHSPE).

The GED, short for tests of General Educational Development, is available nationwide. Designed originally to help high school dropouts finish high school, some homeschoolers take the GED because approximately one-third of colleges require it when an applicant lacks a diploma from an accredited high school.

Catherine's daughter, who attends Brevard College (FL), took the GED. "It was the easiest way to satisfy the requirements of the college," says Catherine. It paid off handsomely. Catherine's daughter was placed on the dean's honors list, which qualified her for a 50 percent tuition discount.

QUICK & EASY

To view some sample GED test questions, visit www.petersons.com /testprep/ged.html.

Other homeschoolers pointedly ignore the GED. Kara, a homeschooling mother of four, writes, "I consider a GED an insult to graduating seniors. Our homeschoolers were not dropouts, as implied by that test." Judy, whose daughter now attends the University of Rochester, agrees. "Our daughter refused to take the GED. She felt that her forty credits from the community college (with a 4.0 grade point average) adequately described the level of her education."

Some families avoid all testing. Shelley, whose sons are attending Iowa Western Community College, explains, "All of my children seem to be very poor test takers. It is very discouraging to me and to them. I have stayed away from standardized testing, because I know our children know more than the test results demonstrate."

Depending on where you live, you may encounter an age-limit problem with the GED. This varies from state to state. Some states allow GED administration to students as young as 16. Other states, hesitant to "compete" with public schools, restrict access until students reach the ages of 18 and even 19. Kate describes the situation in South Dakota: "Our son was not eligible to take the GED in our state until he finished his first year of college. South Dakota will not let homeschooled students under 18 take the GED. They even go so far as to say homeschoolers cannot take the GED until June of the year their age mates graduate from high school."

For age limits and more information about the GED in your state, contact a local library, community college, or adult education center. All can point you in the right direction. Do note that a completely revised GED is planned for January 2002. If your homeschooler will take the GED, be aware of this cutoff date so that you don't use obsolete preparation materials.

Some states offer, in addition to the GED, the opportunity to test out of high school. As an example, California law says that the certificate of proficiency awarded on passing the California High School Proficiency Examination "shall be equivalent to a high school diploma." It was designed not for dropouts but for teenagers ready to leave school before the age of 18. A few other states have similar tests—for example, Michigan, New York, and Pennsylvania. Pennsylvania also offers

MONEY SAVER

Do not have your homeschooler take the GED unless it is absolutely necessary. It does involve, after all, time and money. Talk to colleges of interest before you make any assumptions about requirements. Even if they say they require a GED, ask for a waiver and point out the other evidence of your student's preparation, such as SAT and ACT scores and completed community college classes.

> Diplomas, whether homemade or issued by an accredited school, do not matter nearly so much as your other documentation, such as logs, reading lists, portfolios, and transcripts.

a process by which homeschoolers can earn a state-approved diploma.

How students test for a diploma constantly changes, so you should contact your statewide homeschool support organizations for current information.

To sum up, almost everything your homeschoolers do is a learning activity. Reports to government agencies and possibly also to umbrella schools—together with goals for high school at home—will dictate your record keeping. Diplomas, whether homemade or issued by an accredited school, do not matter nearly so much as your other documentation, such as logs, reading lists, portfolios, and transcripts. At best, the diploma presents an opportunity for you to honor your homeschooler's achievements and recognize a rite of passage.

SIMPLE STARTING POINTS

+ List your teenager's current nonacademic activities. Translate these into educationese, preferably with a group of homeschooling teens and parents. This brainstorming activity can be entertaining and reassuring while helping you create plenty of data for portfolios and transcripts.

+ If you haven't already, begin keeping some records. Try a daily log of activities for one month. Evaluate whether the resulting document is useful for your situation. Create a set of file folders to retain documents associated with different activities and academic subjects. Begin a reading list.

+ Consider the diploma options. Discuss with your teenagers whether and how you will award a diploma. What criteria seem most important to you? What criteria matter most to your teenager?

✦ If your teen will be taking the GED or other state diploma-granting test, plan to prepare for it over the next one to three years. Locate resource materials (books and CDs) at your library and in the study guide section of any large bookstore.

RESOURCES

Note: See chapter 1 for GED testing resources.

Books

Cohen, Cafi. *Homeschooling: The Teen Years.* Prima Publishing, 2000.

Duffy, Cathy. *The Christian Home Educators' Curriculum Manual,* Volume 2. Grove Publishing, 1997.

Pride, Mary. *The Big Book of Home Learning: Junior High Through College, 4th edition, Volume 3.* Alpha Omega Publications, 1999.

Shelton, Barbara Edtl. *Senior High: A Home-Designed Form-U-La.* Available from the author at 182 North Columbia Heights Road, Longview, WA 98632.

Web Sites

Brown's Graduation Supplies, 870-932-4832: http://brownsgrad.com

High School Subject Reviews: http://www.learningshortcuts.com/new1ReviewsC.html

Record-Keeping Systems

Home School Organizer, 334-634-1849: http://www.homeschoolorganizer.com/HSOWelcome.htm

HomeSchool Easy Records, 888-328-7587: http://home.earthlink.net/~vdugar/index.html

HomeSchool Organize!, 703-791-2794: http://members.aol.com/hfsoftware/hspress.html

Homeschool Record Keeper, 908-638-8667: http://fp97.inet-images.com/salem/

Homeschooler's High School Journal, 7–12, Rainbow Resource Center, 888-841-3456: http://www.rainbowresource.com

7

COMPILING A PORTFOLIO

In This Chapter

✦ Portfolio pluses

✦ Contents

✦ Organization

✦ Simple starting points

✦ Resources

© EyeWire

"If you evaluate me from a traditional standpoint, I'm not going to look very good, but if you take time to sit down and look at what I did, you see I have a lot of strengths. I don't have a high school diploma, didn't take standardized tests, but I've done a fabulous amount of work in a lot of related subject areas. It's a different set of strengths."

—Christian McKee, homeschool graduate.

*H*ISTORICALLY, you heard the term "portfolio" and formal education in the same sentence only when reading about collections of artwork, photography, writing, and other creative endeavors.

Portfolios in regular schools became the rage in the early 1990s, not just for art and writing but for all academic subjects. Teachers kept work samples in individual student folders and then evaluated the contents at regular intervals to check progress. Reformers touted portfolio reviews as a realistic form of assessing performance, an alternative to nerve-racking tests.

Some schools still compile student portfolios, and a few of these use them to assign grades. Most institutions that enthusiastically adopted the practice have discontinued it due to personnel and time constraints. It is a lot more work to assemble and evaluate twenty-five portfolios than to administer one multiple-choice test.

In the 1980s and early 1990s, homeschoolers adopted the idea of portfolios to such an extent that several state homeschooling statutes list "portfolio review" as an acceptable assessment.

Take Colorado, for example. For their every-other-year evaluations, homeschoolers in the Rocky Mountain State have two choices—administer a standardized test, such as the Iowa Test of Basic Skills, or obtain a portfolio review by a credentialed teacher or other person deemed qualified by state law. Families whose children do not test well and parents who do not believe in standardized testing welcome alternatives such as portfolio assessment (although most homeschoolers would prefer no state-mandated assessment at all).

PORTFOLIO PLUSES

THE ADVANTAGES OF portfolio review go far beyond eliminating the frustration associated with standardized testing. Many homeschooling families compile portfolios, even though no one outside the family will ever see them. Portfolios, like scrapbooks and photo albums, "show" rather than "tell." In a résumé, you can talk about your teenager having written a published article, created a business-related Web site, or won an art competition. In a portfolio, you can show the products of his efforts—the article, the Web site, or photos of the artwork.

Another advantage? No one compiling a portfolio thinks about speaking educationese—in other words, translating home education into school subject categories. Portfolios, probably better than any other documentation you can create, reflect how you homeschool and the results. Unschoolers and many eclectic home educators appreciate the freedom to report homeschooling exactly as it occurred, without the constraints of producing "what colleges want."

Unfortunately, what most colleges say they want are transcripts. Large state colleges and universities that see huge numbers of applicants every year cannot cope with anything else. Small private colleges, on the other hand, may view portfolios positively. And some small colleges—especially those that emphasize self-directed learning—prefer portfolios to transcripts. Still others know that the portfolio best reflects homeschooling. The Kansas State University Web site has a special page for homeschoolers on which it says, "Course descriptions or portfolios of your work are accepted in place of an accredited diploma."

In the 1980s and early 1990s, homeschoolers adopted the idea of portfolios to such an extent that several state homeschooling statutes list "portfolio review" as an acceptable assessment.

That said, all homeschooling families—those using traditional methods, unit study advocates, unschoolers, and eclectic home educators—will want to consider making portfolios even if they do not intend to submit one with their children's college applications. Why? Consider the following points.

Portfolios As Organizational and Record-Keeping Aids

Lori in Michigan, whose children were enrolled in Clonlara School, an independent-study program that requires portfolios, explains, "We have a large three-ring notebook for each child, and we throw everything in it over the year—programs, papers written, awards received, test scores, letters of recognition, newspaper articles, artwork, and so on. At the end of the year, our teenagers organize it; I don't."

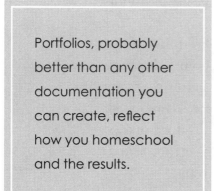

Portfolios, probably better than any other documentation you can create, reflect how you homeschool and the results.

Lori, whose daughter completed her first year at Brandeis University (MA) on the dean's list, continues, "During the high school years, we organized our portfolios chronologically, with the most recent items to the front. Then we thoroughly cleaned up and organized the contents once or twice a year. At this point, we added photos as well."

Lori next explains how they used the portfolio as part of the college admissions process: "My daughter organized her portfolio for

HOW WE DID IT

I kept the daily log Florida requires, listing books used, work completed, and so on. I have one large three-ring binder with a short course description of each credit our son has earned, along with photographs, certificates, and other documents. We did not use the portfolio when applying to Florida Gulf Coast University, but I am certain that my son will use it in the process of obtaining a nomination to the United States Naval Academy.

—PAM IN FLORIDA

graduation in an alphabetical fashion: A for awards, B for biography (personal notes), C for college search, and so forth. We did not use my daughter's portfolio in and of itself for college admissions. Rather, we pulled from it the listing of awards, experiences, and so on for scholarship and college application forms. And we went through the portfolio prior to college admissions interviews."

The First Step in Writing a Transcript

Lori's children's independent-study program wrote their transcripts. If you will be writing your own, portfolios provide an initial way to organize your data and documents.

Mini-Portfolios

Mini-portfolios can supplement transcripts and other paperwork you eventually submit with a college application. If your homeschooler operated a business, published a Web page, excelled at a sport, volunteered with the local fire department, or produced an award-winning science project, a mini-portfolio can make quite an impact at certain colleges.

> If your homeschooler operated a business, published a Web page, excelled at a sport, volunteered with the local fire department, or produced an award-winning science project, a mini-portfolio can make quite an impact at certain colleges.

Substitute Résumés

Sometimes résumés (see chapter 5), especially those written expressly to report extracurricular activities, become indistinguishable from portfolios. When our teenagers wrote their résumés, they attached copies of supporting documentation. My son reported in his résumé that he won an award in Civil Air Patrol and attached a copy of the award. He listed participation on a U.S. diving team and included photos, practice logs, diving meet schedules, and a letter of recommendation from his coach.

Reporting Unschooling or Interest-Initiated Learning

Alison McKee hammers home this point in *From Homeschool to College and Work: Turning Your Homeschooled Experiences into College and Job Portfolios.* No other documentation reports unschooling as well as a portfolio.

In her book McKee includes excerpts from her son's college application portfolio. Under the heading "English," she writes: "The study of English, including reading, writing, speech, and attendance at a wide variety of theatrical performances, has always been a nat-

---

SUGGESTED PORTFOLIO CONTENTS FROM OGLETHORPE UNIVERSITY, ATLANTA, GEORGIA

1. A summary detailing the years of high school study

2. An academic assessment including the following:

   a yearly listing of subjects studied

   textbook titles (if used)

   assignment descriptions

   writing samples

3. A list of all extracurricular activities

4. Recommendations from individuals with direct knowledge of the student's academic achievement, extracurricular activities, or character and maturity

5. Documentation of honors and awards

ural part of Christian's [her son's] life. Christian is widely read. Not only has he read for his own personal enjoyment, but he has also read aloud to large live audiences and on the radio. Christian's writing experiences are many and varied. They include writing articles for various magazines, keeping a journal, letter and e-mail correspondence, writing research papers, and writing radio copy."

McKee proceeds in this part of the portfolio to list specific reading, writing, and videos they used. She also describes her son's public-speaking experience. Of course, the portfolio, being a portfolio, includes examples of her son's writing.

Christian McKee's principal interests during his teen years were fly-fishing and fly tying. From these seemingly nonacademic topics, he learned aquatic entomology, fish anatomy and physiology, biology of streams, rivers, and lakes, and the history of fishing from ancient times to the present. Compiling his fly-fishing-related activities into a portfolio allowed this unschooling family to say exactly how their son learned without an artificial overlay of classifying everything into school subjects.

Applications to Specialized and Small Liberal Arts Colleges

Some small liberal arts colleges emphasize independent, interdisciplinary studies. They are likely to be more impressed by a portfolio than a transcript. Visual and performing arts colleges will require portfolios to view samples of your student's work. In the new millennium, online portfolios (Web pages) may gain currency. This is an obvious way to display your student's expertise with graphic and Web page design.

Scholarship Applications

"We kept a portfolio on our daughter," Kate explains. "It was mostly a large manila envelope into which we stuffed everything from a single year—photos, papers written, newspaper articles describing her activities, artwork, and so on."

"Originally, this was just for me, a memento," Kate continues. "In her junior year, our daughter expressed interest in Trinity Christian College (IL), a school that requires portfolios from home-schooled applicants. I panicked at first. Then I figured I could make a portfolio from the envelopes of stuff I had saved. In the end she chose not to apply there. However, the contents of the envelopes proved extremely valuable when applying for scholarships. It was a good way to look back and remember what she had done when. We had lots of information about activities, the kinds that impress scholarship committees. I recommend all home educators keep some type of 'portfolio' in high school, if only for scholarship applications. Sometimes we could not remember what she had done when, except to note which envelope contained it."

Generate College Credit

Yes, that's right. A few colleges may grant credit for courses based on portfolio reviews. One example is Thomas Edison State College, in Trenton, New Jersey, which at this time restricts its enrollment to ages 21 and up. Other state colleges have similar programs. Check out Charter Oak College, in Framington, Connecticut, and the Regents External Degree Program, in Albany, New York.

Applying for Work

Most college students will look for paid employment during their college careers, either full-time summer jobs or part-time jobs con-current with college. High school portfolios provide impressive documentation—especially for jobs off the beaten track, such as costume design for theater groups or teaching photography.

CONTENTS

WHAT EXACTLY DO people put in portfolios? That depends who you ask. The state of Pennsylvania, which requires portfolios from home educators, suggests a bare-bones format consisting of three items:

- ✦ A log, made contemporaneously with instruction, which lists reading materials
- ✦ Samples of writings, work sheets, workbooks, or creative materials used and developed by the student
- ✦ Standardized-test results

Of course, these requirements apply to families homeschooling all ages and do not necessarily take into account college admissions. The College Board Web site suggests the following portfolio contents:

- ✦ Completed assignments
- ✦ Research papers and essays
- ✦ Artwork
- ✦ Solved math problems
- ✦ Any tangible schoolwork

Like the state of Pennsylvania requirements, these recommendations begin to give you an idea of portfolio contents. Unfortunately, they are so sketchy, they do not help you create a high school portfolio for college admissions.

The logical beginning of any portfolio is identifying information. Your student's personal data should include name, gender, birth date, address, phone number, e-mail address, and a photo. Expanding this information, you could add a student autobiography, which would serve as background information and as a writing

HOW WE DID IT

Our daughter's portfolio was a three-ring binder. She decorated the front with rubber stamps (one of her "hand crafts.") We had a transcript at the beginning. Then I wrote a short description about each course.

For example, under geometry I wrote, "[Our daughter] used the *Jacob's Geometry* text along with *Key to Geometry* workbooks 1 to 6. English: Each year [our daughter] was required to read at least twenty-five books. Many of these were classics, including three Shakespeare plays, *Jane Eyre*, *The Scarlet Letter*, *Little Women*, and many books of the Bible. Each year she completed a "book study" for a classic and designed a "book study" of her own. She wrote at least ten short (two- to four-page) research papers each year and one longer (six- to eight-page) research paper each year." I also wrote a long summary of her extracurricular activities—volunteer work, youth-group activities, work experiences.

After the summaries, we added a few papers from each course, books lists for each subject, log entries for each course, and our evaluator's letter of evaluation. It looked impressive, because under courses such as fine arts, she had a few research papers on composers. Now, for us these counted as both fine arts and English, but in the portfolio it looked like so much work. We used the same technique with other subjects. Her papers counted as both English and another subject, like history, infant and child development.

—Seth and Karen, Pennsylvania homeschoolers whose daughter attended Westmoreland County Community College

sample. An essay—say, 250 to 500 words—detailing the student's academic and career goals could serve the same purpose.

Test scores matter to many colleges, so test scores have a place in an application portfolio. List results of the PSAT, SAT I, ACT, SAT II, CLEP, and AP tests. Include copies of any other standardized-test scores, such as the Stanford Achievement Test or the Iowa Test of Basic Skills. A pattern of high test scores from grades 7 to 12 will reassure many college admissions officers. Conversely, if your applicant does not test well, omit all mention of test scores.

Information about your homeschool, your student's home-based high school, has a place in your portfolio. You can begin with the numbers—that is, some sort of attendance record. Add outlines of your daily schedule, or list the activities for several days when your teenager accomplishes a lot.

For more on your school, consider adding a document that describes the educational philosophy of your homeschool. Although discussing your theories of learning may sound difficult, there is no need to immerse yourself in educational double-talk. Instead, just answer one of two questions:

1. Why did you begin homeschooling and why do you continue?

2. What is a typical day like in your homeschool?

Answering either of these questions usually will allow you to address educational philosophy in easy-to-understand, concrete terms.

Include records of subjects taught. These might be typical high school subjects—or not. You can list English, math, science, and history, just as you find on most high school transcripts. Alternatively, you can list items like rocketry, historical costume design, horses, reptiles, filmmaking, songwriting, political fund-raising, astronomy, and animal rescue—all activities with which I associate the faces of real homeschoolers. Of course, you can also create a combination list, with traditional and real-world subjects.

Under each subject, you should describe the activity and cite materials used. Your descriptions may include photos and illustrations. Materials and resources run the gamut: textbooks, real books, videos, games, computer programs, field trips, volunteer work, classes, conferences, camps, and so on. Report them all. Some portfolios include optional test scores or grades for each subject.

Work samples comprise the major parts of most portfolios. Samples of academic work come to mind first. Certainly you will include well-written paragraphs, essays, and papers; science laboratory reports; foreign-language essays; solutions to difficult math problems; descriptions of history and geography research projects; and photos showing hands-on science investigations and physical education activities. Be selective. Pick representative examples of your student's best work—not everything you have saved.

Think beyond typical academics. Any of the following can demonstrate your student's accomplishments:

QUICK & EASY

Create a place to put extracurricular items and work samples, even if it is only a shoe box. Label it with your teenager's name and today's date, and start collecting all documents and photos relating to your teen's education.

+ Artwork

+ Photography

+ Tape or video recordings

+ Internship and apprenticeship records

+ Newspaper clippings

+ Awards

While some portfolios will have an academic section, others—particularly those from unschoolers—may not.

The focus of these portfolios will be an activities section. Included here will be descriptions of extracurricular activities, such as the following:

+ Community activities (Bible studies, concerts, plays, sports, community drama productions, travel)

+ Community service

+ Classes (first aid, CPR, art and music lessons, 4-H classes, community cooking classes)

As we discuss more fully in chapter 10, outside evaluations of all homeschooled college applicants are extremely important. For that reason, you will want to include letters of recommendation from adults outside your family who have worked with your homeschooler. These might be camp counselors, music teachers, coaches, volunteer and work supervisors, even neighbors and friends. In addition to letters, these people—especially coaches and job supervisors—may have completed evaluation sheets. Include these, if you have them.

Poorly organized, everything-but-the-kitchen-sink efforts will bore your audience—college admissions officers and scholarship committees.

HOW WE DID IT

We kept a portfolio. We had a file drawer with folders for each subject being studied, as well as folders for newspaper articles, awards, and so on. As things came into the house, we just threw them into the correct folder (theater tickets and programs into the English folder; award certificates into the awards folder; SAT scores into the testing folder; lab notebook into the chemistry folder; audiotapes of guitar in the music folder).

Finally, we selected representative materials from each folder to put together the graduation portfolio. We used a binder and put everything in plastic page protectors. We organized it with a section at the beginning for a résumé, awards, and college plans and succeeding sections for each subject, plus work experience and volunteer experiences.

—LANA, HOMESCHOOLING MOM, EXPLAINING HER PORTFOLIO ON AN ONLINE DISCUSSION BOARD

Finally, as chapter 5 relates, admissions officers avidly peruse reading lists. Be certain to include one in your portfolio. Your teen's annotations on a reading list would be even more impressive.

End-of-year summaries, written either by the parent or student, are often found in portfolios. In addition to recapitulating academics and activities, yearly summaries might include areas of growth you and your teenager have noted.

SAMPLE PORTFOLIO ORGANIZATION

PORTFOLIO # 1

- ✦ Table of contents
- ✦ Personal statement
- ✦ Academic records by subject
- ✦ Test scores
- ✦ Résumé
- ✦ Documentation for two major activities

PORTFOLIO #2

- ✦ Portfolio highlights (keyed to page numbers)
- ✦ School profile
- ✦ Narrative
- ✦ Reading list
- ✦ Narratives and exhibits for two major activities
- ✦ Letters of recommendation

PORTFOLIO #3

- ✦ Table of contents
- ✦ Personal statement
- ✦ Transcript, chronological by year
- ✦ Academic work samples
- ✦ Test scores
- ✦ Résumé
- ✦ Documents to support résumé
- ✦ Awards
- ✦ Letters of recommendation

You could put everything listed here into your portfolio, but that's overkill. Poorly organized, everything-but-the-kitchen-sink efforts will bore your audience—college admissions officers and scholarship committees. You want, instead, to select those items that make your points most succinctly and powerfully.

To give reviewers concise overviews, include a table of contents and summary documents, such as transcripts, résumés, and portfolio highlights summaries. To add impact and power to your portfolio presentation, report everything briefly and focus in depth on no more than three special projects or subjects—academic and nonacademic. Explore these fully, with work samples, photos, evaluation sheets, programs, published writing, and so on. Demonstrating a variety of approaches to this special subject will increase impact. If you are touting your homeschooler's writing skills, include several types of writing—essays, reports, research papers, letters, poetry, illustrated stories, book and movie reviews, Web page writing, and so on.

Alison McKee makes an excellent point about deciding what to include. She writes, "The first and foremost question that must be asked when it comes time to compile and write up a final document is: To what audience am I marketing myself? The term 'marketing' may sound a bit commercial, but in fact that is what any portfolio is: a self-marketing tool. . . . For those headed to college or technical school, it is wise to have a basic understanding of the entrance requirements . . . likewise for those who are looking at admissions to art schools, drama schools, schools of music or conservatories."

ORGANIZATION

NO ONE BEST WAY to assemble portfolios exists. The most popular display format is a three-ring binder, with documents and other items in sheet protectors. For actual college applications, you may prefer photocopies of everything that goes into the binder, reducing the portfolio to a more easily mailed ten- to one-hundred-page document. Also, consider a new-millennium format. Although it was not possible ten years ago, you can now create a Web page portfolio. You can put documents, writing samples, even audio and video clips on-line, available to college admissions officers at a mouse click.

> Although it was not possible ten years ago, you can now create a Web page portfolio.

Artists and musicians and dancers submitting their work will have portfolio organization and content (such as audio and videotapes) dictated by the institutions to which they apply. They should ask about specifics, which will differ from college to college, and follow directions exactly.

Think carefully about portfolio organization. Title pages (including date the portfolio was completed), tables of contents, explanatory introductions, and portfolio highlights summaries belong up front, as does personal information. You will probably not need every one of these introductory pages. Just consider what a college admissions officer needs to see. Make it easy for her to find your address, summary academic record (a transcript, in some cases), or your standardized-test scores, if applicable.

Within the main body of the portfolio, you can organize chronologically by school year. Or you can arrange materials according to subjects covered—for example, English followed by math, then science, and so on. You can incorporate work samples with the subject descriptions or in separate sections.

Above all, do not feel overwhelmed by descriptions in this chapter. They exist mainly to provide ideas for a wide range of situations. We hope the ideas here also encourage you to keep documents and work samples and other items that that you currently think are only scrapbook filler. If your homeschoolers apply to competitive colleges or for scholarship dollars at any college, you will need the information.

SIMPLE STARTING POINTS

✦ Think "portfolio," even if you do not plan to make one for college admissions. List the items that you would include for your teenager.

✦ What is your homeschool's educational philosophy? Discuss the answers to these two questions with your teens: (1) Why did you begin homeschooling and why do you continue? (2) What is a typical day like in your homeschool?

✦ With your teenager, examine ten to twenty work samples. Discuss which ones reflect his best effort. Which ones would you put into a portfolio for college admissions? For employment?

✦ Go hands-on. Have your teenager make a mini-portfolio for one of her hobbies or interests or strong academic subjects. What will it include? Try various ways of organizing the information. Have a friend review and comment on the product.

RESOURCES

Books

Gelner, Judy. *College Admissions: A Guide for Homeschoolers.* Poppyseed Press, P.O. Box 85, Sedalia, Colorado 80135, 1989. Out of print but worth reading, especially if you will use a portfolio for college admissions. Try libraries and used-book stores.

Grace, Kathy, and Elizabeth F. Shores. *The Portfolio Book: A Step-by-Step Guide for Teachers.* Gryphon House, 1998.

Kimeldorf, Martin, and Pamela Espeland. *Creating Portfolios: For Success in School, Work, and Life.* Free Spirit Publishing, 1994.

McKee, Alison. *From Homeschool to College and Work: Turning Your Homeschooled Experiences into College and Job Portfolios.* Bittersweet House, P.O. Box 5211, Madison, Wisconsin 53705, 1999.

Web Sites

"Preparing a Homeschool Portfolio," at Homeschool Family Times: http://www.homeeducator.com/FamilyTimes/articles/teach.htm

"High School Portfolio of Educational and Community Activities," at the Republican Christian Academy home page: http://www.csranet.com/~vlmckie/ravport.htm

"Student Portfolios: Classroom Uses," United States Government Department of Education Office of Research Consumer Guide: http://www.ed.gov/pubs/OR/ConsumerGuides/classuse.html

8

WRITING A TRANSCRIPT

In This Chapter

+ Transcript information

+ Official transcripts

+ Simple starting points

+ Resources

© EyeWire

"[We need to] communicate his nontraditional education in the traditional terms outsiders will understand."

—Debra Bell, *The Ultimate Guide to Homeschooling*

*H*OMESCHOOOLERS use transcripts to apply for jobs, internships, apprenticeships, and military enlistment. Primarily, though, homeschooling teenagers use transcripts as part of their college applications. More than 90 percent of United States colleges and universities that require academic summaries request that you send them transcripts.

Transcripts make it easier for admissions officers, scholarship committees, and financial aid offices to evaluate your homeschoolers and compare them with other applicants. When you submit a portfolio, you ask colleges to understand homeschooling on your terms. When you write a transcript, you translate home learning into their terms, into educationese.

Students applying to most large state colleges and universities will have no choice about the portfolio-transcript issue. The admissions staffs at these schools see thousands of applicants each year. They cannot commit the time (usually at least an hour or two) necessary for thorough portfolio review. Instead, they need summary academic information in a brief, easy-to-review form—in other words, as a transcript.

> When you write a transcript, you translate home learning into their terms, into educationese.

Schools with conservative educational philosophies also generally prefer transcripts to portfolios. Portfolio submissions do not coincide with their view of how people learn best—with assignments, texts, lectures, exams, and grades. When our son applied to the United States Air Force Academy (CO), the United States Naval Academy (MD), and West Point (NY), we never considered submitting a portfolio. The lockstep education at these schools indicates that they prefer students who show that they can play the lockstep game.

Even at noncompetitive colleges and universities and at two-year community colleges, you may need a transcript—not for admissions but instead for financial aid applications. Financial aid offices often require grade point averages and high school credits for the big-money awards.

Other reasons to write a transcript for community colleges exist, even though most do not require them. Sometimes, having one allows the academic counselors to understand homeschooling better, make positive recommendations to the financial aid office, and suggest the best placement in classes.

Helen, a curriculum-based home educator whose daughters now attend community college in Arizona, comments, "It is a professional point for us to give a detailed transcript. We need to show with pride what we have accomplished, in a way that is meaningful to the college folks. Since so many scholarship applications also require a transcript, we found we needed to prepare one even for community college."

While some homeschoolers will look better with a portfolio presentation of their accomplishments, others will stand out with a transcript. As an example, let's say the terms "well-rounded" and "multitalented" describe your teenager. He has racked up lots of independent-study and college credits. In addition, you have translated almost everything he has done into educationese. In that case your student will look better with a transcript.

> Even though the product seems designed to report only textbook learning, a transcript works for all homeschooling approaches.

In contrast, homeschoolers who have developed one or two talents or projects or activities in great depth, and who have simultaneously ignored the recommendations to take foreign language or three years of math, may do much better with a portfolio.

Home educators find several other reasons to write transcripts, sometimes beginning as early as grade 7. If producing a transcript for an 11-year-old seems premature, many recommend beginning the practice no later than grade 9, the first year of high school. Families find they use transcripts to obtain student work permits, reduced driver's insurance rates, and admission to special educational programs, such as Aviation Challenge at Space Camp or Talent Search, a college credit program at regional universities such as Johns Hopkins University (MD) and the University of Denver (CO).

Writing a transcript does not commit your teenager to traditional-approach homeschooling or school-at-home. Even though the product seems designed to report only textbook learning, a transcript works for all homeschooling approaches—traditionalists; unit-study and project-oriented homeschoolers; unschoolers, who espouse interest-initiated learning; and eclectic home educators, who use multiple approaches.

Transcripts intimidate many families. They know that colleges scrutinize them closely, and they worry about credibility. Their questions cover the gamut: "Won't colleges see parents as biased and view the resulting transcript with doubt?" "Why should college admissions officers put any stock in homeschool credits or grades?" "What if we don't use the correct format?" Related questions also arise: "How can we give credits and grades if we never operated that way?" "How do we calculate grade point averages and class rank?" "What should we include in course descriptions?"

In this chapter we answer technical questions and show you how to create credible and impressive documents. Remember that most colleges will review transcripts and test scores first. It is worth your while to write credible transcripts and put your best foot forward.

In addition, we include at the end of this chapter actual copies of home-brew transcripts with identifying information removed. Here you will see that no set format exists. All transcripts look different. Among the varied documents admissions officers receive from public and private high schools, your homemade transcript will not stand out like a weed in an otherwise well-tended garden. In fact, your docu-

> Among the varied documents admissions officers receive from public and private high schools, your homemade transcript will not stand out like a weed in an otherwise well-tended garden.

ment may look more impressive than many of those generated by small schools with tight budgets.

TRANSCRIPT INFORMATION

LET'S GET SPECIFIC. Remember, first and foremost, a transcript is a list of academic coursework completed and in progress. It may also include credits and grades for the courses plus other information discussed below.

For our purposes here, it is easiest to separate transcript information into mandatory items found on nearly all transcripts, and optional items.

Mandatory information:

+ Title
+ Date transcript issued
+ Student name and other identifiers
+ Name and address of school
+ Names of completed courses

Optional items, found on some transcripts:

+ Credits and explanation of the credit-granting system
+ Course descriptions
+ Dates courses taken or completed
+ Grades and explanation of grading system
+ Grade point averages
+ Class rank
+ Courses taken in outside institutions (transfer courses)
+ Standardized-test scores
+ Reading lists
+ Narratives

Mandatory Information

It is easy to get lost in course descriptions and grade point averages. Before that happens, make certain you have the basics:

Title

Although it may seem superfluous or too obvious to discuss, create a title for your transcripts. Our survey respondents used the following titles:

- ✦ Homeschool High School Transcript
- ✦ _____ Academy Official High School Transcript
- ✦ Official Transcript _____ Senior High
- ✦ Homeschool Transcript
- ✦ High School Transcript
- ✦ _____ Christian School Transcript
- ✦ Permanent Record

Note that all but one include the magic word "transcript." As we pointed out in chapter 5, homeschoolers should always include some document with "transcript" in the title, even if it is a portfolio or narrative. Certainly, if you write a transcript, call it that.

Date Issued

Although not every transcript bears an issue date, you should consider it required information. For most homeschoolers issue date matters, because transcript content will change every few months. Colleges may ask you to submit a current transcript at the beginning of the application process and an update three to six months later. An issue date near the top of the document allows admissions officers to discern immediately the difference between your two transcripts and, of course, focus on the more recent.

Identifiers

All documents—transcripts, essays, résumés, narratives, portfolios—should have identifying information on every page. This identifying information begins with the student's name. Other student identifiers our survey respondents added include one or more of the following: address, phone number, e-mail address, date of birth, gender, and social security number. Almost all high school transcripts now list the social security number, because most colleges and universities use this number as a secondary identifier.

School Name

Somewhere near the top of your transcript, give your homeschool a name. The principal controversy seems to be whether or not to feature the word "homeschool" prominently. We sent the transcripts of both our children in from "Desert-Mountain Homeschool." Out of eleven applications, we did not experience any discrimination—or even any questions, for that matter. We knew that college admissions officers try to create diverse student bodies, and we felt that prominently featuring our teenagers' homeschooling would help.

> All documents—transcripts, essays, résumés, narratives, portfolios—should have identifying information on every page.

Other families make their transcripts similar to documents from small private schools. They don't want the issue of homeschooling confusing their teenager's application. They send transcripts from "Eagle's Nest Academy" or "La Escuela Garcia" or "Goodacre School" (using a family name) or "Elm Street Christian Preparatory School." If you have not yet given your homeschool a name, pick one, and use it on the transcript.

Courses

All transcripts will include the names of courses. Everyone knows that colleges will understand titles such as "world history,"

"English," "algebra," and "chemistry." In addition, don't be afraid to color outside the lines. More-specific names, as well as nontraditional courses, are not only acceptable but preferred.

> We have seen all of the following on homeschooling transcripts: aviation, fly-fishing, history of baseball, sign language, astronomy, modern children's literature, martial arts, and music theory.

Janice and Bill, whose son was admitted to the University of Kansas on a Provost Scholarship, explain, "Remember that you should use titles for classes that are descriptive. Not 'home economics' but instead 'dressmaking,' 'tailoring,' 'cooking casseroles,' 'bread baking,' 'child care,' and 'interior decorating.' Specific subject names, rather than general, all-encompassing subject titles, show more in-depth study and give a clearer idea of what the student actually covered."

Janice continues, "Not 'history 1,' and 'history 2' but instead 'the world wars,' 'colonial America,' 'Middle Ages.' Not 'literature' but instead 'Christian novels,' 'the modern novel,' 'Shakespeare and other playwrights,' 'English literature,' 'mythology,' 'fantasy and fairy tales.' 'Real' high schools use these terms, and it makes a transcript more fun! We are professionals. We need our end product to the world to be of professional quality."

In addition, course titles can include subjects and activities you would never find on a transcript from a regular school. Examples? We have seen all of the following on homeschooling transcripts: aviation, fly-fishing, history of baseball, sign language, astronomy, modern children's literature, martial arts, and music theory.

Optional Data

Can you submit a transcript *without* credits and grades and class rank and subjects listed by semester? Yes, you can. It all depends on the school. Assess how much time the admissions staff will have to review your materials. Also, determine whether or not the college makes admissions decisions using numerical formulas that incorpo-

HOW WE DID IT: TRANSCRIPT CONTENT

Here is the organization of one successful effort:

Title: Official Transcript

Student name and address

First contact name and relationship

Second contact name and relationship

Contact phone: home and work

School address and phone

Gender

Date of birth

Social security number

Four blocks for grades 9 to 12, labeled with year, school (homeschool), and grade; each lists subjects, divided into two semesters, with letter grades and credit received.

Below each block is a spot for earned credits and GPA for that year.

Explanatory notes: (H) indicates honors course, * indicates research-based course of study continuing for more than one year, ** indicates a two-year course

School head—line for signature and date

Cumulative grade point average (GPA)

Class rank

Graduation status

Graduation date

Bottom of page: Operated in accordance with Wyoming Statutes 21-4-101 and 21-4-102.

All of this is organized artistically on one side of an 8 1/2-by-11-inch sheet of paper. The format was patterned after the local public schools official transcript, but it is not an exact copy and has been customized to portray our school situation. Most people would probably eliminate "class rank."

—LEO AND PENNY, WHOSE HOMESCHOOLED SON WAS ADMITTED TO THE UNIVERSITY OF WYOMING

HOW WE DID IT

Our transcript includes the following:

✦　heading with name, address, and phone number

✦　name of homeschool with note to our curriculum affiliation

✦　years of each grade level

✦　courses taken

✦　bibliography

✦　brief course descriptions

✦　grades and credits

✦　listing of extracurricular activities and jobs

In reviewing my daughter's transcript today, I see some areas that I could expand upon. I did not include extracurricular activities for tenth and eleventh grades, but they were essentially similar to the activities listed for freshman year. Nonetheless, the admissions director of Lourdes College (OH) was impressed with it. Hocking College (OH) accepted it without further inquiry or clarification.

—RHONDA IN OHIO

rate grade point averages. As discussed previously, smaller, private colleges have more latitude and will be more accepting of nongraded courses than large, public universities.

If you decide to include one or more pieces of optional information, here are some tips to smooth your path.

Credits

Some of our survey respondents assigned units or credits. Others omitted credit information, relying instead on book lists, course descriptions, or narratives to give admissions officers an idea of the depth and breadth of their studies. Either system is equally acceptable. You will probably run into problems with omitting credits only when a college says it absolutely must have a calculated grade point average.

Refer to chapter 6 for an explanation of what counts and ways to generate credits. Generally, one credit equals a one-year high school course; one-half credit corresponds to a half-year or one-semester course. Families that keep good records seldom have trouble generating the average number of credits most high schools require for graduation—namely 20 to 25, roughly five to six classes for each of the four years of high school.

Many homeschoolers, like our family, discover an embarrassment of riches when they total everything. They can easily document 40 to 60 credits and actually have to omit courses to make the transcript believable. It is not that homeschoolers are smarter than everyone else, just that home education itself is very efficient.

If you have not kept records, it is usually not difficult to reconstruct what probably happened—either in terms of seat time or other measures discussed in chapter 6. With our son we did rough estimates of seat time, based on our knowledge of his working habits. For example, he completed the *Saxon Algebra II* book lessons and problem sets. We knew that each problem set took him about an hour. We figured he completed more than 120 problem sets, for an excess of 120 hours. Based on that, we granted him one credit for algebra, because we used the conversion one credit equals 120 hours.

> It is not that home-schoolers are smarter than everyone else, just that home education itself is very efficient.

If you include credits, you should also include an explanation of your credit-granting system. In the footnotes to your transcript, you might write, "One credit equals 150 contact hours" or "One credit represents the equivalent of a two-semester high school course" or "One credit represents covering all the materials outlined in the

HOW WE DID IT

Sample course descriptions from various survey respondents:

ENGLISH

Text: *Warriner's Grammar and Composition, Third Course,* by John E. Warriner. A combination of composition and literature analysis is covered. Spelling and vocabulary words are incorporated into the lessons. Literature elements included main conflict, character traits, characterization, theme, plot, and point of view. Books used for analysis included *Where the Red Fern Grows, Lilies of the Field,* and *Merchant of Venice.*

PHYSICS (AP) AND LAB

Lessons include Newton's laws, statics, dynamics, thermodynamics, optics, DC currents, waves, electromagnetics, and special relativity. Simple experiments and demonstrations relate physical concepts to everyday life. Two in-depth laboratory units—on electronics and optics—provided hands-on experience with real-world applications. Text: *Physics: An Incremental Approach,* by John Saxon. Lab manuals: *Experiments in Physics,* by Janice Van Cleave, and *First Steps in Electronics,* by Kathleen Julicher.

CONSTITUTIONAL LAW

Case-study emphasis for the study of the Constitution and its interpretation. Historical background of the Constitution, the Constitution as higher law, executive and congressional authority, limitations on judicial authority, religious freedom, are topics covered. Text: *Constitutional Law for Christian Students,* by Michael Farris.

DRAMA

Roles:

Polonius. *Hamlet*

Orlando. *As You Like It,* performed on "The Green," Colorado Shakespeare Festival

Witch, Mercutio, Lady Capulet, Friar, Puck, Summer Shakespeare Trio: *Macbeth, Romeo and Juliet, A Midsummer Night's Dream*

Performances Attended:

Twelfth Night; Much Ado about Nothing; The Taming of the Shrew; The Skin of Our Teeth

IMPRESSIONIST ART AND ARTISTS

In May the Barnes collection of Impressionist masterpieces came to the Kimball Art Museum, in Fort Worth. In preparation for attending the exhibit, we investigated the lives and styles of prominent Impressionist painters, studied Monet and Gauguin in depth, and reviewed the role of Impressionism in the modern art movement. Soon after, our daughter began her long association with the Fort Worth Museum of Science and History, volunteering from eight to twelve or more hours per week. The educational benefits were many.

PHYSICAL EDUCATION

Inline skating, downhill skiing, snowshoeing, rock wall climbing, swimming, hiking

course description." The exact criterion you select is not as important as honesty and consistency.

Course Descriptions

Some transcripts include course descriptions. Others do not. For applications to the more competitive colleges and universities (Stanford University [CA], Harvard University [MA], for example), you will need course descriptions to explain the content and scope of your homeschooling. Generally, you will not need descriptions for independent-study program courses and college classes.

As with transcripts, no set format for course descriptions exists. Refer to the prefaces, introductions, and tables of contents of books your teen uses. Review promotional literature and Web sites for your learning materials. These sources often provide phrases that will help you describe course content.

Alternatively, you can ignore textbooks and simply describe what your student learned and how he learned it. Include the references to any helpful books, videos, computer programs, and community resources. Course descriptions need not be lengthy. Three to six sentences will usually do the trick. Sometimes the best course description is a simple list. For one of our physical education course descriptions, we wrote, "Cross-country skiing, hiking, martial arts, biking, and swimming."

Some families also find it helpful to read high school and college course descriptions, just to get a feel for how to write them. The end-of-chapter Resources provide several Web sites where you can read these on-line.

Dates

As you review the transcripts throughout this chapter, you will see that some families list courses by semester. Others find it difficult to say that courses were taken fall semester or spring semester or even within one school year, so they simply list completion dates.

Either method is equally acceptable. If you prefer, you need not list dates at all.

Grades

Similarly, you will note that some homeschool transcripts include grades. Others omit them. Letter grades—A, B, C, D, F—are most commonly used. Here are other possible grades:

+ Percentages

+ P/F for pass/fail

+ Excellent, good, satisfactory, unsatisfactory

If you include grades (remember, they are optional), you should also provide an explanation of your grading system. You can use letters to define percentages or—vice versa—percentages to define letters. For example, A = 91–100 percent, B = 81–90 percent, C = 71–80 percent, and so on. If you prefer more subjective assessments, you can define your letters with terms such as A = mastery, B = above average, and so on.

Some families assign grades as their students complete the work. Others assign grades only when it comes time to write the transcript. When asked how he assigned grades after the fact, David Colfax, author of *Homeschooling for Excellence,* said, "I gave my kid straight A's. Isn't that what you would give yours?" Of course, he was not entirely serious. Certainly, his sons' standardized test scores and performance at Harvard University validated the A's and indicated that their learning at home equaled that of any student who received straight A's in school.

We also gave our children straight A's after the fact. In our case, only subjects they mastered made it to the transcript. We defined

> All homeschooling parents, as the principals of their own small private schools, can grant grades any way they deem appropriate.

mastery level as deserving an A. All homeschooling parents, as the principals of their own small private schools, can grant grades any way they deem appropriate.

"We did provide grades (twelve came from outside sources—the community college or her driver's education teacher)," writes Judy, an unschooling mother. "We explained that the grades, other than those from outside sources, were not a part of our 'program' and were given after the fact based on a mastery system (A = mastery, B = comprehension, C = basic understanding; with nothing less, as the student would have continued until at least a basic understanding was attained)."

Grade Point Average

If you homeschool using a traditional approach, your grades probably reflect averaged results of proctored tests, assignments, and research papers. Once you have added grades to transcripts, you may

HOW WE DID IT

All colleges my daughter applied to required transcripts. Our transcript format lists courses by year and keeps track of credits and grade point averages (GPA) per year and cumulatively. I used a grading scale suggested in several college handbooks and explained it in the footnotes of the transcript: A = 4, A– = 3.7, B+ = 3.4, and so on.

I had heard that some people just use the whole numbers, which seems too simple a scale. My husband felt that some of the grades I gave her were too strict, especially the biology grade (B–). I was vindicated by her first semester of college GPA, which was a few hundredths [of a point] off from her cumulative high school GPA. So I guess I did pretty well!

—RUTH, HOMESCHOOLING MOTHER OF THREE WHOSE OLDEST DAUGHTER WAS
ADMITTED TO CALVIN COLLEGE (MI) AND HILLSDALE COLLEGE (MI)

want to calculate a grade point average. Although it may sound complicated, the procedure for this calculation is a lot easier than mentally figuring a 15 percent tip. Just follow these steps:

1. Assign points to each grade as follows: A = 4, B = 3, C = 2, D = 1

2. Multiply grade points by credits. For example, if your student has three A's, three B's, and one C for seven one-credit classes, you would have:

    3 × 4 = 12 (3 A's times 4 points for each A)

    3 × 3 = 9 (3 B's times 3 points for each B)

    1 × 2 = 2 (1 C times 2 points for each C)

3. Total the grade points, and divide the result by the number of credits:

    12 plus 9 plus 2 equals 23; 23 divided by 7 credits equals 3.3 GPA

A perfect GPA, 4.0, represents straight A's. A 3.0 GPA is a B average, a 2.0 GPA a C average. In this age of grade inflation, some high schools now make it possible to earn GPAs of 4.1 or 4.4. How? They beef up the grade points for difficult advanced placement courses, as follows: A = 5, B = 4, C = 3, and so on. You, of course, can take a similar tack, especially if your student completes advanced placement high school work.

Ruth, whose daughter now attends Hillsdale College (MI), comments on GPAs: "I have spoken with many homeschooling moms who think the grade point average is all-important. It is not. In fact, for a homeschooled student, the GPA is suspect. Our daughter's SAT score validated her GPA, but this might not always be the case. The teaching parent is, by definition, biased. Admissions people know this. Homeschooling parents and students in high school should keep this in mind and not put all their eggs in the GPA basket."

Yes, you can work the numbers and generate almost any GPA you wish. Admissions officers may take the information with a grain of salt, or they make take it seriously. Most will put more weight on course descriptions, essays, letters of recommendation, and SAT and ACT test scores.

Class Rank

Class rank, of course, has little meaning to homeschoolers. Your student, after all, is first in his class of one. Although it seems ridiculous to include a homeschooler's class rank on a transcript, sometimes you have to go along to get along. Judy explains, "We were

HOW WE DID IT

The transcript we wrote was entitled "[Family Surname] Home School Transcript." It had the student's name, social security number, date of birth, address, and sex. I gave titles to the courses, along with grades and credits. I also included a grade point average. I indicated which courses had been taken at community college and which at the language institute. I factored in the grades from the community college classes as regular high school credits and did not attempt to weight the grades in any way.

I wrote the transcript because we were planning to apply to large state universities. I figured that anything that simplified the process for them would be welcome and more likely to result in a positive outcome for our son.

I also recommend that homeschoolers play by the school's rules and not ask for unnecessary exceptions. It is up to the homeschooler to show the school how her portfolio or transcript matches the school's requirements. The school will not spend a lot of time to figure out how to make it fit unless the student presents some truly exceptional qualities.

—SERENA, HOMESCHOOLING SINCE 1992
USING A SEMISTRUCTURED APPROACH

specifically asked to provide class rank even though it was 1 of 1. The dean of admissions at Virginia Tech said it would ease their job, because our daughter would better fit into the process."

You can also provide a class rank based on an SAT or ACT score. Note the overall percentile part of the score report, and assign your homeschooler a class rank of 100 minus the percentile number "out of 100." For example, if your homeschooler's overall percentile rank on the SAT is 91, assign him a class rank of "9 out of a class of 100," and add the notation "based on the SAT score percentile."

Outside Courses

What if your homeschooler's background includes a combination of college courses, classes from independent-study courses, and homeschool courses? Should you put them all on the same transcript? You certainly can, if you prefer. We listed all work on the same transcript and called it a "master transcript." Then we attached copies of the transcripts from outside institutions. The format allowed admissions officers to view everything on two pages. They could then review the details—homeschool course descriptions and external transcripts—in the attachments.

Other Optional Data

The last optional items—standardized-test scores, reading lists, and narratives—may make valuable additions to your transcript. Or your teenager may apply to an institution where the information makes no difference. Include this data only if you believe it is not reported elsewhere and it enhances the overall presentation.

OFFICIAL TRANSCRIPTS

HIGH SCHOOLS ISSUE "official" transcripts directly to colleges. To understand what they mean by "official," it helps to define "unofficial." An unofficial transcript is a copy of a high school transcript submitted to a college by a student, not by the high school. Unofficial transcripts are suspect because—having been in the possession of the student or other third party—they may have been altered.

Often high schools emboss, stamp, sign, or otherwise change the original transcript so that it is difficult to alter and reproduce. This helps colleges know that the transcript came directly from the high school.

You can make your homeschool transcripts official in the same way that colleges do, although—for obvious reasons—your official designation does not carry the same meaning. Some parents sign and date transcripts. Others, going further, get their signatures notarized, as several of our survey respondents did. You can also have an embossed seal made up (about $25) and use it to make your transcript "official."

Most college admissions officers, once they realize your document comes from a homeschool, will not care about the transcript's being official. Should you wish to downplay homeschooling, you might want to experiment with various means of making the transcript look as though it came from a private school—including investing in an embossed seal.

As you put together your transcripts, don't agonize too much over mistakes. We probably made a dozen or more errors—usually in the form of omissions—in the transcripts of our two teenagers. Even so, both were admitted to their first-choice colleges. Do your best to present an honest and positive report of your homeschooler's accomplishments. Try to be consistent in your reporting and format. That is all it takes.

SIMPLE STARTING POINTS

✦   If you haven't already, give your homeschool a name. Ask for suggestions from your entire family.

✦   List the optional items you would like to include on your transcripts.

+   Discuss reporting grades on the transcript with your teenager. What system makes the most sense for your situation?

+   Try writing one course description today. Review the examples in this chapter, and try a narrative description and a simple "list" description.

RESOURCES

Blank Transcripts

Bob Jones University Press, Greenville, SC 29614-0001, 800-845-5431

CLASS Lesson Planner, from The Sycamore Tree, 2179 Meyer Place, Costa Mesa, CA 92627, 800-779-6750

Web Sites

Course descriptions from St. Francis Catholic Home School: http://www.geocities.com/Athens/2026/coursdesc.html

Florida course descriptions: http://www.firn.edu/doe/bin00001/crscode/crshome.htm

High school transcript (sample) from St. Francis Catholic Home School: http://www.geocities.com/Athens/2026/transcrp.html

Transcript worksheet: http://members.aol.com/usteach/downloads/HScoursestudy.doc

+   +   +

All the descriptions in the world cannot take the place of real transcripts.

What follows are five transcripts that worked. You will see that each homeschooling family used a different format. These are not model transcripts, only examples of what worked for each family for college admissions.

OFFICIAL TRANSCRIPT
Senior High

STUDENT DATA

NAME: Last, First, Middle
ADDRESS:
CITY/STATE/ZIP:
PARENTS:
BIRTHDATE:
SOCIAL SECURITY NO:

HOMESCHOOL DATA

NAME:
ADDRESS:
CITY/STATE/ZIP:
TELEPHONE:
REGISTERED:

ACADEMIC RECORD

Course/Class Titles	Course Code	Credit	1996-1997 Freshman	1997-1998 Sophomore	1998-1999 Junior	1999-2000 Senior
English: English I	1001310	1	C			
English II	1001340	1		C		
English III	1001370	1			B	
English IV	1001400	1				A
World Literature	1005300	1		A		
Math: Algebra I (taken in 8th grade)	1200310	1	B (8th)			
Algebra II	1200330	1	B			
Geometry	1206310	1	B			
Trigonometry	1211300	1				
History: Geography	2103300	1				
World History	2109310	1			A	
Florida History	2100350	½		A		
AmericanHistory	2100310	1				A
U.S. Government	2106310	½				
Economics	2102310	½				
Science: Biology	2000310	1	B			
Fundamentals of Chemistry	2003330	1		A		
Physics	2003380	1				

Course	Course #	Credit					
Physical Education: Personal Fitness (LHS)	1501300	½			A		
Beginning Weight Training (LHS)	1501340	½				A	
Intermediate Weight Training (LHS)	1501350	½				A	
Advanced Weight Training (LHS)	1501360	½				A	A
Fitness Lifestyle Design (LHS)	1501310	½				A	
Fitness Issues for Adolescence (LHS)	1501320	½				A	
Team Sports (LHS)	1503350	½				A	A
Fine Arts: Acting I	0400370	1				A	
Stagecraft I	0400410	1	A				
Art History I	0100330	1	A				
Other: Leadership Techniques	2400310	1				A	
Critical Thinking & Study Skills	1700370	½				B	
Career Research & Decision Making	1700380	½				A	
Drivers Education (LHS)	1900310	½		A			
Agritech I	8106820	1		A			
Old Testament Survey	2109390	½		A			
New Testament Survey	2109400	½				A	
Electronics	8730010	1		A			
Health I, Life Management Skills	0800300	½		A			
Personal, Social, & Family Relationships	0800330	½		A			
Spanish I	0708340	1	B				
Keyboarding & Business Skills (FHS)	8200320	½				A	

Total Credits Earned	8	9 (17)	8(25)
GPA for Year	3.125	3.78	3.81
GPA Overall since 9th grade	3.125	3.47	3.58

HOMESCHOOL TRANSCRIPT

FALL SEMESTER	SPRING SEMESTER

GRADE 12
(Planned Curriculum)

Advanced Composition, Indiana University Correspondence	English: World Literature
Calculus	Calculus
World History	World History
Chemistry	Chemistry
Science Lab: Group Problem Solving	Science Lab: Group Problem Solving
Violin, Private Lessons	Violin, Private Lessons
Music History	Music History
Symphony	Symphony
	Theater: Shakespeare
Classes at University of Colorado:	
German 3010 (Advanced Speaking & Writing)	German 3020 (Continuation)

GRADE 11

English			English	
Advanced Math			Advanced Math	
U. S. History			U. S. History	
Geography: Asia			Theater: Shakespeare	
Physics			Physics	
Biology/Microbiology Lab			Biology/Microbiology Lab	
Violin, Private Lessons			Violin, Private Lessons	
Fiddle, Private Lessons			Fiddle, Private Lessons	
Youth Symphony			Youth Symphony	
Classes at High School:				
German 5 (C.U. College Credit)	A		German 5 (C.U. College Credit)	A
Composition	B			

Honors: Inducted into Delta Epsilon Phi, German Honor Society

GRADE 10

English			English		
Algebra 2			Advanced Math		
Renaissance History			Colorado History		
Drama			Theater: Shakespeare		
Violin, Private Lessons			Violin, Private Lessons		
Youth Symphony			Youth Symphony		
Photography Class			Biology/Microbiology Lab		
Pre-International Baccalaureate Classes at		High	Classes at High School:		
German 4	A		German 4		A
Biology	B				

GRADE 9

English			English	
Algebra 2			Algebra 2	
Medieval History			U. S. History: Post Civil War	
Geography: Africa, Indonesia			Theater: Shakespeare	
Violin, Private Lessons			Violin, Private Lessons	
Youth Symphony			Youth Symphony	
Ceramics Class			Drawing Class	
Pre-International Baccalaureate Classes at		High School:		
Intro to Chemistry & Physics	A		Intro to Chemistry & Physics	B
German 2	A		German 2	A

Home School High School Transcript
[STUDENT NAME]
[ADDRESS]
[PHONE]
Date of Birth:
Place of Birth:
Soc. Sec. #:

Course Title	Grade	Credit	Points
----- 1989/90 -----			
Physical Science	B	1	3
----- 1990/91 -----			
Biology with lab	A	1	4
World Geography	A	1	4
Current		2	4
Cumulative		3	3.66
----- 1991/92 -----			
Algebra I	A	1	4
World History	A	1	4
Current		2	4
Cumulative		5	3.8
----- 1992/93 -----			
Music Appreciation	A	1	4
Music Theory	A	1	4
Piano Performance	A	1	4
Oklahoma History	A	1/2	4
Algebra II	A	1	4
U.S. Government	A	1/2	4
Literature	A	1/2	4
Writing/Grammar	A	1/2	4
Current		6	4
Cumulative		11	3.9
----- 1993/94 -----			
Music Theory	A	1	4
American History	A	1	4
French language	A	1	4
Writing/Grammar	A	1/2	4
Literature	A	1/2	4
Piano Performance	A	1	4
Current		5	4.0
Cumulative		16	3.83
----- 1994/95 -----			
Economics	A	1/2	4
Advanced Mathematics	A	1	4
French language	A	1	4
British Literature	A	1/2	4
Philosophy		1	4
Organ performance	A	1	4
Writing/Grammar	A	1/2	4
Current		5 1/2	
Cumulative		21 1/2	3.96

Course Title	Grade	Credit	Points
----- 1995/96 -----			
Understanding /Times	A	1	4
French language	A	1	4
American Literature	A	1/2	4
English	A	1/2	4
Organ performance	A	1	4
Sociology (SNU)	A	3 hours	
American History II (SNU)	A	3 hours	
Current		4	4.0
Cumulative		25 1/2	3.96

Summary by subject area

Science
Physical Science with lab	1
Biology with lab	1

Math
Algebra I	1
Algebra II	1
Advanced Math	1
(Algebra III, Trig, Geometry)	

English
Literature	2
Writing/Grammar	2

History
World History	1
World Geography	1
Oklahoma History	1/2
U.S. Government	1/2
American History	1
Economics	1/2

Music
Music Appreciation	1
Music Theory & Composition	2
Piano Performance	2
Organ Performance	2

Foreign language
French	3

Other
Understanding the Times	1
Philosophy	1

Test Scores

PSAT
Year	Verbal	Math	S.I.	S.I.%
1994	70	68	208	98%

ACT
Date	English	Math	Reading	Science	Composite
4/9/94	32	29	35	27	31

SAT
Date	Verbal	Math	Total
10/95	770	720	1490

Other Information

GPA 3.96   total credits 25 1/2   1996 National Merit Scholar
Graduation date: 5/17/1996
Principal's signature _____

ACADEMY   1996-1997
Official High School Transcript

STUDENT:
DATE OF BIRTH:
SS Number:

9TH GRADE	1st Qtr	2nd Qtr	3rd Qtr	4th Qtr
English I	95 A	96 A	96 A	93 A
Algebra I	91 A-	93 A	93 A	91 A
Government and Economics, US	93 A	93 A	95 A	96 A
Spanish I	99 A+	97 A	98 A	97 A
General Science	93 A	92 A	96 A	94 A
Alabama History	96 A	99 A+	95 A	95 A
Typing	95 A	95 A	95 A	95 A
Bible	95 A	95 A	95 A	95 A
Phys Ed	95 A	95 A	95 A	95 A
Health	95 A	95 A		

OFFICIAL TRANSCRIPT
Academy

STUDENT DATA

NAME: Last, First, Middle
ADDRESS:
CITY/ST/ZIP:
PARENTS:

BIRTHDATE: SEX: [M , F]

SCHOOL DATA

NAME:
ADDRESS:
CITY/ST/ZIP:

TELEPHONE:

ACADEMIC RECORD

COURSE/CLASS TITLE	DATE	CREDIT	GRADE	G.P.A.
English - Intro. to Lit.	5/96	1	A	4.0
World Lit.	5/97	1	A	4.0
American Lit.	5/98	1	A	4.0
Grammar/Writing	12/98	1	A	4.0
Modern Novels I	1/99	½	A	4.0
Math - Algebra I	5/96	1	A	4.0
Algebra II	5/97	1	A	4.0
Advanced Math (Geometry/Trig)	5/98	1	A	4.0
PreCalculus	8/98	½	A	4.0
Science - Basic Science	5/96	1	A-	3.7
Biology	5/97	1	A-	3.0
Intro to Chemistry	5/98	½	A	4.0
Botany	5/98	½	A	4.0
Physics	7/98	1	A	4.0
Social Studies - Geography	5/96	1	A	4.0
Alabama History	5/96	½	A	4.0
World History	5/97	1	B+	3.7
U.S. History	5/98	1	A	4.0
Government	1/99	½	A	4.0
Physical Education - Basketball, Soccer, Fitness, Dance		3	A	4.0
Fine Arts - Music Education		3	A	4.0
Biblical Studies		3 ½	A	4.0
Electives -				
Forestry	5/97	1	A	4.0
Spanish	5/98	1	A	4.0
Video Production	5/98	2	A	4.0
Construction	12/98	2	A	4.0
Driver's Education	5/97	½	A	4.0
Computer Skills I/II	97,1/99	1	A	4.0

GRADE POINT EQUIVILANTS

A = 4.0   A- = 3.7   B+ = 3.3   B = 3.0   C+ = 2.3   C = 2.0

CUMULATIVE SUMMARY

TOTAL CREDITS	G.P.A.
33	3.95

College Test Scores

SAT	ACT
1460	29

Class Rank

Top 5%

Signature of Principal_____   Date_____

High School Transcript

Smith, Jane Marie   **1/1/81**   *Final Report*
Student's Name   DOB

Jane Marie Smith
1234 Maple Avenue
Anytown, VA 22000
(703) 123-4567
DOB: 1/1/81
SS#: 111-22-3333

6/15/99	3.96
Date	Cumulative GPA
5/28/99	28
Graduation	Total Credits
	1 of 1
	Class Rank

SUBJECT AREA	Semester 1	Semester 2	honors	SUBJECT AREA	Semester 1	Semester 2	honors
ENGLISH				**FOREIGN LANGUAGES**			
9	A	A		Latin III	A	A	
10	A	A		French I & II (FRE 101 & 102)	A	A	cc
11 - Emphasis on American Literature	A	A		French III & IV (FRE 201 & 202)	A	A	cc
12 - Emphasis on British Literature	A	A		French V (FRE 233) literature & civilization I	A		cc
Shakespearean Literature	A	A	h	French VI (FRE 298) grammar & writing		A	cc
MATHEMATICS				**SCIENCE**			
Algebra I with Geometry	A	A		Chemistry	B	B	h
Algebra II with Geometry	A	A		Horticulture	A	A	
Precalculus with Geometry	A	A		Ecology Lab (BIO 299) plant communities		A	cc
Calculus/Analytic Geom I & II (MTH 173 & 174)	A	A	cc	University Physics I & II (PHY 241 & 242)	A	A	cc
				Introduction To Space Science (ES 100)	S		cc
SOCIAL STUDIES				**OTHER SUBJECTS**			
World Geography	A	A		Computer Science/Information Systems	A	A	
Ancient History	A	A	h	Web Design	A		
American History - Through the Civil War	A	A	h	Programming in C & C++		A	
American History - After the Civil War	A	A	h	Speech	A		
Economics	A	A	h	Drama		A	
American Government		A		Home Economics	A	A	
				Driver's Education		A	
				Physical Education	A	A	

h - honors courses; cc - courses taken at Northern VA Community College or U of Alabama

Grading System
A = Mastery
B = Comprehension
C = Basic Understanding

Honors & Achievements: _National Merit Scholar, AIME Qualifier_

AHSME: 1996 **81** 1997 **93** 1998 **106** 1999 **96** ; Bronze & Silver Medal

PSAT: 10/97 v**70** m**78** w**71** SAT: 5/98 v**720** m**720** SAT: 11/98 v**780** m**730**

9

DAZZLING

APPLICATION ESSAYS

In This Chapter

✦ Explaining home education

✦ Essay tips

✦ Self-directed learning

✦ Essay for West Point

✦ Samford University submission

✦ Shakespeare's influence

✦ Lessons learned

✦ Simple starting points

✦ Resources

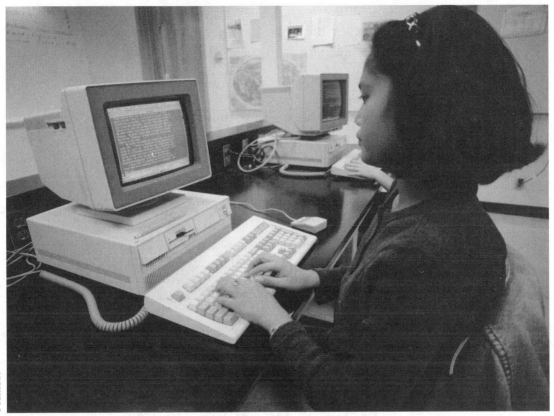

"The better the college, the more heavily they weigh the essay."

—Gayle Moskowitz, guidance counselor
and school social worker

*A*pplication essays matter, in some cases more than test scores and transcripts. Several colleges—Sarah Lawrence (NY), for example—rank the application essay as the primary source of information. Northwestern University (IL) considers transcripts first and essays second—ahead of the college entrance exams—in rating applicants.

You may think that big state colleges have no time to read essays. Don't bet on it, though. Even the University of Michigan, which receives approximately 25,000 applications each year, reads every essay.

Some colleges make the essay optional or read it only in borderline cases. Ted O'Neill, the University of Chicago (IL) dean of admissions, says, "Often [test] scores are in the same acceptable range, the kid's done well in the same classes everybody else has taken, and it's the essay we finally refer to."

Even schools that read essays only in borderline cases probably read every essay from homeschoolers. Because of the presumed bias

AGNES SCOTT COLLEGE (GA) ESSAY QUESTIONS

✦ Are there any significant experiences you have had, or accomplishments you have realized, that have helped to define you as a person?

✦ What social or political issue most concerns you and why?

✦ What has been the most significant event in your life?

✦ What cultural work (literature, music, art, or dance) has had the most significant effect on your life?

✦ The topic of your choice.

in homeschool transcripts, admissions officers usually give more attention to other documentation—test scores, letters of recommendation, interviews, and essays.

That said, many colleges do not require essays at all. Most two-year community colleges and many open-admissions and marginally competitive colleges fall into this category.

You will learn what individual colleges require when you receive their blank applications. Somewhere on the application—if the college requires it—you will see short-answer questions and requirements for longer essays of roughly 250 to 1,500 words. More competitive colleges may require up to three essays. In addition, some colleges require specific essays about the how and why of home education—only from homeschoolers, of course.

EXPLAINING HOME EDUCATION

WHAT DO COLLEGES WANT in these essays to explain homeschooling? Wheaton College's (IL) Homeschool Information Form includes the question "What factors led to your decision to home school?" Huntington College (IN) has a Web page devoted to homeschooled applications. It says, "Your application essay is especially important. . . . We ask students to write about themselves—why they chose homeschooling. . . . Take some time with this essay."

In general colleges want your teenager to answer the same questions you have already answered many times for your friends, neighbors, and relatives:

+ Why does your family homeschool?

+ How does your family homeschool?

+ What are the benefits and disadvantages?

ESSAY TIPS

ALTHOUGH WE WILL devote most of the space in this chapter to essays written by real homeschoolers, we offer first a few essay-writing tips:

Answer the Question

Your homeschooler will not get to first base, and certainly won't be admitted, if he ignores the topic. When he completes his essay, make certain that he addresses the question.

Create an Emotional Impression

The Cambridge Essay Service, which helps develop and edit college application essays, says, "The essays are . . . read by harassed

WHEATON COLLEGE (IL) ESSAY QUESTIONS

1. In a two-page essay, describe the beginning and development of your faith and its impact on your life.

2. How do you see yourself as a good match to Wheaton's academic and spiritual environment?

3. Select one topic below and write a two- to three-page essay:
   - ✦ If you could spend an evening with any person (other than Jesus Christ), whom would you choose and why?
   - ✦ How have your cultural experiences developed your personal identity and your worldview?
   - ✦ Select a creative work—a novel, film, poem, musical piece, or work of art—which has influenced you in some way. Discuss its effect on you.

admissions officers who are looking for an impression. That impression is mostly emotional. The reader of your essay is reaching *an emotional conclusion about you, not an intellectual conclusion about your topic* [emphasis mine]. And the very best emotional conclusion that reader can reach is: 'I really like this kid.'"

Avoid the Generic

"Big idea" topics—the Constitution, racism, the Middle East, gun control, and freedom of the press—generally do not make memorable essays. Although some essay questions may seem to suggest that applicants should write about big ideas, writers should avoid that temptation.

"Big idea" topics—the Constitution, racism, the Middle East, gun control, and freedom of the press—generally do not make memorable essays.

Instead, encourage your teen to focus on small, personal subjects and events that reveal something about her and her life. Your college applicant should follow the advice of many published authors, "Write what you know." What your teenagers know best are their lives, families, and interests. To brainstorm more specifically, sit down with your teen and make lists under each of the following categories:

+ accomplishments
+ distinguishing qualities
+ attributes
+ skills
+ influential books, movies, and works of art
+ strong personality traits
+ strong beliefs
+ important activities
+ dreams for the future

Use the resulting lists to find appropriate essay topics.

Be Concrete

In "How to Avoid the Big Mac Syndrome," which appeared in *U.S. News and World Report,* Parke Muth, assistant admissions counselor at the University of Virginia, deplores what he calls McEssays, all depressingly the same, not unlike McDonald's hamburgers. He characterizes McEssays as "essays usually five paragraphs long that consist primarily of abstractions and unsupported generalizations."

Muth explains, "If an essay starts, 'I have been a member of the soccer team, and it has taught me leadership, perseverance, and hard work,' I can almost recite the rest of the essay without reading it. Each of the three middle paragraphs will give a bit of support to an abstraction, and the final paragraph will restate what has already been said. A McEssay isn't wrong, but it's not going to be a positive factor in an admission decision."

Employ Effective Rhetoric

The Cambridge Essay Service recommends two effective and simple rhetorical devices least used by college admissions essay writers. These are dialogue and facts.

Directly quoting people you mention in your essay creates an immediate, unforgettable impression. Contrast the following two examples:

"Throttle up," he said as the plane gathered speed.

He told me to throttle up as the plane gathered speed.

Facts—as opposed to vague statements—add interest. For example, "I live in a small town on the central California coast," is not nearly as effective as "I live in Arroyo Grande, California, a hilly coastal town of 15,000 people—mostly retirees—midway between San Francisco and Los Angeles."

Encourage your teenagers to use dialogue and facts, rather than vague generalities. Give the reviewer reading hundreds of essays clear mental images.

UNIVERSITY OF CHICAGO (IL) ESSAY QUESTIONS

Respond to three questions:

1. How does the University of Chicago, as you know it now, satisfy your desire for a particular kind of learning, community, and future? Your response should address with some particularity your own wishes and how they relate to Chicago.

2. Describe a few of your favorite books, poems, authors, films, plays, music, paintings, artists, magazines, or newspapers. Feel free to touch on one, some, or all of the categories listed or add a category of your own.

3. Four essay options; here are two:

   ✦ "Landscape is a slippery word. It means more than scenery painting, a pleasant rural vista, or ornamental planting around a country house. It means shaped land, land modified for permanent human occupation, for dwelling, agriculture, manufacturing, government, worship, and for pleasure."—John R. Stilgoe, *Common Landscape of America, 1580–1845*

   In light of Stilgoe's definition of landscape, think about the landscape (or cityscape) in which you live. In an essay, tell us how this landscape defines and is defined by you and your community. How does it reflect the society in which you live? How has the landscape changed or been altered since you've lived in it?

   ✦ The late-eighteenth-century popular philosopher and cultural critic Georg Lichtenberg wrote, "Just as we outgrow a pair of trousers, we outgrow acquaintances, libraries, principles, etc. . . . at times before they're worn out and at times—and this is the worst of all—before we have new ones." Write an essay about something you have outgrown, perhaps before you had a replacement—a friend, a political philosophy, a favorite author, or anything that has had an influence on you. What, if anything, has taken its place?

Edit and Revise

Your teenager should treat the college application essay as a serious writing project. Take at least one to two weeks to brainstorm topics and approaches to various questions. In addition, for an outstanding product, he should revise the essay several times over several weeks.

> Your teenager should treat the college application essay as a serious writing project.

Get Outside Opinions

Give your teenager's essay to several friends, neighbors, relatives, and adult mentors for comment. Listen carefully to their reactions, and encourage further revisions as needed.

Do consult the Resources for more ideas and in-depth tips about writing college application essays. We devote the remainder of this chapter to five products, college application essays written by real homeschoolers.

SELF-DIRECTED LEARNING

THE AUTHOR OF the following essay has been homeschooled for most of her life. Her family at first used unit studies and an eclectic approach and finally switched to unschooling—except for grade 9. Our homeschooler explains, "The first six months to a year of high school, I was worried that if I didn't do certain subjects a certain way, I wouldn't get into college, so I had literature, vocabulary, and grammar textbooks for English. I'd soon had enough of that. I still read the literature book for an interesting selection of stories, but that was it. I took some classes (French, calculus, and physics) at our local community college and studied other subjects mainly on my own, reading from textbooks and nonfiction books from the library. I also took part in math, writing, and book discussion clubs."

This homeschooler now attends the University of Rochester, in New York. Here is her application essay:

The most significant experience of my life has been homeschooling. It is the experience that colors and flavors every part of my life. My life has never been divided into the two parts, school and out of school, because I've never used a standard curriculum for each grade or been confined to a schedule. The result has been that I've had freedom to take charge of my own education.

I've had freedom from the traditional setting of learning and haven't been confined to a desk. Some of my earliest memories are of sitting on stairs reading aloud with another homeschooled friend, of making pictures of trains out of celery and peanut butter, and of relaxing on the lawn with my math problems. Field trips came up two or three times a week, and as I grew up in the D.C. area I had the opportunity to explore history through monuments, museums and houses.

I've had freedom from time constraints. I could start studying a subject any month of the year. My "school year" could start late in September because of a vacation, or I could work through the summer on a subject I didn't feel like I had completed. I could take night classes at the community college and I could sleep in the next day.

Even with my more recently busy schedule because of community college courses, I could skip a day of my studies to go to a museum, and if I got absorbed in something I didn't have to put it down and move on at the ring of a bell.

I've had freedom to pursue my own interests, especially in languages. For as long as I can remember I've been interested in French, and homeschooling allowed me to begin my studies in kindergarten. My French tutor moved away and I began studying Latin when I was eight. Math is another language and I've been able to pursue this interest on my own, then through an interest club and finally at the local community college. Programming is yet another language. At the beginning of high school I had the opportunity

QUICK & EASY

Use college application essay questions as writing practice during your teenager's last couple of years of homeschooling. Find these questions on the applications posted at college and university Web sites or by simply requesting applications from several different colleges.

to take an informal robotics class and now am teaching myself some C and C++.

I've had the freedom to make my own choices and direct my own education. I've chosen to use a traditional language arts curriculum, to belong to a peer writing club for feedback on my fiction, to study Shakespeare with a Shakespearean actress over a period of six years, to use a distance learning option to study calculus, and to take French and physics at our local community college. Some of these choices have been challenging, but I've always managed to find what I've wanted and have learned from the decisions.

For me, freedom in education has come through homeschooling, but even among homeschoolers this amount of freedom is not the norm. What I do has been called unschooling but that term seems unsatisfactory to me. Unschooled . . . not schooled, they could almost be synonymous, and without much stretch of the imagination you could come up with uneducated. A much more accurate term, and one I have now chosen for myself, is an autodidact. It doesn't have the negative connotations of "unschooler" and it describes what I am: a self-taught person. While my mother has always been there helping, counseling, providing resources, and guiding me throughout my life, I was the one who taught myself the things I've learned. Better yet, an autodidact is something that I don't have to stop being merely because I graduate and go off to college and join the workforce.

Having learned how to learn, an autodidact is something I can be for life. I think that is the most significant idea homeschooling has impressed upon me: Freedom to learn what you want is there forever.

ESSAY FOR WEST POINT

NEXT WE HEAR from a successful applicant to the United States Military Academy, at West Point, New York. His mother briefly describes their home education as follows: "Our goal as home educators is to manage and direct the student away from a teacher-dependent focus to a predominantly self-taught, internally motivated concentration of study." Here is the application essay, written by a member of the 2001 class at West Point:

Since I was a child, I have had the desire to be in the military. Like most boys, my ten-year-old friends and I were fascinated with guns. We always loved dressing up in camouflage, getting our homemade wooden rifles, and running into the woods to go fight the "bad guys." The weapons we played with were handcrafted by young, eager hands to vaguely resemble the "great machine guns of World War II." Realistically, they were crudely made pieces of wood that in any ten-year-old's mind looked like a real weapon. We also had the opportunity to organize a club we called U.S.M.C. (United States Marine Club). This club basically organized what we had been doing for months, by making fake military scenarios (mock battles) and by trying to stop the who-shot-who fights.

As I grew older and moved away, the desire to be in the real army never went away, although the desire to "play army" has been greatly diminished. I, now, look toward my future, as I currently undergo my final year in high school, and with it at my fingertips I know that the army is what I want to pursue. I have learned that the army is not "going out and fighting bad guys," but is a way of life that teaches discipline, respect, principle, and integrity to those it trains. My desire is to seek knowledge by gaining a higher education, and with that knowledge pursue a career in which I can excel.

The United States Military Academy will not only accomplish that goal completely, but it will also further my understanding of honor, courage, and discipline, words with great meaning when applied to one's character. I have always looked with awe upon the men in gray, and now I have the opportunity to pursue a cadetship for myself.

As a competitive swimmer I have put a lot of effort and time into the goals I have set for myself, and have, in turn, been rewarded with such traits as diligence, determination, and perseverance. I have also developed a love for the sport, and would count it an honor not only to be a member of the Corps of Cadets, but also to swim for Army Swimming and Diving. The Academy is a place where I can learn and train to be a soldier, to be pushed physically as well as mentally, and to seek excellence in all areas of life.

I also desire to be a part of tradition, to carry on for past generations, to experience now what it was like then, and to do the things that those I have looked up to have done. Attending the United States Military Academy is something I know is worthy of striving for, and as a West Pointer I know I would be able to stand tall and proud with an exemplary character others could look up to. I know it would be an invaluable experience that would make me proud to be a member of the Long Gray Line.

SAMFORD UNIVERSITY SUBMISSION

THIS NEXT ESSAY comes from the daughter of a family home-schooling primarily for religious reasons. She had been home-schooled since 1991. In 1997 she applied to the University of Mobile (AL) and Samford University (AL) and won admission to both.

When my pastor first asked our youth group to help with the local Baptist Association Vacation Bible School (VBS), I just rolled my eyes and groaned. I thought, "Oh, great, I get to spend a week of my summer teaching obnoxious kids who want to do anything but sit still and pay attention." Reluctantly, I agreed to help.

On the first morning of VBS a dark foreboding came over me. I dreaded the day ahead of me. I prayed, "Lord, I want to wipe out this selfish attitude; please give me the strength to do that. In everything I do today I want to bring glory and honor to Your name. Thank you for giving me this opportunity." A tremendous peace came over me. All dread left me as if a mighty wind had blown straight through my soul and wiped away all the negative thoughts.

As the director was telling us the plans for the day, he mentioned that we would be working at an adult day care before we started VBS. I didn't know what to think as I heard this and I was nervous. I thought an adult day care was a place where elderly people played dominos all day, not realizing it was a center where physically and mentally handicapped adults stayed during the day. I wasn't sure of what the men and women living in the day care would do when a group of boisterous teenagers came barging into their quiet day.

We prepared some songs, practiced handling our puppets, and worked out a few skits, but we still felt like we didn't know what we were doing. We had barely begun to set up everything in the center when a group of both young and old came scurrying through the door. As I watched them, an older lady walked up to me, held out her hand, smiled, and said to me in a quiet voice, "I want to thank you young people for coming. You will never know how much this means to us."

I turned around and saw my friends looking at me. They heard what the woman had said. We were all thinking the same thing. We knew these people did not care whether we sang on the right key, or whether we made mistakes with our puppets. They knew we had given our time to come and share with them. My thoughts had been that we would be giving something to the adults and that we would be the ones teaching them. But it was, in fact, the adults in the center who taught us.

That day was perfect for me. I learned that God works through people who are willing to serve others. My attitude at the beginning of that day was not one of service, and I realized that once my heart changed, God was able to work through me and show me wonderful things.

SHAKESPEARE'S INFLUENCE

THE AUTHOR OF the next essay was admitted to Vanderbilt's (TN) Blair School of Music on an honors scholarship. He transferred in his second year and now attends Macalester College (MN), where he also studies music.

Although my professional goals are musical, I also enjoy directing and acting in plays, preferably Shakespeare. Theater has had a big influence on me. I tend to absorb the personality of my characters to the point where I incorporate their mannerisms into my daily life. When I played Caliban, it became a running joke at the dinner table that it was not me but Caliban, the downtrodden monster, hunched over a bowl of gruel. But Caliban and others had only a mild effect on me. It was playing King Lear's Fool that changed my life or at least my lifestyle.

First, I loved the Fool's rhymes, sayings, and clever metaphors. The Fool plays with language constantly, a pastime that I also relish. Words, along with music, represent one of the mediums I use to express myself and unleash my creativity. Besides playing with words, the Fool is also the only one in the play who knows the truth and can say it without being banished. I, too, like to mix playful jest with more serious thoughts about reality.

Foolery is spontaneous. A Fool often needs off-the-top-of-the-head humor. My extensive improvisation presents a perfect musical analog. In improvisational music one must feed off the moment, acting quickly and skillfully, but retaining the meaning and purpose of the music.

But these aspects of the Fool did not change my life. It was the fool lifestyle, the fool finesse, that did it. My friends say I have never recovered

UNIVERSITY OF VIRGINIA
ESSAY QUESTIONS

1. College of Arts and Sciences. What work of art, music, science, mathematics, or literature has surprised or unsettled or challenged you, and in what way?

   School of Architecture. If you could change the current architecture of your school, what change(s) would you make?

   School of Engineering. What experiences have led you to choose the School of Engineering?

   School of Nursing. What experiences have led you to choose the School of Nursing?

2. Answer one of the following questions. Limit your response to half a page, or approximately 250 words.

   ✦ Look out any window in your home. Given the opportunity, what would you change about what you see?

   ✦ Besides the computer, what technological development has had the greatest impact on human society?

   ✦ "The past is never dead. It's not even past." So says the lawyer Gavin Stevens in Faulkner's *Requiem for a Nun*. To borrow Stevens's words, what small event, from either your personal history or the history of the world, is neither "dead" nor "past"?

   ✦ Does discrimination still exist? What experience or event has led you to your conclusion?

   ✦ What is your favorite word, and why?

3. Please submit a final piece of writing on any subject you choose. Limit your response to one page, or approximately 500 words.

from the role of the Fool. They say I play the Fool all the time, which is not an unwarranted opinion, because I try to spout jokes, riddles, and witticisms at all times.

I have taken it to heart to be a fool. This does not mean that I simply fool around. It means that I know the importance of hard work and the benefits to be derived from it, but strive to approach all my endeavors with enthusiasm, with gusto, and with humor. While my professional aspiration is to become a great musician, my equally important personal goal is to be a true fool.

The Fool's life is a good one, filled with laughter and mirth. However, the Fool also knows the stark truth of life—that we're born and then we die. The Fool is not deterred. He boldly strides into the face of the great mystery and gives a cosmic laugh. In my life, I strive to do the same. After all, as I like to say, "Life's too mysterious; don't take it 'serious.'"

LESSONS LEARNED

THE AUTHOR OF the next essay was homeschooled from grades 2 through 12. When asked why she wanted to go to college, she responded, "I think that I had always assumed that I would go to college, because it's what you do after high school. As the time drew closer, however, and I discussed it with my parents, I realized that I had always loved learning and wanted to continue my education and that I wanted the preparation and experience necessary to get a good job later." She is now a sophomore at Hillsdale College (MI).

"You're so shy," my friend Beth complained.

"I don't think so," I disagreed, but Beth wasn't convinced.

"Oh, yes, you are. Remember when I first met you, how quiet you were?"

Maybe Beth's opinion of me wasn't too surprising. After all, compared to Beth, who as an eighth-grader used to introduce herself to strange mothers on the playground in hopes of getting a babysitting job, anyone might be considered "shy." In reality, though, I'm not shy and never have been. As a toddler, I let out a constant stream of talk—even when no one was listening. I talked about everything I did and saw.

When I was a little older, I remember that when my parents had friends visiting, I would sit in a corner of the living room without saying a word, scarcely daring to move, hoping against hope that my mom would forget to send me to bed and I could stay up and listen to the conversation. Even better was going for walks with my dad, so we could talk about things. My dad used to make up stories for me.

"Guess what happened to me yesterday," he would say. "I went to visit the ants that live in that anthill."

"Oh, tell me about it," I would beg. "Tell me—from the beginning."

I still love conversation, no matter what the subject—and the deeper and more complex the discussion, the more I love it. This year my parents, along with some other homeschooling parents, started a discussion group for homeschooled high schoolers. Our meetings are the highlight of my week. I like exchanging ideas and opinions with my friends. Meeting new people and finding new things to talk about is one of the things I look forward to most about college.

Perhaps it's because I love conversation that I value truth so much, for what kind of discussion can you have with someone who is not telling the truth? Honesty is something that has always been important to me. Many years ago I made a promise to myself that I would never tell lies. I don't remember why I did it. Maybe I was inspired by a story I had heard or read, maybe by a lesson I was taught at home or at Sunday school. I do remember that ever afterward when I was tempted to lie, I would say sternly to myself, "Remember—you promised!" Honesty became such a habit with me that even now I doubt that I could tell a lie with a straight face. I can't claim to have kept my promise perfectly. I have said less than the whole truth sometimes, occasionally something that wasn't entirely true. Most of the time, though, I've been truthful.

From the time I was little I liked to be neat and orderly. I was always sorting things—arranging my crayons in rainbow order, lining up my dolls from largest to smallest. It's a standing family joke that each Christmas I hang my ornaments on the tree in order starting with my "Baby's First Christmas" ball and ending with the newest ones.

Just as neatness is important to me, I always want things to be just so no matter what I am doing. If I draw a picture and something is out of proportion, I can't rest until I've fixed it. I get frustrated when I'm playing the piano and my fingers aren't strong enough to play a trill quickly or controlled enough to play a chord softly. I'm the kind of person who reads instruction manuals cover to cover and keeps all the dollar bills in a wallet facing the same direction.

Sometimes my neatness can be a blessing, but sometimes it's a curse, as when I had to teach myself to write a little less perfectly in order to get my math papers finished on time. In the same way, God has given me all of my personality, and I can't change it, but I can learn to use it for good. I need to use my orderliness not to become an uptight perfectionist, but to always strive to do my best; to learn not to talk too much, but to listen to others as well; and to uphold the truth in all things.

All of these essays were written by real people. They recount real events in the author's lives, and—in several cases—we experience the authors' real impressions. They show growth, leadership, learning, and character. Regardless what question they were asked, these applicants drew on personal experiences to generate answers. The essays reflect, above all, the incredible diversity of homeschoolers and the individuality of their authors.

SIMPLE STARTING POINTS

+ Have your teenagers keep daily journals beginning in grade 8. When it's time to write a college application essay, they can page back through their lives to find an appropriate incident to relate.

+ Discussion often precedes good writing. Visit five to ten college Web sites and find their on-line applications. Read and discuss the essay questions with your teenagers.

+ Get a little help from your friends. At your local homeschool support group, ask if anyone has college application essays that they can share.

+ Some college applications ask you to create your own essay question and answer it. Brainstorm "ideal" questions with your teenagers.

RESOURCES

Books

Burnham, Amy, et al. *Essays That Will Get You into College.* Barron's Educational Series, 1998.

Curry, Boykin. *Essays That Worked: 50 Essays from Successful Applications to the Nation's Top Colleges.* Fawcett Books, 1990.

Georges, Christopher. *100 Successful College Application Essays.* Mentor Books, 1991.

McGinty, Sarah Myers. *The College Application Essay.* College Entrance Examination Board, 1997.

Stewart, Mark Allen. *The Best College Admissions Essays.* IDG Books, 1997.

Van Raalte, Susan D. *College Applications and Essays.* IDG Books, 1997.

Web Sites

"Writing the College Application Essay," at the College View site: http://www.collegeview.com

"Your College Essay," at College Board Online: http://www.collegeboard.org

The Cambridge Essay Service, Cambridge, Massachusetts, 617-354-2242: http://world.std.com/~edit

College Gate Essay Editing Service: http://www.collegegate.com/index.shtml

10

OUTSIDE EVALUATIONS: RECOMMENDATION LETTERS, COLLEGE ADMISSIONS TESTS, AND COLLEGE CLASSES

In This Chapter

✦ Recommendation letters

✦ College admissions tests

✦ Scholastic Assessment Test II: subject tests

✦ Test preparation

✦ College courses

✦ Simple starting points

✦ Resources

© EyeWire

"In the absence of a conventional transcript, alternative ways of showing achievement can be crucial, especially at highly selective institutions."

—Bruce Hammond in "Will Homeschooling Hurt
Your Child Later On?" at the Parent Soup
Web site, http://www.parentsoup.com

At many schools your list of classes or transcript will suffice for admissions. For the most competitive colleges and universities, however, outside evaluations of your homeschoolers' accomplishments move front and center. "Naturally, antennae go up when it's a school of two, and the teacher is your mama, and the principal is your daddy," explains John Albright, senior associate director of admissions at the University of Georgia.

Even with Mom as teacher and Dad as principal, homeschoolers have many options for outside evaluation. The most common include letters of recommendation, college admissions tests, and grades in college classes. You will need all three for applications to highly selective colleges.

Letters of recommendation serve two purposes: First, they substitute for the commonly requested counselor and teacher recommendation. In addition, letters of recommendation from adults outside your family provide outside assessment of your teenagers' character traits and independent descriptions of their achievements.

Moving from verbal evaluations to cold, hard numbers, standardized tests—such as the Scholastic Assessment Test I (SAT) and the ACT Assessment—lend credibility to transcripts. The Preliminary Scholastic Assessment Test (PSAT) provides admissions officers a preview of the SAT score and serves as the qualifying test for the National Merit Scholarship Program.

Additional tests, the Advanced Placement (AP) and College Level Examination Program (CLEP) tests, allow schools to grant your students college credit and sometimes place them in sophomore- and higher-level courses. Decent scores on these college-credit tests enhance chances of admission to selective schools. Outstanding scores almost guarantee admission and big financial aid awards.

Finally, grades in college classes act as independent corroboration of your homeschooler's abilities and accomplishments. Our son—not unlike many high school homeschoolers—completed more than 20 college credits at both the Community College of Aurora and the University of Denver. After he earned "B's" in the difficult first-year laboratory physics sequence at the University of Denver at ages 16 and 17, Air Force Academy (CO) admissions officials probably believed that he really had earned his homeschool "A's" in math up through trigonometry.

Read on to learn the details behind accumulating this data. If your child is middle-school age, it's not too early to start. Your teenager can begin acquiring letters, preparing for tests, and even taking college classes as early as grade 8.

RECOMMENDATION LETTERS

HOMESCHOOLERS MOST FREQUENTLY use letters of recommendation as substitutes for the counselor's, principal's, and teacher's recommendations that competitive colleges request.

Beginning in grade 8, your homeschoolers should request recommendation letters from any adult with whom they work, in both academic and nonacademic settings. Think 4-H and scout leaders, volunteer program directors, employers, coaches, music and dance teachers, homeschool support-group leaders, tutors, church choir directors, pastors, rabbis, youth-group leaders, and college teachers.

> Beginning in grade 8, your homeschoolers should request recommendation letters from any adult with whom they work, in both academic and nonacademic settings.

Denise, whose son was admitted to the highly selective Stanford University (CA), says that their family requested letters from her son's community college physics and English professors and also from a summer internship mentor.

Julie's son won admission to Vanderbilt (TN). She reports, "He got letters from his violin teacher, German teacher from school,

HOW WE DID IT

All our daughter's applications asked for letters of recommendation, both college applications and scholarship applications. Because of where we lived, in a remote area, and her limited choices of activities, the people she could ask to write these were also limited in number. Because my husband is a pastor, she didn't have that option to choose from, either, as they were supposed to be written by non–family members.

She asked her piano instructor (from whom she took lessons for five years and who knew her very well), one of the church youth-group leaders, and adult friends from church that she worked with at vacation bible school.

—RUTH, WHOSE DAUGHTER WON A NATIONAL MERIT SCHOLARSHIP

science project mentor, and math and science club leaders. These last two were homeschool dads with whom he had worked."

Ruth, homeschooling since 1987, recommends that students ask people for recommendation letters several weeks in advance of the due dates. She says that both she and her husband have fielded requests from applicants who have given them a week's notice, barely enough time. Give busy adult mentors a month or two, if possible.

When your homeschoolers request letters, three additional items will help the recommender:

✦ A copy of the relevant parts of the application. With this the writer can see exactly what the university or scholarship program has requested, as well as the correct name and address for their submission.

In addition to requesting recommendations during the mad rush of completing applications, we encourage homeschoolers to begin

HOW WE DID IT

Our son had adults he knew well write letters of recommendation. His piano teacher of ten years wrote a recommendation. The 4-H extension agent wrote letters for both applications and scholarships. After our son took a college course (while in high school), he asked that professor to write letters for scholarships.

—KATE, A SOUTH DAKOTA HOMESCHOOLING MOM

requesting letters in grade 8. Often it is difficult to find people one or more years after your teens have worked with them. It is also challenging for the adults to recall specific events one or two years in the past. Get letters at the same time your teens are working with these adults. Request them now, not later.

✦   A résumé or list of activities. The person writing the recommendation may know your homeschooler as a violinist, martial arts student, hockey player, church choir member, or volunteer worker. At the same time, they may be unaware of all his other accomplishments. Give them more to rave about and provide phraseology for the letter with a brief résumé or activities list.

✦   A stamped envelope in which to mail the letter to the student or directly to the college or university.

Ask adults who work with your teenagers for any period of time—a day to several years—for their impressions. If they seem positive, request a general college letter of recommendation. Each year, you should be able to file two or three of these with your teenager's portfolio and extracurricular materials. These letters—obtained in advance of need—often work perfectly for college applications.

LETTER OF RECOMMENDATION

[Letterhead of Center for the Performing Arts]

To whom it may concern,

I have had the pleasure of working with Jennifer Smith since she was a very young girl and have watched her grow into a very special young lady. As a student she has always been hardworking and attentive. As a student teacher, she is dependable and diligent and always responsive when I ask for help.

Jennifer is bright and creative, and I highly recommend her for any scholarship.

Very truly yours,

[Name]
[Title]

Sometimes a coach or volunteer supervisor or other adult may hesitate to write a recommendation. This can be especially confusing if the person seems otherwise enthused about your teenager. Remember that some people dislike writing. Others do not have time. In these cases, offer to write the letter. Then he or she can review the draft, make changes, and sign it.

Include at least three items in any letter of recommendation:

✦ How the adult knows the student. "I was Jeff's first flying instructor in single-engine aircraft."

✦ What skills, accomplishments, and character traits the recommender has observed. "Tamara's enthusiasm for new tasks and her ability to communicate well with patients are assets to the hospital volunteer program." The letter should also contain examples that support the generalizations.

✦ The recommendation. "I highly recommend Jason for your challenging program." You can begin or end the letter with this type of statement.

LETTER OF RECOMMENDATION

[Letterhead of Cooperative Extension Office]

[Date]

To whom it may concern,

I highly recommend Christine Jones for consideration as a scholarship recipient.

I am so impressed with Christine. I have spent considerable time with her the past year and a half. She enrolled in the Green County Leadership Institute and graduated from the seven-month course in May 1998.

The course was designed for adults. It included skills building, community-based experiences, and an individual leadership assessment. In all cases, Christine excelled. Her being the only youth in the program concerned me. But Christine's maturity and personality allowed her to fit in well, actively participate in discussions, and get involved in activities.

The Cooperative Extension Service was invited to conduct a student leadership assessment for Jefferson High School students. After working with Christine in the institute, I thought she would be very capable of assisting me with the planning and implementation of this project. We met with school personnel and students last spring. We met during the summer to create new scenarios related to youth issues. Christine was responsible for finding four role players and setting up the training. During the assessment this fall, she was the lead facilitator.

In every way, I found Christine to be very responsible and organized. She is an extremely motivated young lady and showed a great deal of initiative in the project. We assessed twelve students, and the resulting evaluations were very positive.

On a personal note, I have become very fond of Christine. She is a joy to be around. She is very cheerful and enthusiastic. She's extremely bright and competent.

She deserves a scholarship for how hard she works and excels. Please consider Christine for a scholarship. If you have any further questions, please call me at [phone number].

Best,

[Name]
University Extension Educator

COLLEGE ADMISSIONS TESTS

FIRST THINGS FIRST. Although we will discuss college admissions tests in this section, you need to know up front that your homeschoolers may not need to take them. Most two-year community colleges and many noncompetitive colleges do not require test scores.

In addition, an increasing number of colleges and universities have made SAT or ACT scores optional. FairTest is a nonprofit advocacy organization that, according to its Web site, "is working to end the abuses, misuses, and flaws of standardized testing and ensure that evaluation of students and workers is fair, open, and educationally sound."

> At this writing, FairTest lists 284 four-year colleges and universities that have eliminated or reduced SAT and ACT requirements for admission into bachelor's degree programs.

At this writing, FairTest lists 284 four-year colleges and universities that have eliminated or reduced SAT and ACT requirements for admission into bachelor's degree programs. Schools on this list include Allen University (SC), Bates College (ME), Hawaii Pacific University (HI), Wayne State University (MI), and the University of Houston (TX). Some schools on FairTest's list may use SAT and ACT scores for academic advising or only for out-of-state applicants.

Homeschoolers who do apply to institutions that require college entrance tests should know that their predecessors have done well. In 1999 2,219 students identified themselves on the SAT as homeschooled. They scored an average of 1083 (verbal 548, math 535), 67 points above the national average of 1016 (1600 is a perfect score).

In addition, in 1999 3,616 homeschoolers took the ACT, scoring an average of 22.7. The national average was 21 (36 is a perfect score).

With that good news, let's take a look at the different standardized tests applicants take prior to and during the college application process:

+ Preliminary Scholastic Assessment Test (PSAT)

+ Scholastic Assessment Test I: Reasoning Test

+ ACT Assessment

+ Scholastic Assessment Test II: Subject Tests

+ College Level Examination Program (CLEP) and Advanced Placement (AP) tests

Preliminary Scholastic Assessment Test (PSAT)

The first standardized test your homeschooler may encounter, the PSAT, is optional. No applicant needs a PSAT score for admission to any college or university. Nevertheless, your teen may want to take this test—for two reasons.

First, as a shorter, supposedly simpler version of the SAT I, the PSAT functions as a practice SAT. Students take the PSAT under real testing conditions and receive scores that predict the SAT I score. The PSAT has verbal, math, and writing sections. Each section is graded from 20 to 80, with 50 being an average score. Students receive two-digit scores on each section—for example, 63 verbal and 57 math. If you append a zero to these scores, you have the estimated equivalent SAT score—in this case 630 verbal and 570 math.

Second, the National Merit Scholarship Corporation uses the PSAT to rank students for the National Merit Scholarships—hence the alternate name for the PSAT, the National Merit Scholarship Qualifying Test (NMSQT). Only a small percentage of examinees win these scholarships. If your homeschooler has previously scored in the ninety-fifth percentile or above on a standardized test, he or she might be competitive. The National Merit Scholarship administrators calculate a "selection index," using the math, verbal, and writing scores. This favors students with verbal strengths over those with mathematical talents.

Fewer than one percent of students nationwide qualify for National Merit Scholarships. Even so, homeschoolers have proven they can win these awards. The National Merit Scholarship Corporation selected as semifinalists 70 students in 1998 who identified themselves as homeschoolers—137 in 1999, and 150 in 2000. Understand, though, that most students—including most homeschooled teens—receive scholarships and loans elsewhere—primarily through college financial aid offices (see chapter 12).

The PSAT is given only in October of each year (in the 1999–2000 school year, for example, on two Tuesdays and two Saturdays). Unlike the SAT I, the PSAT is a school-based test. Your homeschooler must sign up for it through a local public or private school. Contact high school counseling offices in the spring to ensure that you do not miss September sign-up deadlines. When your student registers, make certain you get a PSAT/NMSQT Student Bulletin, which will contain a sample test.

Many students take the PSAT both their sophomore and junior years. However, only the score attained in what the student identifies as his junior year counts for the scholarship competition.

Scholastic Assessment Test I: Reasoning Test (SAT I)

According to the test-administering organization, the College Board, "The SAT I is a three-hour, primarily multiple-choice test that measures developed verbal and mathematical reasoning abilities related to successful performance in college." Test content consists of three verbal sections and three math sections plus one "equating" verbal or math section, which does not count toward the student's score. The test makers use the equating section to develop new questions and compare current and older versions of the test.

The SAT I is one of two principal college admissions tests, the other being the ACT, described below. More than 90 percent of competitive colleges in the country require either an SAT I or an ACT score. Side comment: Do not confuse the SAT college admissions test with the Stanford Achievement Test, a grades 1-to-8 achievement test with the same initials.

SAT I scores run from 200 to 800. The College Board reports average scores of 505 verbal and 511 math for college-bound seniors in the 1999–2000 school year. Most students take the SAT I either late in their junior year or early in their senior year. Many teens take the SAT I more than once, some up to three to six times. Most experts agree that students do not significantly improve their scores after taking the test three times.

For the 2000–2001 school year, there are seven Saturday test dates, October through June. Registration deadlines precede test dates by four to five weeks. Sunday test administrations are offered for those whose religion precludes Saturday testing. Homeschoolers register for the SAT independent of any school. Register on-line or via regular mail with materials you obtain from any high school counseling office.

MONEY SAVER

For test preparation, visit the College Board Web site SAT Learning Center, which has real SAT questions and answers, plus a diagnostic test.

ACT Assessment

According to the ACT Web site, "The ACT Assessment is designed to assess high school students' general educational development and their ability to complete college-level work." Tests cover four skill areas—English, mathematics, reading, and science reasoning. Scores on each part range from 1 to 36. The ACT composite score is the average of all four scores. Average scores each year hover in the 21–22 range.

Although the ACT, like the SAT I, is touted as a general-abilities test, many say that the ACT requires slightly more recall of specific information. Colleges that require admissions tests usually request either the SAT I or the ACT. The ACT is more popular in the Midwest and Southeast; the SAT I, more often preferred everywhere

HOW WE DID IT

Leo and Penny, homeschooling parents who used a self-designed home-schooling program, describe the results of their son's high school achievement test and college admissions test:

"Our son got the following scores on various tests:

✦ Tests of Achievement of Proficiency (TAP, grade 10), composite in the ninety-ninth percentile [note: the TAP is the high school version of the Stanford Achievement Test, given in grades 1 to 8]

✦ PSAT/NMSQT: Selection Index 198, ninety-sixth percentile, received a National Merit Letter of Commendation

✦ SAT: 1390

✦ ACT: 33 composite, ninety-ninth percentile"

else. Home educators whose students are applying to colleges that accept the results of either test may want to experiment with sample tests at home to determine which to focus on.

Some homeschoolers take both the SAT and the ACT. Maria in Oklahoma, mother of two National Merit Scholarship finalists, explains, "Our sons took both the ACT and the SAT as well as the PSAT. They took the PSAT for practice and for scholarship potential. They took the SAT for scholarship applications. They took the ACT because most colleges in our area of the country prefer this test."

For the 2001–2002 school year, there are six Saturday ACT testing dates, September through June, with provisions for Sunday testing similar to those for the SAT. Just as with the SAT I, your homeschooler can register for the ACT Assessment independently, either on-line or by regular mail. Obtain hard-copy registration materials at any high school counseling office.

Scholastic Assessment Test II: Subject Tests

The SAT II Subject Tests are one-hour tests in specific subjects such as U.S. history, world history, biology, chemistry, Spanish, French, literature, writing, and math. (If you applied to college fifteen or more years ago, you might recall that these were then called Achievement Tests.) Scores for the SAT II Subject Tests range from 200 to 800, just as they do for the SAT I.

Except for colleges that have discriminatory policies toward homeschoolers (see chapter 1), only the most competitive colleges in the country require SAT II test results. These colleges—Harvard (MA), Stanford (CA), and the University of California, Berkeley, for example—request that applicants submit scores from one to three SAT II Subject Tests. The writing test is requested most frequently.

HOW WE DID IT

Our son took the SAT I and five SAT II Subject Tests—writing, math IC, math IIC, U.S. history, and German with listening.

We used score withholding for strategic release of scores. Since he had historically been a poor test taker, we had him take a College Insights course, which gave him lots of practice and more confidence.

He scored in the upper 600s, pretty much across the board, although the math scores were a bit lower. He could probably have retaken the tests and brought those scores up, but chose not to, since they were not so important for music school.

—JULIE IN COLORADO, WHOSE HOMESCHOOLED SON
WAS ADMITTED TO VANDERBILT UNIVERSITY (TN)

MONEY SAVER

Earn a CLEP or AP "scholarship." Have your homeschooler prepare for and take one or more CLEP and AP examinations to shorten time in college and save money.

If your teens will apply to high-powered academic schools, they should prepare for these tests as part of their high school curriculum. Generally, students take SAT II's as they complete the applicable subject matter. In some cases this might be as early as the end of your homeschooler's sophomore year.

Even if your teenager applies to moderately competitive schools that do not require SAT II results, she may want to take one or more of these tests anyway—for two reasons: First, these scores lend credibility to a transcript or portfolio and help with both admissions and financial aid. Second, because SAT II tests focus on specific subjects, test preparation is more likely to raise an SAT II score than an SAT I score. Even after preparation and taking practice tests, many students cannot raise their SAT scores out of the mediocre range. They should consider studying specific subjects, such as chemistry or history, to produce an eye-catching SAT II score.

College Level Examination Program (CLEP) and Advanced Placement (AP) Tests

What if your teenager could begin college as a sophomore and take just two to three years, rather than the usual four to six years, to obtain a degree? College Level Examination Program (CLEP) and Advanced Placement (AP) tests offer this money-saving and timesaving opportunity to all—including homeschoolers.

CLEP is the most widely accepted credit-by-examination program in the United States. There are 34 subject-specific CLEP exams—biology, history, and Spanish, for example. Approximately 2,900 colleges and universities grant anywhere from 3 to 12 college credits for satisfactory results. Study guides are available from the College Board or in the study-guide section of any large bookstore.

According to the College Board Web site, "AP gives you the chance to try college-level work in high school, and to gain valuable skills and study habits for college. If you get a 'qualifying' grade on the AP exam, there are thousands of colleges worldwide that will give credit or advanced placement for your efforts." AP college-level subjects include English, economics, music theory, physics, calculus, and about two dozen others.

You need not take a special AP course to take an AP test. Although at least two organizations now offer AP courses to home-schoolers worldwide, you may prepare any way you like.

Homeschoolers often ask whether it is better to focus on AP or CLEP tests. That depends on where your teenager applies and what his ultimate goals are. In addition, not every school recognizes CLEP and AP results, and not every school gives credit in the same way. Ask admissions counselors which tests rate most highly at their schools.

TEST PREPARATION

ONE SATURDAY MORNING early in my senior year in 1967, I joined my classmates in the school cafeteria for the SAT. Other than attending our usual high school classes, none of us had prepared for this test. Indeed, preparation courses were largely unknown. We all took the test once, and that was that.

Things have changed. Enter "college admissions tests" into any Web search engine, and you will see that the test-preparation business now runs into the millions of dollars. It feeds off the fear we discussed in chapter 2—namely, "Go to college, have a good life," except that now it's "Get good test scores, go to college, have a good life."

HOW WE DID IT

Our daughter's preparation for the PSAT and the SAT—which she took first as an eighth-grader to participate in the Center for Talented Youth program and twice more in high school—was working through the book *Cracking the SAT*. She found this "course" both helpful and amusing. Her PSAT score qualified her to enter the National Merit program. Her senior-year, third-time-at-the-test SAT score was 1590. Her ACT score was also high. I highly recommend preparing for tests and taking them more than once.

—RUTH, WHOSE DAUGHTER WON A NATIONAL MERIT SCHOLARSHIP

Homeschoolers—sometimes more than others—need to adequately prepare for college admissions tests. In addition to regular preparation—information about the content and format of the tests—homeschooling teenagers may need practice with basic test-taking skills.

> In addition to regular preparation—information about the content and format of the tests—homeschooling teenagers may need practice with basic test-taking skills.

Diane Flynn-Keith, editor of *HomeFires,* a national homeschooling publication, explains, "I am preparing my son for college entrance exams right now. He has never taken tests. The single hardest thing has been to acclimate him to the idea of sitting still for three hours. We had to start with twenty-minute intervals and work up. Also, he makes careless errors. My son is not used to correcting his work, proofreading, and so on. He is learning to do that now."

"A significant challenge for him was getting a lot of ink on paper for an essay," Diane continues. "He has never been required to sit and write long essays. He can type at lightning speed. But when it comes to ink on paper, he was too slow to be able to get his thoughts onto the paper in the twenty- to thirty-minute time frame of some standardized tests. We have been doing many exercises to increase his speed."

For all homeschooling families, preparation is everything. Few teens can walk into these tests cold and ace them. Preparation takes work and time. Your teens need you to guide them through the process.

Begin with the free materials available locally. Pick up registration and preparation booklets from any high school counseling office (or read them on-line at the College Board and ACT Web sites). They contain sample tests, which you can use to acclimate your student to typical exam questions. Plan to prepare over the course of one to three years. Skills develop best with what educators call "distributed practice"—that is, practice in small chunks over a long period of time.

In addition, you may want to invest in one or more book and CD-ROM preparation courses (see Resources). Many homeschoolers, accustomed to independent study, use these. Beyond at-home independent study, some homeschoolers use private SAT and ACT preparation courses, now offered in most communities.

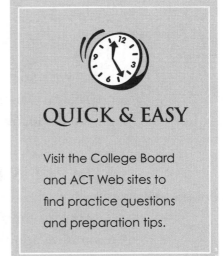

QUICK & EASY

Visit the College Board and ACT Web sites to find practice questions and preparation tips.

As Diane Flynn-Keith says, "Giving your teens the tools and practice they need so that they can take the tests and score well—without a lot of stress—is not only critical; it is the kindest and most humane thing you can do for a student—especially one who isn't used to it."

Finally, if your homeschooler has a documented learning or physical disability, all of the test makers have provisions for adapting their tests appropriately. You can find details at their Web sites or by contacting them directly.

COLLEGE COURSES

WHILE NOT APPROPRIATE for every homeschooler, A's and B's in college classes also provide independent evaluation of your homeschooling—sometimes better than tests. While good SAT scores correlate with college success, good grades in college classes *show* college success.

Consider college classes concurrent with your high school homeschooling for all teenagers—not just the academic superstars. Think about college classes especially for poor test takers. This group of homeschoolers can negate the impression of a mediocre SAT score with "A's" in two to four college classes.

> While good SAT scores correlate with college success, good grades in college classes *show* college success.

Always begin college classes with a "good" subject, a subject in which your teen has a lot of confidence. Start with a single class on-line or at your local community college.

Letters of recommendation, college entrance tests, and college courses—use one or more to enhance your homeschooler's academic profile. Plan to provide these external evaluations to silence the admissions officers before they express their doubts.

SIMPLE STARTING POINTS

✦   List adults from whom your teenager might request letters of recommendation right now.

✦   Visit the College Board and ACT Web sites. Read and have your teenager try some SAT and ACT practice questions.

✦   If your teenager will be taking the SAT or ACT, make a timeline for registering for and taking the tests. Be certain to allow time to take tests twice.

✦ Pick up a local community college catalog at your library, and review the course listings with your teenager. Does it make sense to take a course there next semester?

RESOURCES

Books for Test Preparation

Buffer, Elizabeth, et al. *Cracking the SAT II: English Subject Tests 1999–2000*. The Princeton Review, 1999. See similar titles for other subjects.

College Entrance Examination Board. *10 Real SATS*. College Entrance Examination Board, 2000.

Ehrencraft, George, et al. *Barron's How to Prepare for the ACT: American College Testing Assessment Program,* 10th edition. Barron's, 1998.

Robinson, Adam, and John Katzman. *Cracking the SAT and PSAT 2000 (Annual): With Sample Tests on CD-ROM*. The Princeton Review, 1999. See also the CD-ROM version.

Rodman, David. *SAT II: Writing 2000–2001 (SAT II Writing)*. Kaplan, 2000. See similar titles for SAT II Math, Chemistry, and so on.

Rubenstein, Jeff. *Crash Course for the SAT: 10 Simple Steps in Less than One Week*. Princeton Review, 1999.

CD-ROMs for Test Preparation

Compton's Learning: Score Builder for the SAT/ACT. Creative Wonders.

Kaplan SAT, ACT, and PSAT Deluxe 2001. Encore Software.

The Princeton Review: Inside the SAT, ACT, and PSAT 2000 Deluxe. The Learning Company.

College Admissions Testing

ACT: ACT Registration, P.O. Box 414, Iowa City, IA 52243, 319-337-1270: http://www.act.org

The Advanced Placement Program (AP), The College Board, 45 Columbus Avenue, New York, NY 10023: http://www.collegeboard.org

College Level Examination Program (CLEP): *The Official Handbook for the CLEP Examinations,* published by the College Board, P.O. Box 6601, Princeton, NJ 08541: http://www.collegeboard.org

FairTest: National Center for Fair and Open Testing, 342 Broadway, Cambridge, MA 02139, 617-864-4810: http://www.fairtest.org

PSAT: Given only in October through private and public high schools; contact a high school counselor's office in August or early September for registration information; for general information, call 609-771-7300

SAT Services for Students with Disabilities, P.O. Box 6226, Princeton, NJ 08541-6226, 609-771-7137

SAT I and SAT II: College Board SAT, Princeton, NJ 08541, 609-771-7600: http://www.collegeboard.org

AP Courses

Apex Learning (on-line Advanced Placement courses), 800-453 1454: http://www.apexlearning.com/

Pennsylvania Homeschoolers' Association (on-line Advanced Placement courses nationwide): http://www.pahomeschoolers.com/courses

Part Three

THE ADMISSIONS PROCESS

11

UP CLOSE AND PERSONAL:

CAMPUS VISITS

AND INTERVIEWS

In This Chapter

✦ Campus visits

✦ Interviews

Simple starting points

✦ Resources

*"They weren't leaving [other colleges] because the
English Department was no good. Their reason was
'I just didn't feel comfortable there.'"*

—Dan Lundquist, dean of admissions,
Union College, New York

Choosing a college without visiting is like purchasing a home without seeing it in person. Colleges, classes, and student bodies may appear outstanding in view books. Nevertheless, crime-ridden neighborhoods surround some beautiful campuses. Other colleges have crowded classrooms, inaccessible professors, and cultures that emphasize partying—all of which can reverse positive impressions conveyed by promotional literature.

College view books—like real estate ads—will never show your teenagers the disadvantages of individual schools. And make no mistake; all schools have problems. To find them, your teens have to move into a hands-on mode. They have to visit.

Although most colleges and universities no longer require them, many homeschooled applicants make interviews part of these visits. Interviews help homeschoolers in the same way as test scores, recommendation letters, and grades in college classes. Through interviews, admissions personnel create yet another independent evaluation. More important, in one-on-one conversations admissions representatives can move beyond the paperwork and see for themselves the results of homeschooling.

Don't skip this chapter if your teenager is only 13 or 14 years old. At that age you can profitably investigate colleges through informal visits and begin preparation for awkward interview questions. If you have an older teen, time is of the essence. In this chapter, we discuss making the best possible impression and visiting to gather information available no other way.

CAMPUS VISITS

"INTUITION RULES WHEN it comes to the college visit," writes Charlotte Thomas, the career and education editor at Peterson's, a company that provides college admission and financial aid information for students, parents, admissions officers, and guidance counselors. "Nothing substitutes entirely for walking the campus, sitting in classes, talking to students, eating the food, and sleeping in the dorm. You can't get the experience secondhand."

When to Visit

Visits fall into two categories—those in the window-shopping stage and those in shopping-list stage.

The window-shopping stage comes first and can begin as early as age 13 or 14. Of course, at this age many parents say, "But my child has no specific career goals. We don't know if college will figure into his plans, let alone which colleges he might apply to."

Window-shopping visits can help. Almost all students staring into an unknown future consider college. And more than 90 percent end up trying it, at least for a year. While studying alternatives (see chapter 2) can help your teenager decide about college, so can getting a feel for academia. Your children first begin to develop this "feel" when they informally tour campuses and see some students bent over books in the library stacks and others playing soccer on carefully groomed athletic fields.

Certainly, tour local colleges throughout your homeschooler's high school years even if your teenager is not considering them. Remember, it's free. More significantly, during these visits your teenagers can begin to list and discuss what they like and don't like. You will get inklings of preferences when they comment on both the important and seemingly trivial:

- ✦ "Everybody wears Birkenstocks. This is not for me."
- ✦ "I love the large outdoor sculptures."
- ✦ "This campus is too big. How will I meet any people here?"
- ✦ "The students seem genuinely friendly and interested in their studies."
- ✦ "I could attend a concert or play every day here."

HOW WE DID IT

Our daughter visited a couple of campuses informally while she was younger, and this gave her some familiarity with what she liked and didn't like.

During her junior year we visited a couple of colleges of possible interest that were decidedly different (large versus small, private versus public), specifically Duke University (NC) and Virginia Tech (VA). We took the group tours and went to the admissions officers' talks.

During the summer between her junior and senior years, we went on a (camping) tour, visiting six or seven campuses, and later visited a couple of other, more local schools. These were all schools she was strongly considering. The visits eliminated several schools from her list. One of the schools far down on the list moved to the top. After paring down the list, she revisited the University of Rochester and Virginia Tech. She attended classes, talked to the departments about specific interests and how they would mesh with their programs, and spent a night in a dorm.

—JUDY, WHOSE DAUGHTER NOW ATTENDS THE UNIVERSITY OF ROCHESTER

These initial look-see visits can help your homeschooler narrow down colleges to which he wants to apply. As you move into more serious planning with older teens, you will want to schedule visits to specific campuses, both nearby and more distant.

Campus visits fall into four categories:

- ✦ Informal walks
- ✦ Group tours
- ✦ Individual days and overnights, which include class attendance
- ✦ Special one- to six-week summer programs

Informal visits involve showing up and taking your own walking tour. Most campuses provide maps at strategic locations, making it easy to find your way around. Alternatively, find the visitors center or admissions office and ask for a map or even a self-guided walking tour. If you mention that you will be checking out the cafeteria, they may even provide free meal tickets.

On these expeditions, you can visit the library, the bookstore, the student center, and any recreational areas. You should also walk the halls of one or two instructional buildings, read bulletin board postings, and grab a copy of the campus newspaper.

Almost all colleges schedule regular group tours—for prospective students as well as for families and the general public. Simply call or e-mail the admissions department to make a reservation. Group tours provide a chance to ask questions of admissions representatives. Of course, the tours always hit the best parts of the college.

What about those sites not on the group tour? To get the lowdown on any campus, your homeschooler will want to attend classes, eat in the cafeteria, and stay in the dormitories. Above all, she will want to talk to current students, off the record. Most colleges now have programs to accommodate requests for visits like this, either for all applicants or for admitted students still trying to decide between two or three different colleges.

Finally, your homeschooler should consider attending summer academic and sports "camps" or "sessions" at colleges of interest. Many schools have special programs designed for high school students. When he was 16, our son attended a three-week residential course at the University of Denver (CO) called "The Making of An Engineer." He got college credit and more than a

> Almost all colleges schedule regular group tours—for prospective students as well as for families and the general public.

MONEY SAVER

Carpool those first college visits. Work with your local homeschool support group and arrange for groups of three to six teenagers to preview local and more distant colleges together.

HOW WE DID IT

I have found that the summers between grades 10 and 11 and 11 and 12 are a good time to search for summer camps at universities of interest. They give teenagers a chance to get to know the staff and the campus. My 16-year-old daughter just returned from a harp camp at Eastman School of Music (University of Rochester, NY). It changed her whole outlook on the college selection process. My oldest daughter went to an engineering camp at her first-choice college the summer before her senior year and scratched it from her list.

The harp camp did two things for my younger daughter. First, it helped her define her goals. Second, it gave her a chance to think critically about what she wanted in a college experience. Before harp camp, our daughter thought that going to a top school like Eastman was maybe something she could do, but she wasn't sure. Her teacher here encouraged her, but our daughter wasn't too confident about how her skills would stack up. Then she went to the camp and met some current students (who were very good!) and some incoming freshman. She realized that after two more years of practice she will be very competitive. She was really invigorated by this.

Previously, she had been more concerned with the individual teacher she would be working with. She really connected with the head of the harp department at Eastman, but our daughter was less than enthralled with the location of the campus in downtown Rochester, the distance from the main campus, and the amount of orchestra time the harpists get. Now she can't wait to get out and look at the other music schools on her list and determine if there's a school that will meet all her desires.

Similarly, when our older daughter spent a week at Michigan Technological University (MI), she found out the fabulous labs and facilities were mainly for the grad students. The underclassmen she met had never seen many of the labs. Some of the professors didn't know their students' names even though the school wasn't that large. That was a big turnoff. It's difficult to learn these kinds of things in an afternoon visit.

—SERENA IN OHIO

bird's-eye view of the campus and professors. Of course, the professors got to know him as well.

Ideally, your homeschooler will visit campuses for one to three years before applying to college, as well as during the application process. If he has to decide among several campuses after admissions, you may schedule additional visits at that time. Many selective colleges schedule weekends for admitted students in April and May. Your student should attend these, finances permitting.

How to Visit

During the earlier, informal tours and the later, "do I want to live here?" overnight visits, your teenager needs a how-to manual to get the most out of the experience. Here we present a few tips:

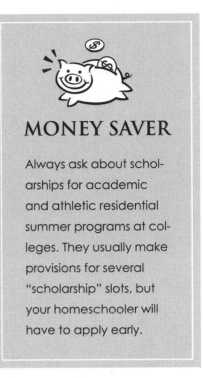

MONEY SAVER

Always ask about scholarships for academic and athletic residential summer programs at colleges. They usually make provisions for several "scholarship" slots, but your homeschooler will have to apply early.

HOW WE DID IT

We visited three schools—Pensacola Christian College (FL), Auburn University (AL), and Bryan College (TN)—on weekends when the colleges had planned activities. Our son visited classes, stayed in the dorms, and talked to admissions people. I found these weekends helpful, because the colleges had seminars for both students and parents.

For a first-time college parent, I had a lot to learn. Going to these planned weekends exposed me to what they felt I needed to know. To prepare, I read catalogs, asked questions, met people, and noted e-mail addresses. This research helped me ask better questions.

—DARIA, HOMESCHOOL MOM WHOSE SON WAS ADMITTED TO ALL THREE COLLEGES THEY VISITED

✦   Check the calendar. Visit when classes are in session. Avoid holidays and summer so that your homeschoolers can get a feel for the campus culture. Visiting during the instructional year provides the best opportunity to have all questions answered. If you have to schedule a visit between semesters, don't despair. Any visit is better than none. Go and do the best you can.

> Visiting during the instructional year provides the best opportunity to have all questions answered.

✦   Prepare. Your student should prepare for any college visit by reading a college's mission statement, usually available at its Web site and in its promotional literature. She should know up front the most popular majors and which two or three activities people most associate with the college—from football to television production to religious education.

For tours and day visits or overnighters, your applicant should prepare two lists of questions. On the first list are questions for admissions personnel and professors. On the second list are questions for current students.

HOMESCHOOL GRADS SAY

Get to know the school you plan to attend. I didn't really think that much about what the schools were like, how the people were, and what the personality was. The reality of living on campus escaped me the first time around. There was a lot of false advertising in the form of glossy brochures. Try to find clearly what benefits each school offers and what sort of things you would get out of it.

—STEVE, WHO BEGAN AT VANDERBILT (TN)
AND TRANSFERRED TO MACALESTER (MN)

HOW WE DID IT

People start initial visits in spring of junior year. You can also visit during the summer, but that will usually mean that there are no classes in session, which is one way to get a feel for a place. For an initial visit, though, that wouldn't be absolutely necessary. This leaves time in the fall of the senior year for follow-up visits to top-choice colleges. It also allows those first experiences to filter around in the brain for a while, providing adequate time for the decision process to take place.

—RUTH IN PENNSYLVANIA

✦ *Must-sees.* Your student should have a core itinerary, things he checks at every college he visits. This itinerary will vary. Musicians will gravitate toward the practice and concert facilities. Scientists will want to see laboratories. Athletes will inspect the gym and playing fields.

✦ *Inside scoop.* The best way to learn about Australia or France or Nigeria is to live there. It is the same with colleges. Although your homeschooler cannot live there for an extended period of time, she can schedule day, overnight, and weekend visits. During these visits, she may attend classes, shadow a student, meet professors, eat in the dining facili-ties, sleep in a dormitory, work out in the gymnasium, and so on.

Best of all, prospective students can talk to current students in unsupervised environments and find out what the college is really like. The sidebar on page 240 contains a list of questions. Review and edit this list with your homeschooled teen.

✦ Evaluation and follow-up. Urge your homeschooler to make notes during his visit and then follow up on things that interested him. Some students may even want to take photos to help them remember settings and people. Your teen can

QUESTIONS TO ASK DURING A CAMPUS VISIT

Here are a few questions for current students, questions you will seldom see addressed in a college view book:

✦   What do you like best here?

✦   What do you dislike most?

✦   Would you choose this college again? Why or why not?

✦   Do you feel safe walking around campus alone at night? In the daytime?

✦   Do you have problems getting classes?

✦   How responsive is the administration to student concerns? Can you give me some examples?

✦   What role do athletics play in student life?

✦   How do you feel about the college's rules and regulations?

✦   How many students are in your classes?

✦   What organizations do you belong to and why?

✦   What spiritual outlets do you take advantage of?

✦   What do students here do on weekends?

then call or e-mail individual students, department heads, and admissions officers to inquire further.

Charlotte Thomas suggests that students always write thank-you notes. She explains, "It won't get you admitted, but it sure will get you noticed."

INTERVIEWS

INTERVIEWS ARE marketing opportunities, a time for your homeschooler to sell herself and make homeschooling seem like a normal educational alternative. Although poor interviews seldom preclude admission, solid interviews look good to admissions committees and can make a difference, especially if your teenager has deficiencies on other parts of her application.

A few colleges have mandatory interviews. Our son applied to the United States Air Force Academy and United States Naval Academy. He had interviews not only with academy liaison officers but also with committees from our congressman's and senators' offices. Although not requiring them, some small liberal arts colleges prefer to interview all candidates, as do some specialty colleges that offer unique programs and majors.

At most colleges, interviews are optional. Admissions officers admit that interviews seldom

> Although poor interviews seldom preclude admission, solid interviews look good to admissions committees and can make a difference, especially if your teenager has deficiencies on other parts of her application.

provide a thumbs-up or thumbs-down in admissions. Nevertheless, most homeschoolers should take advantage of any opportunity for the staff to get to know them. College personnel may not know any

HOW WE DID IT

We went to admit weekends at University of Virginia (the Echols Scholar Weekend) and the Stanford Admit weekend. Our son wanted to see which one gave him a warm, fuzzy feeling. The University of Virginia was comfortable. Stanford was all warm and fuzzy! In both cases, there were sessions for parents and students, and students spent at least one night in the dorm. Stanford did an excellent job with this—sessions about advising, housing, academic lectures. They even brought out the marching band!

—DENISE IN VIRGINIA

homeschoolers personally. That lack of familiarity can breed distrust and confusion in the best of us. The interview removes doubts about "normal people" homeschooling by presenting admissions staff members with a "normal" person who happens to have been homeschooled.

That said, a few homeschoolers should avoid interviews. Some students freeze up when they feel someone is putting them on the spot. In such cases it is always better to skip an optional interview than to risk making a bad impression.

Your homeschooler may have one or more of three different types of interviews—alumni interviews, group interviews, and personal interviews.

Many colleges use former students from all over the country to help with interviews and recruiting. Alumni interviews often occur close to your home, instead of on a campus hundreds to thousands of miles away. This advantage may be offset by the fact that alumni interviewers have variable training and enthusiasm for the job. Sometimes they know what they are doing, sometimes not. In either case, the alumni representative completes an evaluation report that becomes part of the application.

Student group interviews are often conducted during college visits. Usually an admissions staff member presents an overview of the college, and students ask questions. Group interviews focus on providing information, rather than evaluating students. Colleges seldom use them to assess applicants.

Personal interviews work differently. They can be both informational and evaluative. Informational interviews require applicants to direct the conversation. Often they begin with

MONEY SAVER

Homeschool reviewer Mary Pride alerts us to "video visits." She writes: "Call VIDEC [800-255-0384, www.videc.com] to request a free video visit to any one of about fifty private colleges. [Eleventh- and twelfth-graders] may request as many as four video-tapes at a time." Some of the colleges your homeschooler can preview this way include Vanderbilt University (TN), Hillsdale College (MI), Emory University (GA), Southern Methodist University (TX), and Tulane University (LA).

HOW WE DID IT

We took a five-college tour with three homeschoolers. At the first college all three were interviewed. This was the first such experience for each, and they were nervous, big time! By the third college, they were more confident. They had come up with some questions to ask the campus tour person and knew pretty much what they would be asked in the interviews: Why do you want to come here? What are your goals, activities, and interests?

We parents learned throughout this process as well. I have seen since then, in how-to-apply-to-college articles and books, some suggestions of questions for a student to have ready to ask in an admissions interview.

Our son is more reserved than our daughter and will be starting the application and campus visits process this spring. We intend to help him with some interview practice to equip him a little better than we did our daughter. It's a good idea to know about the college ahead of time, to appear informed, and to have questions at the ready.

—Ruth, homeschooling mother of three in Pennsylvania

the interviewer's saying, "What can I tell you about this school?" In an evaluative interview, applicants are encouraged to discuss their academic work, activities, and personal goals. Typically, the interviewer will write a summary, which will become part of the student's application package.

Best Foot Forward

Regardless of the type of interview your homeschooler faces, a little preparation will go a long way. Here are a few tips for a successful experience:

✦ *Prepare for questions about home education.* Although the word "homeschooling" no longer draws blank looks, you never know when your teenager may have to overcome the perception that only backwoods hippies and religious fanatics homeschool their children.

Judy explains, "Duke University (NC) was the only college we dealt with that required an interview. Our daughter did not feel it went very well. The recent graduate who interviewed her seemed to want a typical student and seemed to feel that homeschoolers were weird."

Your teenager should be prepared to explain how and why your family homeschools. At the same time, instruct your child to avoid negative comments about traditional schooling. Instead, she can focus on the positives of home education. Often simply describing a typical day does the trick.

> Although the word "homeschooling" no longer draws blank looks, you never know when your teenager may have to overcome the perception that only backwoods hippies and religious fanatics homeschool their children.

✦ *Take the paperwork.* Seldom do interviewers have the student's application materials. Your homeschooler should bring copies of transcripts, résumés, portfolios, or similar documents. An applicant should not overwhelm interviewers but instead leave them with a concise summary of accomplishments. Our son took a copy of his résumé to all interviews. It served as a reminder for interviewers writing their evaluations. In addition, it included activities not discussed in the interview.

✦ *Do the homework.* Your applicant should have some basic information about the school before he interviews. He should know the college's academic strengths and prepare a few questions about specific departments and programs. Interviewees should avoid obvious questions that any view book would answer, such as, "Do you have a biology major here?" Instead, they can focus on questions about internships, student government, and performance

SAMPLE INTERVIEW QUESTIONS

Be prepared. Have your teenager practice answering these questions in an interview format.

- ✦ So, you're homeschooling. Tell me about it.
- ✦ Why does your family homeschool?
- ✦ How does your family homeschool?
- ✦ What are the benefits of home education?
- ✦ What are the disadvantages of homeschooling?
- ✦ What kinds of growth would you like to see in yourself over the next four years?
- ✦ What would your adult mentors say is your greatest strength as a person and as a student?
- ✦ What are your weaknesses as a student?
- ✦ What books have you read in the past year that have special meaning for you?
- ✦ What events in your life have been most crucial?
- ✦ What do you see as "the good life" twenty years from now?
- ✦ Last year we had fifteen thousand applicants and accepted only three thousand. Why should we accept you?
- ✦ What are you looking for in a college?
- ✦ If you didn't go to college, what would you do instead?
- ✦ How do you see yourself here on our campus and in our community? What part will you play?
- ✦ In your opinion, what is a college education?

opportunities, for example. Above all, an applicant should never project indifference toward a school, even if it is not his first choice.

✦ *Choose words carefully, and watch body language.* At-home practice can substantially improve your teenager's interviewing skills.

Applicants should avoid slang as well as conversation fillers such as "hmm," "you know," and "like." Even something as simple as giggling too much can detract from an evaluation.

Body language can convey immaturity and poor speaking skills. Teach your homeschooler to establish and maintain eye contact and, at the same time, avoid nervous habits such as tapping feet, chewing nails, drumming fingers, or twirling strands of hair.

✦ *Dress for success.* Your homeschooler should wear neat, comfortable attire for interviews. When in doubt, overdress. Better yet, call ahead of time and ask about appropriate attire. A well-groomed appearance conveys character. A sloppy presentation conveys just the opposite.

✦ *Be on time. Not early. Not late. On time.* Showing up more than ten minutes early conveys a lack of confidence. Lateness slows the interviewer down and says, "I have no regard for your time."

QUICK & EASY

Practice sample interview questions at home and videotape the results. Watch the videotape and assess word choice and body language.

✦ *Be honest.* This seems obvious, but you should emphasize to your homeschooler that she should not say she loves Shakespeare when she prefers science fiction. Pretending may make your teenager sound impressive, but experienced interviewers will expose it almost every time. If your homeschooler says that she worked more than 200 hours in the library volunteer program, she had better be able to remember the name of her supervisor. Homeschoolers should not try to guess "the right answer" to questions. Instead, encourage your teenager to be herself.

"Being oneself" extends to weaknesses in the academic record or extracurricular activities. Your homeschooler should admit deficiencies, if they come up, and try to put them into perspective.

HOW WE DID IT

Our daughter was interviewed by Cornell (NY), our son by Rose-Hulman Institute of Technology (IN) and also by Kettering University (MI). The interviews lasted between one and two hours and were basically conversational. At our son's interview for Rose-Hulman, we were also in the room and participated, which I thought was unusual.

Our older two children had to discuss why they were homeschooling, but the younger ones did not, probably because there are so many homeschoolers now.

—KARA, MOTHER OF FOUR GROWN-UP HOMESCHOOL GRADUATES, AGES 20 TO 26

Here is an example: "We had a difficult time studying foreign language. We tried Spanish and failed miserably. Then we switched to Latin. That worked better, I think, in part because such marvelous Latin self-instructional materials have been produced for homeschoolers. Our goals have been to develop a reading knowledge of Latin and to read some of the classics in the original. My Latin vocabulary is not extensive, because our program emphasized studying the structure of the language, as well as its history. I do feel that Latin has helped a lot with my English grammar and vocabulary."

> Your homeschooler should admit deficiencies, if they come up, and try to put them into perspective.

✦ *Make it a conversation.* An interview is a two-way street. Your homeschooler should answer the questions asked, of course. At the same time, he should not wait for the interviewer to spoon-feed him every question. Colleges want applicants who are self-assured enough to talk about themselves and their lives. Your teenager should practice keeping the interview conversational, not speaking too little or dominating the conversation by speaking too much.

✦ *Follow-up afterward.* Everyone appreciates thank-you notes. Interviewers are no different. Colleges remember written appreciation, and notes help reinforce positive impressions. Remind your student to write down the interviewer's full name so that she can properly acknowledge the time. If follow-up questions occur to your homeschooler after the interview, she should contact her admissions counselor.

> Colleges remember written appreciation, and notes help reinforce positive impressions.

College visits and interviews are hands-on research opportunities, essential complements to the research suggested in chapter 4. Begin with honesty and common courtesies. Preparation and follow-up will allow your homeschooler to have positive experiences and enhance his chances of admission to any college or university.

SIMPLE STARTING POINTS

✦ Begin visiting local colleges and universities, even those you know your homeschooler will never apply to. Take self-guided walking tours, or sign up for group tours.

✦ Call local colleges and universities and ask if your teenager can observe several classes. This will help build her database of likes and dislikes.

✦ Research residential summer programs and special programs for high school students at both local and more distant colleges that your teenager may someday apply to. Contact the admissions office and ask to be transferred to whoever conducts summer programs.

✦ Conduct practice interviews at home. Use some of the questions from this chapter. Try this several times over a period of several months. Give your teenager time to practice and improve.

RESOURCES

Books

Nemko, Mary, and Deborah Zembe. *You're Gonna Love This College Guide.* Barron's Educational Series, 1999.

Ripple, G. Gary. *College Pursuit: Making the Most of Your Visit and Interview,* 8th edition. Octameron Associates, 1999.

Schneider, Zola. *Campus Visits and College Interviews: A Complete Guide for College-Bound Students and Their Families.* College Entrance Examination Board, 1990.

Spencer, Janet. *Visiting College Campuses,* 5th edition. Princeton Review, 1999.

Yale Daily News. *The Insider's Guide to the Colleges, 2000.* Griffin Trade Paperback, 1999.

Web Sites

About.com Campus Visit Page and Interview Pages:
http://collegeapps.about.com/education/collegeapps
Collegiate Choice Walking Tour Videos:
http://www.collegiatechoice.com/

12

FINDING MONEY

In This Chapter

✦ Money for college 101

✦ College financial aid offices

✦ Private sources

✦ Reserve Officer Training Corps (ROTC)

✦ Athletic scholarships

✦ Overlooked budget alternatives

✦ Simple starting points

✦ Resources

"Sticker shock when you go to a new-car dealer is nothing compared to your shock when you read the tuition prices of most private universities—$20,000 or more per year! Of course, most parents don't pay that much. Colleges have financial aid plans so that the less you make, the less you pay. If you're poor enough, you can actually afford it!"

—Howard Richman, of the Pennsylvania homeschoolers in "Colleges without Walls"

*A*ll kidding aside, college is like homeschooling, in that everyone who wants this type of education for their children can manage it—one way or the other. But you don't get something for nothing. College, like homeschooling, costs money.

Unfortunately, those costs have been escalating for the past twenty years. Since 1980, average tuition at four-year colleges has more than doubled, after adjusting for inflation. At the same time, the median family income for parents of college-age children has increased just 12 percent.

Those statistics concern all families, but the numbers may engender more alarm than necessary. According to Terry Hartle, senior vice president at the American Council on Education, "Americans overestimate the price of higher education and underestimate the amount of financial aid that's available."

In other words, we tend to assume the worst. The next time you see a headline about high college costs, read the article to see what schools they cite as examples. Then remember that only a small fraction of students attend schools with the heart-stopping charges of Harvard (MA), where annual expenses now top $32,000.

In contrast, nearly 70 percent of undergraduates attending four-year colleges choose lower-cost, public universities. According to a College Board survey, more than half of full-time undergraduates attend bachelor-degree-granting schools that charge less than $4,000 in tuition and fees per year.

Many private schools don't deserve a bad rap, either. Ruth explains, "Although it is generally true that private schools cost more, people should keep in mind that private schools also often have more financial aid to spread around to fewer students. It might end up that the final 'package'

> According to a College Board survey, more than half of full-time undergraduates attend bachelor-degree-granting schools that charge less than $4,000 in tuition and fees per year.

at a private college is more favorable than what a large state university offers."

And there's more good news. Need-based aid—grants, loans, and work-study assistance awarded based on a family's demonstrated inability to pay full costs—has increased substantially over the past ten years. Living from paycheck to paycheck is not the sole criterion for need-based aid. Many middle-income families—those with incomes from $25,000 to $70,000 per year—find that their students qualify.

Finally, in efforts to attract top students, second- and third-tier private colleges are handing out more merit scholarship money than ever before. Approximately 10 percent of the freshmen at Washington University in St. Louis, Missouri, have merit scholarships, which cover half to all of their tuition, plus a $2,500 stipend toward room and board.

Although the situation is not as grim as many would have you believe, you will need to understand the financial aid process and plan ahead to assure that your homeschooler receives the maximum money available.

MONEY FOR COLLEGE 101

FINANCIAL AID can be divided into two categories—gift aid and self-help aid. Two forms of gift aid—money that your student need not pay back—consist of grants and scholarships. Colleges usually award grants based on financial need, and the ultimate source is often the federal government. In contrast, colleges award scholarships based on academic, athletic, or artistic merit. In some cases financial need also enters into the scholarship qualification. One form of gift aid, ROTC scholarships, requires service in the army, navy, marines, or air force after college. Failure to complete the service changes the gift into a loan, which must be repaid.

Self-help aid comes as loans and student employment. Loans, of course, must be repaid with interest. On the plus side, loan payments

HOMESCHOOL GRADS SAY

I had no problems applying for financial aid. I got the forms, filled them out, sent them in, and voilà. When I was accepted to the college, I was immediately granted extra aid, supposedly due to my SAT scores.

—DANIEL, WHO NOW ATTENDS MOUNT IDA COLLEGE (MA)

usually do not start until after the student graduates. Employment can be federal and state work-study programs, teaching and research assistantships (usually confined to graduate students), and regular part-time employment during the academic year or in off periods, such as summer and the winter holidays.

Below we discuss major scholarship, loan, and work-study conduits—places where you begin your money-for-college search. These include college financial aid offices, private sources, the military for Reserve Officer Training Corps (ROTC) scholarships, and athletic departments (yes, homeschoolers do win athletic scholarships).

We conclude the chapter with a list of too often overlooked budget alternatives—strategies to earn college degrees for less than $5,000 or at least cut expenses substantially at any college.

Even if you cannot complete your tax forms until March or April, submit the FAFSA as early as you can after January 1, using estimated income information.

COLLEGE FINANCIAL AID OFFICES

WHEN YOU REQUEST application forms from colleges, ask for scholarship and other financial aid forms at the same time. About 95 percent of student aid comes from three sources—the federal government, state governments, and colleges and universities themselves. Most of this money is funneled through college financial aid offices, which makes them the logical place to begin.

Families must complete and submit the Free Application for Federal Student Aid (FAFSA) for virtually all forms of need-based aid. Most colleges suggest submitting the FAFSA as soon as possible after January 1 of your student's senior year—ideally by March 1 for most state aid—and in any case no later than May 1. The FAFSA requires family tax information for the previous tax year. Even if you cannot complete your tax forms until March or April, submit the FAFSA as early as you can after January 1, using estimated income information.

Ruth emphasizes doing everything early. She writes, "Students cannot win financial aid at a given college unless they have been accepted. Financial aid packages are usually awarded after a certain date. With only so much money to go around, you want to be part of that aid pie when they first cut it. Submit college applications early so that they complete the acceptance process by the time financial aid grants begin."

Once your student has been admitted and colleges have reviewed your FAFSA information, they will crunch the numbers and come up with your financial need based on cost of attendance (COA) and expected family contribution (EFC). The COA includes tuition, fees, room and board, books and supplies, travel, and personal expenses. EFC is exactly what it sounds like, the amount the financial aid gurus say that your family can afford. EFC—taking into account funds provided by both parents and students—is affected not only by income but also by assets, family size, and number of children in college.

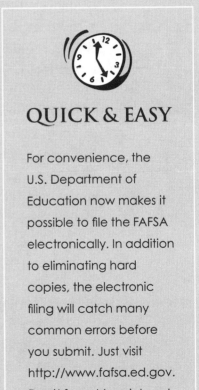

QUICK & EASY

For convenience, the U.S. Department of Education now makes it possible to file the FAFSA electronically. In addition to eliminating hard copies, the electronic filing will catch many common errors before you submit. Just visit http://www.fafsa.ed.gov. Don't forget to print and mail (land mail) the signature page.

It's a simple formula: financial need = COA − EFC. Schools try to meet this demonstrated financial need through a "package" consisting of scholarships, grants, loans, and student employment. For example, Dan and Beth's son's package included Pell grants, work-study assistance, and state grants. Their son also received an ACT scholarship. Of course, the college took this into account when making its financial assistance offer.

Unfortunately, most schools cannot meet the entire demonstrated financial need. The major exceptions are the top-tier, selective colleges, such as Harvard University (MA) and Stanford University (CA), which pledge to meet the needs of all admitted students. Other colleges, due to more limited funds, acknowledge a "need gap" or "unmet need," which your family must make up through student summer or academic-year employment and educational loans, including the federal Parent Loan for Undergraduate Students (PLUS).

Kara, a homeschooling mother of four, explains how this worked in their situation: "Our sons applied for financial aid for Rose-Hulman Institute of Technology (IN) and awaited 'the package.' Because we have a reasonable income, we were not too successful. In addition, I have a problem revealing the kind of information the FAFSA requires. As my husband says, it is like telling them how

HOW WE DID IT

Our daughter applied for financial aid using the FAFSA. She received a grant from the state of Michigan, a Presidential scholarship from Spring Arbor College (MI), and a work-study award. Plan ahead and pray—not necessarily in that order!

—LAURA, AN ECLECTIC HOMESCHOOLING MOM

much you have so they can take 33 percent of it each year. It seemed odd for a four-year-degree program to remove one-third of our reserves every year rather than one-quarter of it, but that's how the expected family contribution came out."

"Rice University (TX), in contrast, has a wonderful endowment," Kara continues. "Once students are admitted, Rice takes care of the rest. We paid for our daughter's incidentals and not much else. Rose-Hulman, on the other hand, did not have the same funding, and we never saw a package that covered the whole 'need.'"

> Refusing federal government aid does not mean that your homeschooler will have to rely entirely on your family resources.

Although previously "financial aid" meant grants and scholarships, it is now just as likely to mean a loan that must be repaid after graduation. Ben Wildavsky in the online article "Is That the Real Price?" writes, "Some financial aid experts worry that, increasingly, access to college is coming at the cost of growing student indebtedness. About half of all students graduate with loans, an average of $12,000 at public schools and $14,300 at private schools."

Some home educators look askance at any federal and state funds, knowing that government money often comes with strings. They oppose taking federal and state funds for philosophical reasons. "I personally do not believe the government has any business paying for my children to go to school," Kate comments. "We did fill out the FAFSA, but only because they required it for our son to get an on-campus job."

Refusing federal government aid does not mean that your homeschooler will have to rely entirely on your family resources. Kate continues, "Our son did apply for every scholarship he could at the school and outside it as well. He won an academic scholarship at Dordt College (IA) based on his ACT score and a departmental scholarship based on his high school records and essay about greenhouses and gardening. He was also awarded two community-based scholarships. Homeschooling families should apply for everything

HOW WE DID IT

For students in the performing arts, participation in state and regional competitions and workshops during their middle and high school years greatly increases their chance of becoming known in higher-level performing arts circles. The University of Wyoming's music department's interest in our son began when he was 14. They telephoned several times over the years for updates on his plans and activities. Even when he was 14, they told us that he could be considered for full scholarship.

—LEO AND PENNY, WHOSE SON RECEIVED A FULL FOUR-YEAR SCHOLARSHIP
PLUS $1,000 PER YEAR TO PURSUE A DEGREE IN KEYBOARD PERFORMANCE

they can find. Although some scholarship competitions are slanted toward public school applicants, you never know when committees will be intrigued by the unusual!"

In addition to the FAFSA information, colleges will factor in your student's academic record, achievements, and activities to consider her for non-need-based scholarships. Merit scholarships are usually awarded for academic excellence. Special-category scholarships might be reserved for "students studying physical therapy" or "sons and daughters of Vietnam veterans," for example. The music, chemistry, or history department with a college may award a departmental scholarship.

Always ask the financial aid personnel about merit, special-category, and departmental scholarships. Usually, the financial aid officers automatically consider all admitted applicants for these awards, but sometimes not—especially if you do not file an FAFSA. In any case, just ask. Better safe than sorry.

Whatever package colleges offer your homeschooler, consider further negotiations. Some colleges will try to better offers from other institutions. Carnegie Mellon University sends admitted students letters inviting them to submit copies of better financial aid offers from other institutions. Last year Carnegie Mellon gave better deals to more than half the nine hundred students who requested a review, with a $3,000 average increase in aid.

PRIVATE SOURCES

"WE DID NOT APPLY for financial aid, but our son did receive academic scholarship offers from every university he applied to," reports Serena, a homeschooling mother of five. "Parents should also look into local scholarships that might be very specific. In addition to his academic scholarships, our son also received one from the country club at which he worked."

As we said above, 95 percent of student aid is accessed through college financial aid offices. The remaining 5 percent consists of private scholarships and student loans from banks. Most private scholarships—from civic organizations, clubs, local businesses, and corporations—are relatively small. As an example, our church this year awarded five renewable $400 scholarships. Although not a lot of money, it will buy books for five students.

To find private scholarships, start right outside your front door. First contact

MONEY SAVER

Ideally, no later than your student's ninth-grade year, check with your statewide homeschooling organizations about how enrollment in "state-approved" home education programs might affect offers at state colleges and universities. Pam, homeschooling since 1986, tells us, "In Florida, homeschoolers who register with the school district for grades 11 and 12 qualify for the Florida Bright Futures Scholarship, which pays for 75 to 100 percent of in-state college tuition. Homeschoolers without documentation of a prescribed course of study must make a composite ACT score of 23 to qualify. With documentation, they qualify with an ACT of 20, as do all students in school. An ACT score of 28 or above qualifies for 100 percent tuition reimbursement."

HOMESCHOOL GRADS SAY

I do not qualify for need-based financial aid. I did receive the Dordt agriculture program scholarship, Dordt academic scholarship, Clinton Township Alumni scholarship, Heritage Loan program, Dordt distance grant, and a work-study job in the Dordt greenhouse. I think I was judged fairly for all the scholarship programs I applied to. The scholarship money paid for about 30 percent of tuition, room, and board.

—TED, A 2000 DORDT COLLEGE (IA) GRADUATE

businesses and organizations with which your family is affiliated. Talk to your spouse's business, the scout troop leader, your children's summer employers, your piano instructor's music teachers' association, and the officers' wives club if you live on a military base.

Then branch out. Many community-service organizations have annual scholarship competitions for awards that might range from $200 to $2,000. You do not necessarily need an affiliation with these groups for your student to apply. According to homeschooling mother Ruth, your two principal enemies are time and self-selection.

> Many community-service organizations have annual scholarship competitions for awards that might range from $200 to $2,000.

"People should start researching early," Ruth says. "Completing college applications and scholarship essays in the fall of our daughter's senior year took a lot of time. She also had regular schoolwork, after all. In doing college application essays, our daughter ran out of time to seek local sources of aid—local industries or businesses, for example."

Ruth adds, "One of the biggest reasons students do not win private scholarships is self-selection. You won't get any money if you don't apply. Let these private scholarship committees decide if you qualify or not."

+ FastWEB: http://www.fastweb.com
+ Scholarship Search by the College Board: http://www.collegeboard.org/index_this/fundfinder/html/ssrchtop.html
+ SRN Express: http://www.rams.com/srn/execsrch.htm
+ CollegeNet Mach25 Scholarship Database: http://www.collegenet.com/mach25
+ Sallie Mae's Online Scholarship Service: http://scholarships.salliemae.com

How do you find private scholarships? Begin with queries at local public and private high school counseling offices. Often they will be willing to give you a list with contact information. Watch your local newspapers for additional announcements. Contact service organizations like Kiwanis and Rotary. Finally, cast a wider net by asking all your friends, neighbors, and relatives to help you find these opportunities.

HOMESCHOOL GRADS SAY

I was awarded financial aid, and was given more than I might have otherwise received, because of being homeschooled. Spring Arbor College gives out points for certain things and awards financial aid based on the number of points. I got 4 for a high ACT, 4 for a high GPA, and 4 for being in the top 10 percent of my class, even though I was the only one in my class. I got all the points possible and was awarded the Presidential scholarship, worth $5,000.

—SUSANNA, A STUDENT AT SPRING ARBOR COLLEGE

MONEY SAVER

Never pay for a scholarship search. Don't believe claims of "untapped financial aid," especially if the advertiser wants your money to search for it. Several free search services online identify scholarships based on your homeschooler's academic profile, activities, and demographic characteristics. Just point and click!

RESERVE OFFICER TRAINING CORPS (ROTC)

IS YOUR STUDENT thinking about an engineering, computer science, chemistry, math, physics, meteorology, foreign-language, or business major? If so, he might want to consider applying for ROTC scholarships through one of the armed services—air force, army, navy, or marines.

Successful ROTC applicants can have all of their expenses paid for two to four years of their college careers. These scholarships also include a small monthly stipend. In return, ROTC recipients spend part of their college summers training and after graduation serve four years in the U.S. armed forces as commissioned officers.

ROTC applicants must qualify not only academically but also physically and medically. As an example, air force ROTC currently requires a minimum of 24 on the ACT or 1100 on the SAT, plus a transcript showing a 2.5 minimum grade point average. It also requires that candidates pass an applicant fitness test involving sit-ups, push-ups, and a mile run. Medically, applicants must meet certain height, weight, and vision standards. The final stage of the process involves even more intensive medical screening to assure that scholarship recipients can handle the physical challenges they will eventually face.

ROTC scholarships can be used only at colleges and universities that have ROTC programs. Naval ROTC scholarships pay only at schools that offer naval ROTC. This holds also for the air force, army, and marine ROTC programs. Obviously, if your homeschooler decides to try for ROTC scholarships, you should make certain that he applies to one or more campuses with the corresponding ROTC program.

Many students apply to ROTC programs with three or four different services. Offers from the various military branches can differ significantly. Our son received ROTC offers that ranged from paying all expenses for two years (army) to covering everything for four years (navy).

The ROTC application process is completely separate from your homeschooler's college and scholarship applications. You can get forms in the financial aid office of any school that offers ROTC. Alternatively, obtain forms at air force, army, navy, and marine recruiting offices.

ATHLETIC SCHOLARSHIPS

THE Home School Legal Defense Association (HSLDA) has done quite a bit of work on the issue of athletic scholarships. Before getting into the details, we should highlight the sobering statistics at its Web site: "There are nearly 1 million high school football players and about 500,000 high school basketball players. Of those numbers, approximately 150 make it to the NFL and only about 50 make it to an NBA team."

Even good athletes have little hope of playing professionally. Clearly the goal of most homeschooled athletes should center on obtaining a solid academic education. To obtain that education, good athletes can and do use sports scholarships to help pay for college.

Currently the National Collegiate Athletic Association (NCAA) certifies to its nine-hundred-plus member schools a student's academic eligibility to practice, compete, and play. The smaller National Association of Intercollegiate Athletics (NAIA), comprised of about a hundred member universities, operates much like the NCAA. The NCAA classifies colleges as Division I, II, or III, based roughly on size, with Division I being the largest. Only Division I and Division II schools offer athletic scholarships.

Homeschoolers have joined the ranks of students with athletic scholarships. HSLDA reports, "During the 1998–1999 academic year, the NCAA approved the academic eligibility of forty-nine homeschool students to receive scholarships at Division I schools and twenty homeschool students to receive scholarships at Division II schools. These homeschool athletes went on to play college basketball, baseball, volleyball, football, wrestling, track, and virtually every sport."

HSLDA advises homeschoolers to ask individual colleges about requirements for their particular sport. Determine also if the college is a member of the NCAA or NAIA. Ask college financial aid offices for paperwork to begin eligibility process through NCAA or NAIA. Athletic scholarship money eventually comes from the colleges, but NCAA or NAIA determines whether the student is eligible.

Homeschooled student athletes complete the NCAA eligibility process just like everyone else—with one exception. Homeschoolers working with the NCAA must go through an initial eligibility waiver process through the NCAA national office—not through their college.

Currently the waiver application requires the following items:

✦ homeschool transcript

✦ ACT and SAT scores

✦ description of homeschooling, the teaching environment

✦ list of text titles

✦ tables of contents for texts for core courses

✦ work samples

In addition, the NCAA requests a parent statement saying that home education was conducted in accord with state laws. Don't be intimidated by this list. It's just red tape, and clearly some homeschoolers have successfully negotiated the process.

OVERLOOKED BUDGET ALTERNATIVES

WE HAVE GIVEN YOU an overview of the financial aid process. Now it's time to consider some overlooked money-saving alternatives. By using some of these suggestions and applying for scholarships and need-based financial aid, you can substantially reduce the cost of college and probably allow your homeschooler to graduate debt free.

Staying Home

Depending on the college your teenager selects, living expenses and transportation can account for up to one-half of costs. Staying close to home—or, better yet, staying home—makes sense. Many homeschoolers choose local colleges for this reason.

Along these lines, beginning at a junior college or a community college and transferring to a four-year school after two years can save thousands of dollars. Need proof? Look at the numbers. For the 1999–2000 academic year, community college average tuition was $1,627; public university tuition, $3,356; and private college or university tuition, $15,380.

> Homeschoolers have joined the ranks of students with athletic scholarships.

There's a bonus to beginning with a two-year junior college. Some state universities award free tuition to students who achieve high grade point averages the first two years in junior college.

Really Good Deals

Consider the unbeatable deals—the four military academies, and colleges such as Berea College (KY), Deep Springs College (CA), and College of the Ozarks (MO). Chapter 4 has a more complete list. All of these schools offer free tuition, and many also offer free room and board. The military academies even pay a stipend for incidental expenses.

In addition, several colleges guarantee tuition for a fifth year of college, under certain conditions. Others promise students that tuition will not rise faster than inflation. Ask about programs like these wherever your student applies.

QUICK & EASY

Families earning less than $25,000 per year often have to convince their children that college is possible. Consider putting spare change in a coffee can labeled "college fund." Although the amount may not make a dent in college costs, it sends a powerful message about the importance of higher education.

Three-Year Degrees

There's no specific reason that college degrees need take four years. That's simply the usual amount of time students can expect to spend. There are several ways to accomplish the same amount of work in a shorter time period and considerably reduce costs. A number of colleges now offer three-year degree programs for some majors. These include the University of South Carolina, Spartanburg; Lake Superior State University (MI); and Drury College (MO).

Similarly, if your homeschooler eventually plans to attend medical, dental, or veterinary school, look for programs that grant the bachelor's and the professional degree together in six or seven years, instead of the usual eight. The Sophie-Davis School of Biomedical Education, also known as the City University of New York Medical School, offers an integrated seven-year program through which students earn their both their B.S. degree and M.D.

Consider implementing your own program-shortening strategies at any college or university. Using Advanced Placement (AP) and College Level Entrance Program (CLEP) tests (see chapter 10), your teenager can test out of a year or more of introductory classes, thus shortening the overall time in college.

Finally, there's the "buckle down" alternative. Some homeschoolers, accustomed to motivating themselves and using their time wisely, find that they can take an extra class each semester beyond what is considered a "full load." These students end up decreasing overall time in college by a year or more, because they fulfill degree requirements sooner.

Work and School

Another way to buckle down? Consider colleges that alternate paying work experiences with attendance at school. Kettering University (MI), which advertises "professional co-op education with a difference," offers work experience in combination with formal instruction in a way that can substantially lower costs.

Of course, your homeschooler can create a similar situation at almost any college by alternating periods of full-time employment with college. One student we know works full-time for six to nine months. Then he takes a full load at college for a semester. Although it will take him six or seven years to finish college this way, he will have paid for it himself and graduate debt free.

Aim Low

Remember those merit scholarships that second- and third-tier colleges award to attract top-notch students? If your homeschooler applies to schools where his SAT score exceeds the average SAT score of those admitted, he may qualify for one of these scholarships.

Even if your student's SAT score lies in the slightly above average range, you may find a private college that will court her with a merit scholarship. Just visit the library and check out any of the college resource books that list SAT scores. If the SAT average of those they admit is under the national average, you have places to begin.

Enlist

All of the military services offer educational opportunities—while soldiers are enlisted as well as after they complete their initial tour of duty. In addition, all of the services are inaugurating new educational programs to make enlistment even more attractive.

Recently, the United States Army began a learn-while-you-serve program, called Army University Access Online. It enables new recruits to earn a college degree within four years *during* active enlistment.

Read Up on Tax Laws

The federal Hope Scholarship went into effect in January 1998. If the family meets certain low-income criteria, college freshman and sophomores (or whoever pays the tab) can have up to $1,500 taken off their taxes.

In addition, anyone enrolling in college can qualify for the lifetime earning credit, wherein 20 percent of out-of-pocket expenses may remain untaxed, totaling up to $1,000 each year. For more information, see the Internal Revenue Service Web site at http://www .irs.ustreas.gov.

With savings, scholarships, loans, student jobs, and other strategies, most homeschoolers can find a way to afford their first-choice college. Henry Ford said, "Nothing is particularly hard if you divide it into small jobs." Researching financial aid is no more than a series of small jobs—if you start early, as all our survey respondents recommend.

SIMPLE STARTING POINTS

+   Get a sample Free Application for Federal Student Aid (FAFSA) on-line or from any college counseling office. Review the data colleges will need to assess your teenager's financial needs.

✦ Read one or more of the financial aid books suggested in the resources. All have excellent ideas.

✦ Visit one or more financial aid Web sites. Many have excellent, in-depth articles that will give you even more ideas for finding money for college.

✦ Discuss cost-saving measures with your teenager. Thoroughly investigate all those that seem to apply to your family.

RESOURCES

Books

Blum, Laurie. *Free Money for College.* Checkmark Books, 1999.

Cassidy, Danicl, and Michael J. Alves. *The Scholarship Book 2001.* Prentice-Hall Publishers, 2000.

College Scholarship Service. *College Costs and Financial Aid Handbook 2000* (serial). College Entrance Examination Board, 1999.

Davis, Helm, and Joyce Lain Kennedy. *College Financial Aid for Dummies.* IDG Books, 1999.

Kaplan, Benjamin R. *How to Go to College Almost for Free.* Waggle Dancer Books, 2000.

McKee, Cynthia Ruiz, and Phillip C. McKee. *Cash for College: The Ultimate Guide to College Scholarships.* Hearst Books, 1999.

Vuturo, Christopher. *The Scholarship Advisor 2000.* Princeton Review, 1999.

Wadsworth, Gordon. *Debt-Free College.* Financial Aid Information Services, 1999.

Web Sites

FAFSA Online. Free Application for Federal Student Aid; Financial Aid Information Page; FAQs, telephone numbers, links to college financial aid offices, newsgroups, and mailing lists: http://www.cs.cmu.edu/afs.cs/user/mkant/Public/FinAid/finaid.html

FastWeb Online Scholarship Search: http://www.fastweb.com

FinAid: The Smart Student Guide to Financial Aid: http://www
.finaid.org

Initial Eligibility Procedures for Homeschooled Student Athletes;
NCAA certification process for homeschooled athletes: http:
//www.ncaa.org/cbsa/home_school.html

Scholarship Resource Network:
http://www.rams.com/srn/scholarships/index.cfm

U.S. Department of Education Student Guide: http://www.ed.gov
/prog_info/SFA/StudentGuide

For Athletes

National Christian Home School Athletic Association, P.O. Box
8060, Wichita, KS 67220, 316-684-6953

National Collegiate Athletic Association (NCAA), Indianapolis, IN,
317-917-6222: http://www.ncaa.org

13

TIMELINES:

PUTTING IT

ALL TOGETHER

In This Chapter

✦ Creating a personalized checklist

✦ Homeschoolers' college planning checklist

✦ Simple starting points

✦ Resources

"Have you noticed it's called the Office of Admissions, not the Office of Rejections?"

—Charlotte Thomas, Career and Education Editor
at Peterson's, a college and career information service

RESEARCHING COLLEGES, keeping records, compiling port-folios, writing transcripts and application essays, visiting and inter-viewing, finding money—these are some of the tasks homeschooling families face when their teenagers apply to college. In addition, other foundational tasks precede those, including planning high school at home, evaluating noncollege alternatives, and preparing for SATs and ACTs.

It can be overwhelming unless you think ahead. As Kara, the mother of four homeschool graduates, reminds us, "Failure to plan is planning to fail." Of course, no one fails outright. Your home-schooler will get in somewhere, because it is relatively easy to get into most colleges.

That said, all applicants improve their outcomes if they accom-plish everything at the earliest possible dates. By thinking ahead, you will enhance your teenager's odds of admission to his first-choice college. In addition, you will increase his chances of qualifying for need-based aid and winning merit scholarships. Encourage your homeschooler to complete everything not just on time but early. Once admitted, this assures him a place near the front of the line for classes and housing.

In addition to thinking ahead, you, the parent, should keep that high school counselor hat firmly in place. Many homeschooling par-ents have found that you will put in more time and effort than most high school counselors ever could. Ruth, whose daughter applied to Hillsdale College (MI) and Calvin College (MI), comments, "Unless a college is proactive in helping them through the process, parents and students need to be on top of the whole thing. Do not wait for information. Go after it with questions. *Assertive* and *aware* are key words."

"Our daughter almost missed the scholarship application dead-line at Hillsdale (MI) because someone there forgot to send us the pertinent information," Ruth continues. "Her admissions counselor was a 23-year-old graduate of the college and the only one who re-

HOW WE DID IT

I agree that parents need to oversee the admissions process. At the same time, students—not parents—should make all contacts and ask all questions. Homeschoolers should avoid using their parents as go-betweens, except when absolutely necessary. The military academies, where our son applied, specifically told us that they did not want to hear from parents. I think admissions officers at highly selective schools feel the same way.

Even though we had been warned against it, we had to intervene at one point. The military academy medical evaluators found an aberrant laboratory value on a blood test. At that point—about December—they rejected our son on medical grounds. We made dozens of phone calls to investigate and eventually learned that the reporting laboratory had made a clerical error. The admissions office reversed the rejection and eventually admitted our son. He graduated from the United States Air Force Academy in 1997.

—CARLEEN, HOMESCHOOLING MOM IN CALIFORNIA

ally appeared to be personally interested in her progress through the hoops. She called two days ahead to check why they had not received our daughter's application. We had to fax it to make the deadline. Had she missed that date, she would have lost the half-tuition scholarship due her for her Merit Scholar status. Always ask the question 'Are there any deadlines in the admissions process we should know about?'"

Kate agrees. She says that homeschoolers should also ask admissions departments if they have any additional requirements for homeschooled students. You may have read all the literature and completed every form. Nevertheless, if the admissions people need additional documents from homeschoolers, it's easy for them to forget to tell you. Ask specifically about this—more than once."

QUICK & EASY

Post a calendar with deadlines in a prominent place in your home—perhaps on the kitchen refrigerator. Note all the important dates. Color code these dates for individual colleges and scholarship programs.

"After students have applied, they should follow up with a phone call to make sure the college 'thinks' they have application materials," Kate in South Dakota adds. "This is especially important if [the student] sent something that did not look like a traditional transcript, such as a narrative or portfolio. Anything can go wrong. For our daughter's application (she is a senior and going through this process right now), her pottery teacher filled out her recommendation form and then forgot to send it. We were unaware of the incomplete application until we asked about it during a follow-up phone call eight weeks later."

We agree with several of our survey respondents, who suggest making both a checklist and a calendar, labeling important dates and deadlines. When you receive college applications and scholarship and financial aid information, they will almost always include timelines and deadlines. Extract that information onto your own records and refer to it constantly.

Of course, deadlines for testing and applications are last-chance dates. Ideally, you want to do everything as soon as possible. Given that, create your own personal deadlines, ahead of the school deadlines. For example, if a college or university requires all applications not later than March 1, try to get everything in by January 1.

CREATING A PERSONALIZED CHECKLIST

THE REMAINDER OF this chapter consists of a generic checklist for grades 7 to 12. Before you read the list, please underline the following two points:

✦   Checklist grade levels are not written in stone and in fact mean little other than to suggest a sequence.

✦   No one will do everything on this checklist.

Let's first discuss grade levels. Many parents give little thought to whether their homeschooler is a freshman or a sophomore. They simply proceed with their activities and curriculum at a comfortable pace. Why shouldn't they? That is one of the principal advantages of homeschooling.

We never worried about doing grade-level work or even identifying our son and daughter as high school freshmen or sophomores. In addition, as it turned out, high school at home did not take our teenagers four years—two to two-and-a-half years was closer to the mark. This may happen to you as well. Your teenagers may graduate "early" or—for various reasons   late.

As eclectic home educators with a strong un-schooling bent, we did not see early graduation coming until we got within a year of its happening. Keep that in mind when you review and re-vise the following checklist.

> We never worried about doing grade-level work or even identifying our son and daughter as high school freshmen or sophomores.

To use the checklist, do not assume that your homeschooler's grade level equals the age-appropriate grade at your local high school. Instead, count backward from the your teenager's projected graduation date. For example, if your child will complete his high school homeschooling in spring 2003, figure that 2002–2003 is her senior year (grade 12), 2001–2002 is her junior year (grade 11), and so on. Like us, you may have to recalculate the graduation date as your student proceeds through her high school years.

To sum up, "grade level" means "sequence" more than anything else, and many readers will adjust checklist grade levels for college admissions purposes. In addition, keep in mind that you will not need to accomplish everything the checklist includes. We are trying to cover a wide range of situations. Every family has different needs and will emphasize different portions of the list.

For that reason, we now turn this chapter into a hands-on exercise. As you read the checklist, check off those items that apply to your teenager and your family. In addition, you will note that we include several blanks at the end of each section. Complete these with additional timeline items peculiar to your situation. In other words, edit the lists to fit your situation, discarding inapplicable items and adding more points for special situations, like musical auditions, NCAA applications, or military academy physical fitness testing.

Then retype your own checklist, individualized for your teenager and your family. Review the checklist year by year, and make alterations as needed.

Finally—as one of our survey respondents notes—no family needs to accomplish the tasks within the suggested grade levels. We suggest an optimal schedule, but it can be altered. Except for some of the academics, you and your teenager can complete almost everything listed for grades 7 through 12 within the last six to twelve months before your homeschooler goes to college. The process is complex enough as it is. Keep what you can use, and ignore the rest.

HOMESCHOOLERS' COLLEGE PLANNING CHECKLIST

Grades 7 to 8

❑ Help your homeschoolers choose several activities that will provide leadership experiences as they reach their upper teens. In most organizations, it takes several years to rise to the in-charge positions. Examples include 4-H, Civil Air Patrol Cadet Program, scouts, various sports, and so on. Choosing several activities now gives your teenager a chance to focus on the one or two that are most productive later.

❑ Begin foreign-language study. Do not delay until high school. Spanish and French and German are difficult, but less difficult for younger learners than their older siblings. Your teenager could actually finish "high school" foreign language before he reaches high school age.

❑ Plan your math sequence for grades 7 to 12 in line with the requirements of colleges where you think your homeschooler may apply. Few who begin algebra in grade 10 will be able to complete trigonometry by grade 12. To take the SAT II math test by December 1 of senior year, students should begin algebra not later than grade 8.

❑ During family trips, make time to tour one or two college campuses. Also, check out several local colleges and universities.

❑ Experiment with different record-keeping systems to determine what works best for your family. You need not keep records full-time at this point.

❑ Keep detailed records of any academic or other work that you may eventually count as "high school." Remember that you—as the principal, teacher, and administrator of your own private school—decide what to count for grades 9 to 12. If your homeschooler completes a high school–level course, such as geometry, in grade 8, you can certainly count it for high school credit if you choose.

❑ Near the end of grade 8, try the verbal portion of a practice PSAT. If your student has

> Your teenager could actually finish "high school" foreign language before he reaches high school age.

> If your homeschooler completes a high school–level course, such as geometry, in grade 8, you can certainly count it for high school credit if you choose.

completed first-year algebra and some basic geometry, try the math part of the test.

❑ Compile a "practice" narrative, transcript, résumé, or portfolio at the end of each year.

(Enter additional grade 7–8 checklist items here.)_____

_____

_____

_____

Grade 9

❑ Plan a full homeschooling schedule around your student's interests, talents, and goals. If you use a formal curriculum, be certain that it doesn't absorb too much time—say, more than four to six hours each day. Your homeschooler should have time for eye-catching activities, fun, and just plain hanging out.

❑ Set up and implement your record-keeping system. Keep all pertinent documentation, not just academic work samples. Retain programs, photos, score sheets, awards, letters of recommendation, and so on.

❑ Begin foreign language if your homeschooler does not already have competency equivalent to two years of high school study.

❑ Begin serious practice for the PSAT, which many tenth-graders take in October. Or get a PSAT preparation course and incorporate it into your student's studies.

❑ Include SAT I and ACT preparation materials in your curriculum. Keep this simple. You can visit the SAT Web site and do the "Question of the Day" together, for example. Many like to drill SAT word lists while chauffeuring their teenagers to activities.

❑ During vacations and nearer to home, visit several college campuses. Take formal tours, and afterward discuss what you saw.

❑ Begin researching colleges, especially if some of the alternative programs described in this book appeal to you and your teenager. Learn which colleges offer special programs such as block scheduling, co-op arrangements with businesses, learning-disabilities accommodations, ROTC, performing opportunities for musicians and actors, scholarships for homeschoolers, and so on.

❑ Request recommendations from any adult who has worked with your teenager. Begin to build a file of letters from employers, coaches, music instructors, church leaders, 4-H and scout leaders, and volunteer program supervisors. Remember, it may be difficult to find these people two years later.

> Your homeschooler should have time for eye-catching activities, fun, and just plain hanging out.

❑ In April or May, locate a public or private school where your homeschooler can take the PSAT the following October.

❑ Have your homeschooler keep daily or weekly journals of activities and events. This makes a great database. Your teen may eventually enlarge on journal excerpts for her college application essays.

❑ At the end of the year, summarize your homeschooler's educational experience. With your teenager, compile a portfolio, write course descriptions, create a transcript, or put together a résumé. Too much trouble? At least create a reading list or write a one- to two-page narrative describing homeschooling that year.

❑ If your homeschooler will be taking specific SAT II tests, decide now which subjects he will concentrate on. Selective colleges generally need at least three SAT II scores by December of the senior year for the admissions and financial aid processes.

(Enter additional grade 9 checklist items here.)_____

_____

_____

_____

Grade 10

❑ Reassess goals and priorities and reevaluate curriculum and activities. Eliminate dead-end activities and academics. Begin new activities.

❑ Continue or begin foreign-language study. When your student applies, competitive colleges will want to see at least two years of Spanish or French or German or other modern language. Very selective colleges will want even more—three to four years.

❑ Take the PSAT in October. Register at a local school in late August or early September. Students may take the PSAT as sophomores and juniors. The sophomore year is a "practice" year. It's the score obtained the next-to-last year (the junior year) of high school that counts for National Merit Scholarship consideration.

❑ Include SAT I or ACT preparation materials in your curriculum. One schedule? Take one SAT I or ACT practice section each week, grade the results, and discuss them.

❑ If your homeschooler will be applying to top-tier schools, such as Harvard and Stanford, he should plan to take an SAT II Subject Test (Achievement Test) in the spring. Save the writing and math Achievement Tests for later. Consider instead an SAT II Subject Test this year in biology, American history, and social studies or a foreign language.

❑ Play the interview game. Have your teenager practice answering typical interview questions at home (see chapter 11). You can call it speech or English.

❑ In the spring, consider having your homeschooler take one class through your local junior colleges or via a college correspondence program. Remember, this is not the time to fill "holes." Begin with classes in areas where your student feels strong academically.

❑ Contact several college admissions offices for view books, or take virtual tours at their Web sites. Plan visits and group tours to those that look interesting. Have your teenager practice drawing up lists of questions to ask.

❑ Research colleges that offer summer residential programs for teenagers. One- to three-week academic, sports, and fine arts programs are all viable options. Discuss having your teen attend one of these programs.

❑ Request letters of recommendation. Again, do not wait until it's time to complete college applications.

❑ Have your teenager keep a daily or weekly journal of activities and events.

❑ Create a reading list, if you have not already. Assess the titles on that list for diversity. Do you see fiction and nonfiction, poetry and plays, and an interesting variety of authors? If not, discuss branching out with your teenager.

❑ At the end of the year, write or update the narrative, transcript, course descriptions, portfolio, or résumé.

(Enter additional grade 10 checklist items here.)_____

_____

_____

_____

_____

_____

Grade 11

❑ Assess accomplishments and the impression your documentation makes. Compare it with requirements at colleges of interest, and make adjustments. To win big scholarship money at any college, exceed its recommended course list at least in one or two areas.

❑ Research and discuss noncollege alternatives with your teenager. Reread chapter 2 and check out some of the resource books mentioned.

❑ If you have not done it yet, include foreign-language study in your academic program. For competitive colleges, it will be difficult to complete the equivalent of two years of academic study after this point.

❑ Attend college fairs. Call local public and private high school counseling offices for times and places. Your teenager should interview as many admissions personnel as possible at these fairs. Always ask about special scholarships for homeschoolers. It never hurts to plant the idea!

❑ Take the PSAT in October. Remember, this test is optional. It provides practice in a real testing situation and—in this, the junior year—eligibility for the National Merit Scholarship competition.

❑ Continue to practice for the SAT I or ACT. Your teenager should intensify her efforts this year. Begin at-home study courses recommended in chapter 10. Have your teenager take an entire practice test at least once every month or two.

❑ Register for the SAT I or ACT in the fall of the junior year. Generally registration precedes the actual testing dates by four to five weeks.

> To win big scholarship money at any college, exceed its recommended course list at least in one or two areas.

> Always ask about special scholarships for homeschoolers. It never hurts to plant the idea!

❑ Take the SAT I or ACT in the spring of the junior year. When you receive the score, talk to your teenager about whether or not it makes sense to prepare further and take the test again in the fall. Compare the test score with average scores of admitted students at colleges of interest.

❑ For applications to very selective schools, practice for writing, math, chemistry, physics, and other SAT II Subject Tests. Also, consider taking AP and CLEP tests.

❑ Schedule SAT II Subject Tests in the spring. Again, registration deadlines will precede test dates by four to five weeks.

❑ Your teenager should consider taking at least one college class each semester. Again, focus on areas of strength. Save challenging courses for the following year.

❑ Make a list of ten to twenty colleges that most interest your homeschooler. With research, visits, and discussion, whittle this list down to three to six to which he will apply. Call, e-mail, or write for their application materials. Ask about acceptable documentation. Do they require additional forms or information from homeschoolers?

❑ Request financial aid forms at the same time. The admissions process at some schools (most notably the military academies) actually begins in the spring of the junior year, so this is not too soon. If it applies, request ROTC forms now.

MONEY SAVER

If your student will be applying to many high-powered schools and scholarship programs, holler "uncle" and invest in a copy machine. You will save a little money on the copies over having someone else do it. Just as important, you will save a lot of gas and time.

❑ Research private scholarships in your community. Ask local high school counseling offices for lists of organizations that award these. Read your local newspaper carefully in the spring to see which community groups award scholarships.

❑ Spend several hours at Internet Web sites such as FastWeb (see chapter 12), researching private financial aid.

❑ Go over the college application materials with your teenager. Make a list of questions for each school.

❑ Practice interviewing, using the questions in chapter 11.

❑ Query colleges—especially local ones and those more distant to which your student might apply—about special summer academic and sports programs for high school juniors and seniors. Make provisions for your student to attend one.

❑ Encourage your teenager to make daily or weekly journal entries. In the spring, review these entries for possible college application essay topics.

> Read your local newspaper carefully in the spring to see which community organizations award scholarships.

❑ Request recommendations from any adults who work with your teenager. Give them a résumé or other paperwork to help them write glowing letters.

❑ Write or update your transcripts, course descriptions, narratives, portfolios, résumés, and reading lists.

❑ During spring and summer, plan family vacations so that you can visit or revisit those schools to which your homeschooler will apply.

(Enter additional grade 11 checklist items here.)_____

_____

_____

Grade 12

Fall

❑ Review recommended preparation at your student's target colleges. Compare this with your documentation. Make adjustments to your academic program as needed.

❑ Homeschoolers should maintain the quality of their academic programs. Consider taking one or two college classes each semester.

❑ Attend any local college fairs offered in the fall.

❑ If you have not previously done so, obtain application materials and financial aid forms from all colleges to which your homeschooler will apply.

❑ If applicable, obtain ROTC application materials, either from college financial aid offices or from military recruiters.

❑ Obtain private scholarship application forms based on the research suggested for the previous year.

❑ Review all of the application materials (for colleges and public and private scholarships), and request—as needed—additional letters of recommendation from music teachers, coaches, volunteer work supervisors, and so on.

❑ Make a calendar on which your homeschooler records dates of school tours, college fairs, interviews, and so on. On this calendar you also should have deadlines for standardized-test registrations, application submissions, merit scholarships, financial aid statements, and so on.

❑ If your teenager has not taken the SAT I or ACT, he should register to take the test as soon as possible. If he is not satisfied with the score, work with some preparation materials and schedule a retest.

❑ If your homeschooler will be applying to highly selective colleges and universities, she should plan to take all SAT II Subject Tests not later than December 1.

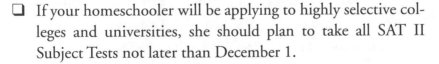

QUICK & EASY

Many applications ask for a photo of the student. Have these made ahead of time. Keep them handy, or you will end up running to the mall for a passport-quality picture at the last minute.

—RUTH IN PENNSYLVANIA

QUICK & EASY

Make photocopies of every application, essay, recommendation letter, form, and document before mailing. Paperwork does get lost. Also, if questions arise with colleges or scholarship organizations, you will have the same thing in front of you as they have.

❑ Schedule interviews, as needed.

❑ Write the application essays. Your home-schooler should allow at least one month to each essay. Ideally, begin essays as soon as your student has the applications. Plan on several rewrites, and have one to three adults review and comment on them.

❑ Submit applications as soon as possible. Waiting until the last minute will reduce opportunities for admissions, scholarships, housing, and so on.

Spring

❑ Beginning January 1, submit financial aid forms.

❑ Complete all private scholarship applications. Submit as early as possible.

❑ Complete federal and state tax returns as early as possible. You will need the information for financial aid forms.

❑ Contact colleges and arrange for day or overnight visits so your student can attend classes and talk to students already enrolled.

❑ Submit updated transcripts, résumés, or portfolios—especially if your student has applied to "reach" schools, where average SAT scores substantially exceed his and he might not be admitted. Include all in-progress courses.

❑ Check with admissions and financial aid officers monthly to make certain that they have received recommendation letters, test scores, and any other required paperwork.

❑ Your student should schedule and take AP and CLEP examinations that might result in college credit.

- ❑ When your homeschooler receives acceptances in early April, schedule additional school visits, if needed. Some colleges offer weekend orientations for parents and students to help them to rule a school in or out.

- ❑ Review and carefully discuss acceptances as a family. Decide on the college that best fits your homeschooler's career, academic, and other goals.

- ❑ When you receive financial aid offers (also in early April), compare them. Negotiate with schools that have made lower offers, citing other, higher offers.

- ❑ Return acceptance notices as soon as possible. With your homeschooler, begin planning for the start of college!

(Enter additional grade 12 checklist items here.)_____

_____

_____

> If your homeschooler will be applying to highly selective colleges and universities, she should plan to take all SAT II Subject Tests not later than December 1.

Thousands of homeschoolers succeed in college admissions every year. We did. You can too. Always get your own information, directly from college admissions and financial aid officers. Never rely on what "somebody told you." Be persistent when difficulties arise. For a successful outcome, plan ahead and stay on top of the process.

SIMPLE STARTING POINTS

✦ Read some of the resource books to compare their planning sequences (written mostly for students who attend school) with the one in this chapter.

> Negotiate with schools that have made lower offers, citing other, higher offers.

✦ Involve your teenagers and encourage them to take control of every part of the process. At the same time, maintain a watchful eye, assisting as needed.

✦ Enjoy your child's teenage years. Planning for college should save you time and energy and allow you to proceed through the process in a relaxed, confident manner.

RESOURCES

Books

Cohen, Cafi. *"And What About College?" How Homeschooling Leads to Admissions to the Best Colleges and Universities,* 2d edition. Holt Associates, 2000.

Good, Jim, and Lisa Lee. *Getting into Any College: Secrets of Harvard Students.* 101 Publisher, 1998.

Hayden, Thomas. *Peterson's Insider's Guide to College Admissions: Find Out What You Really Need to Know to Get into College.* Peterson's Guides, 1999.

Hernandez, Michelle. *A Is for Admission: The Insider's Guide to Getting into the Ivy League and Other Top Colleges.* Warner Books, 1999.

McKee, Alison. *From Homeschool to College and Work.* Bittersweet House, P.O. Box 5211, Madison, WI 53705, 1999.

Mayher, Bill. *The College Admissions Mystique.* Noonday Press, 1998.

Paul, William Henry, and Bill Paul. *Getting In: Inside the College Admissions Process.* Perseus Publishing, 1997.

Rubenstone, Sally, and Sidonia Dalby. *College Admissions: A Crash Course for Panicked Parents,* 2d edition. IDG Books, 1998.

Turner, O'Neal, and C'Neal Turner. *The Complete Idiot's Guide to College Planning.* Macmillan, 1999.

Web Sites

About.com College Admissions Guide: http://collegeapps.about
.com/education/collegeapps/mbody.htm

College Admissions Quick Reference Guide: http://www.collegeview
.com/guidance/admit_glossary.html

14

"HOW DO THEY DO?" COLLEGE EXPERIENCES OF HOMESCHOOLERS

In This Chapter

+ Academics

+ Enthusiasm

+ Value systems

+ Dealing with challenges

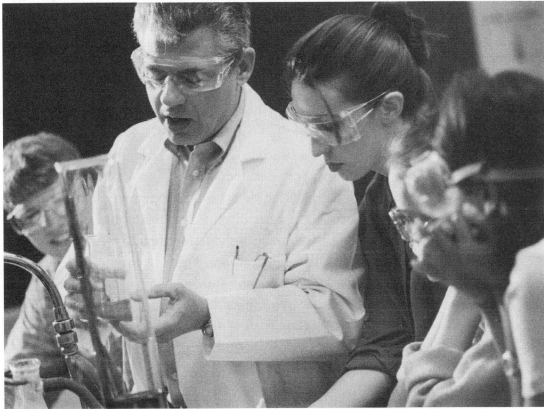

"Homeschoolers emerge as intelligent, confident, responsible adults who overwhelmingly define life success in terms of love and happiness, and look forward to a continuing learning lifestyle in a world of infinite possibility."

—Linda Dobson in *Homeschoolers' Success Stories:
15 Adults and 12 Young People Share the Impact
That Homeschooling Has Made on Their Lives*

"DOING GREAT." That phrase echoes as we scan the parent survey responses to the question "How are your graduate homeschoolers doing in college?" Parents tell us that their homeschooled teenagers—as a group—seem to embrace college classes and activities more enthusiastically than their schooled peers. We even have several accounts of homeschooling alumni who audit additional classes, not for credit but simply because they want to continue a learning lifestyle.

Of course, homeschooled teenagers beginning college face challenges, just like everyone who transitions into a new environment. The general public assumes that those challenges must relate to academic preparedness and fitting in socially. In contrast, our survey respondent parents comment on different adjustments to college. These include learning in classrooms and adapting to group pacing. Our homeschool graduate respondents eloquently describe how their views of parents, family, and education differ from those of their college classmates. A disturbing number talk about dealing with the party (read: drinking) and drug scenes.

ACADEMICS

KATE COMMENTS ON the value of study skills that many high school homeschoolers develop, saying, "Our son had no problems transitioning to college. He did most of his work independently in high school anyway."

"He loves his school, Dordt College (IA), but he looks forward to graduation and coming home to our farm when he graduates," Kate continues. "He wants to work for his dad on the farm and keep up with his greenhouse and gardening business in the summers. He is not sure what he will do in the winter in South Dakota. Maybe he will have his own snow-removal business."

Most homeschoolers do well academically. Maria in Oklahoma reports, "Our son is a senior in college, studying this year in Germany. He has nearly a 4.0 GPA and has been awarded the Outstanding Undergraduate Organ Student award for three years running. He has received several similar awards. He has ranked second or third in national organ performance competitions. He said his major academic adjustment was the amount of writing and time crunch involved in college."

Both of Maria's sons attend the University of Oklahoma. She continues, "Our second son is in his first year of college while living at home. He had a 4.0 GPA his first semester. Classes were generally easier than he expected, although he did have to work. He also had to learn to get his work in on time without Mom prodding him. He has yet to face the dorm, living-on-his-own opportunity."

Beth's children attended Faulkner University (AL). "My two older sons are doing fine," she comments. "They have graduated college with bachelor's degrees. Our first son went on to Auburn University, in Montgomery, Alabama, and earned his master's. Our second son went to Southern Christian University (AL), has completed all the classroom work towards his master's degree, and is working on his thesis."

College graduates, no less. And then what? Beth continues, "Our first son now manages a business, and our second son is a minister. They both thought most of the college work easier than they expected. Our oldest graduated magna cum laude, and our next son graduated as the valedictorian with a 4.0 grade average."

> Laura says that her daughter's principal challenge at Spring Arbor College (MI) was letting professors set the pace, as opposed to setting her own.

Laura says that her daughter's principal challenge at Spring Arbor College (MI) was letting professors set the pace, as opposed to setting her own. It must not have been that difficult, however. Laura writes, "Our daughter is doing wonderfully.

HOMESCHOOL GRADS SAY

It would be easier to explain why I want to be at college now than to explain why I originally wanted to go. I had always assumed that I would go to college, because it is what you do after high school. As the time drew closer, however, and I discussed it with my parents, I realized that I had always loved learning and wanted to continue my education. Also, I wanted the preparation and experience necessary to get a good job. Always close to home in the past, I found it difficult to leave. But I think I also understood that it was time.

College has more than lived up to my expectations. I love being here and will be sorry when my college years are over. My first college classes reinforced how much I love learning, education, and reading. I discovered new passions—Spanish, literature, and, writing, something I had always dreaded before. My art classes reinforced my decision to major in art. I feel sure that this is where I belong.

Getting a job is still in the future, of course. Nevertheless, I know that the education I am receiving is excellent for its own sake and also will give me the background necessary to find a job when I graduate. College is also a time for personal and spiritual growth. I have learned about independence, making my own decisions, relationships, and integrity. I have also learned to conquer my procrastination!

Everybody faces challenges at college. Although homeschoolers have some unique ones, I had no problems adjusting. Going to classes and taking notes were

She made the dean's list first semester, is a student supervisor for work, manages her time well, and has made a network of friends."

Serena's daughter, age 20, received her bachelor's degree in May 2000 in chemical engineering. Regarding her daughter's experience, Serena writes, "My daughter told me that initially she was at a disadvantage in college, because she had not memorized as much chem-

new experiences for me, but I was already used to independent study. I found the most changes in social life. I made some good friends quickly, but I was not used to dealing with the complex tensions that arise from spending so much time with my friends every day.

This is not to say that I have problems with socialization. I have a wonderful group of friends at college who mean a great deal to me. The college environment is just very intense, even for people who were not homeschooled. Naturally it is a bigger change for a homeschooler than for someone who went to public school. It was very different for me to enter this new environment when I previously spent most days at home with my family. On the other hand, my close family relationships and a strong personal identity formed at home helped me to get through some of the minor conflicts that have arisen and to build even better friendships than before.

Homeschooling has given me a foundation and a sheltering home environment in which I formed and strengthened my faith and values before testing them against the world. I still look often to my parents for guidance as I continue to develop and clarify these beliefs. This is not to say that my classmates lack firm faith but perhaps that I have been influenced less by peers and media in forming my beliefs. I have a closer relationship with my family than many of the other students. I write to them more often, ask my parents for advice more, and tell them more about my classes and my activities.

—KARENA, NOW A SOPHOMORE AT HILLSDALE COLLEGE (MI)

istry or math as traditional students. By the second or third semester, this disadvantage was far outweighed by the fact that she knew how to teach herself and puzzle things out when other students gave up in favor of asking the teacher during the next class. After all, she had already taught herself advanced math, chemistry, and physics as a high school homeschooler."

HOMESCHOOL GRADS SAY

I had little trouble transitioning academically. I did well learning on my own, although it took me almost a year to recognize the true value of group study sessions. My social transition was more difficult. Even before homeschooling, in my small New England town, I grew up in a family-based social circle. My transition to age-peer-based social circles was slow.

I believe home education provided me with better study skills (especially independent-study skills) than my classmates. Also, since classes were more of a novelty to me than to traditionally educated students, I believe I was more willing to pay attention and take notes during my first two years.

—CHRISTOPHER, NOW AT MESSIAH COLLEGE (PA)

"Now my daughter plans to get an advanced degree," Serena adds. "Interestingly, Purdue University (IN), which wanted her to take extra SAT II exams for admission as an undergraduate, has now offered her a full scholarship and a generous stipend for her graduate studies."

Liz and Nathan, unschoolers from Connecticut, report on their son's experience at Hunter College (NY), writing, "He's enjoying college and city life tremendously. The day before he started his freshman year, he showed me his books and predicted he'd be on the dean's list. Sure enough, straight A's his first semester and only one B so far."

According to Liz and Nathan, their son was invited to enroll in the Hunter College (NY) Special Honors Curriculum for his sophomore year. In a note home, he wrote, "I'd get to avoid taking any boring classes that they require other students to take, and I would get (yet) another degree when I graduate (making three). I would take trickier (and thus more interesting) elective classes, as well as the Honors Colloquia—nifty interdisciplinary classes, with cool professors and smart kids. It would also be one more thing for you and Dad to brag about."

At college, Liz and Nathan's son is a member of the Hunter Film Society, Students for a Free Tibet, and the Political Science Club. He works as a store clerk one day a week and as an intern at a film distribution company (for which he earns college credit) about ten hours weekly. Commenting on his social adaptation, Liz and Nathan write, "During his growing-up years, he spent a lot of time alone—mostly by choice. He had one or two good friends at a time. Now he is very social and does not seem to have any difficulty adjusting to a huge school with 20,000 undergraduates in New York City."

Interestingly, Purdue University (IN), which wanted her to take extra SAT II exams for admission as an undergraduate, has now offered her a full scholarship and a generous stipend for her graduate studies. What poetic justice, especially since Purdue is not her first choice!

—SERENA,
HOMESCHOOL MOM

ENTHUSIASM

BILL AND JANICE, Christian homeschooling parents, say that their studious, independent son is excited about college. "He immediately joined Campus Crusade (at University of Tennessee) and began to lead music," Janice explains. "He also works with a church youth group, participates in honors program social activities, competes on the crew team, and plays free-for-all soccer. He has his own apartment in a house in the historic district, a hangout for Campus Crusade and similar activities."

Bill and Janice's son also finds time to work and help cover expenses. They explain, "His landlord offered him the position of house maintenance man in exchange for lower rent. Our son has the ability to assure people of his confidence in doing most anything."

HOMESCHOOL GRADS SAY

It seems that no one at my college can read at more than a basic level. And when they read, they don't understand. And when they understand, they don't draw conclusions or fit pieces together. English class is the constant bane of most students I know.

I wanted to go to college to be a designer. College is not for the undecided. Now that I'm here, it seems that people who haven't decided on a goal and just want the college experience are wasting their money and time.

I did not have high expectations, so college beat them. I was antisocial back home, and I am antisocial here, although I have made two or three friends. The food is decent, the living quarters livable. The classes are wonderful. It is amazing to be in courses completely focused to my goals, around people who are both my competition and partners. It is wonderful to stop someone in a hallway and compliment their figure–ground relationship, and have them know what it means. I cannot stress enough how great the classes are. Homeschoolers, if they can, should try to get into smaller, more personal classes. None of mine top twenty people; some have only five. The learning experience is beyond words.

—DANIEL AT MOUNT IDA COLLEGE (MA)

Janice, who runs a homeschooling umbrella school in Alabama, adds, "I have asked several of our son's friends who graduated last year from public school, 'How's college?' Their answer has been 'Oh, it's school, but it's okay.' Several of our son's fellow homeschool graduates—when asked the same question—can hardly contain their enthusiasm. What a difference! I think that homeschool has given these children the confidence to embrace the world and new learning experiences with enthusiasm and clarity even in the midst of worldly teaching. Because of the success I see with these young adults, I am more convinced that high school at home is the best answer for youth."

Sharon has educated her five children at home since the early 1980s, and she currently has two homeschool graduates. Her son opted for a plumbing and pipe-fitting apprenticeship, which includes junior college classes. Her daughter completed her community college degree and currently works for the Home School Legal Defense Association in Virginia. She plans to become a lawyer.

Sharon writes, "Both our son and our daughter are very much in charge of their lives. They seem to know who they are, where they came from, and where they want to go. They are self-motivated and have an excellent work ethic."

Sharon, a conservative Christian, says that both her children found that community college was not always smooth sailing—especially when it came to the social scene. "They had difficulty figuring out how to be a part of the crowd without giving in to the crowd. Our daughter fared better than our son. She struggled to find ways to communicate that maintained her integrity while keeping in the groove of college life. Our son tried to 'go with the flow.' He quickly discovered how easy it is to get into trouble. He learned the hard way."

> Sharon writes, "Both our son and our daughter are very much in charge of their lives. . . . They are self-motivated and have an excellent work ethic."

Sharon's children's experiences with academics mirror those of many other respondents. She says that both her son and her daughter found sitting in classes easier than expected. "They marveled at how the other students travailed in class, taking notes the whole time. They had never learned to do that. At first they thought that they would fail their classes. However, they discovered that they could do well in every class by listening carefully to the teacher's lecture and reading the assignments. They must have looked funny to the teacher and the students as they sat there listening intently, possibly twiddling their thumbs. Nevertheless, they were tops in every class. They did well

HOMESCHOOL GRADS SAY

I did not have any problems adjusting to the life here at Spring Arbor College (MI). Part of it may have been that I had a very studious roommate for the first semester, and I followed her example.

I treat college very seriously and, for the most part, try very hard to get good grades in my classes, an attitude that some students lack. I do not think it is right to come to class in my pajamas or to treat the professors disrespectfully. Not all students have poor attitudes, but the few that do, stand out.

—SUSANNA AT SPRING ARBOR COLLEGE (MI)

because they were not burned out. The classroom scene was new, different, interesting, sometimes exciting, and only occasionally boring."

Shelly's homeschool graduates, like Sharon's children, also attended community colleges. Shelly writes, "We encouraged our first son to start with just two or three classes at Iowa Western Community College, because school had always been hard for him (he probably has a learning disability, although we never had him tested). We wanted to give him a chance to adjust to a classroom setting, studying, and so on. After his first day (in the culinary arts program), he was so excited that he begged to take a full load. His first semester, he earned a 3.0, which pleased us immensely."

Shelly agrees with Sharon, writing, "I believe that one of the reasons our son did so well was that he was not burned out by the classroom."

VALUE SYSTEMS

JUDY'S UNSCHOOLED DAUGHTER had a strong academic background that included 40 credits at their community college.

She entered Rochester University (NY) in 1999 as a homeschool graduate.

Just like Sharon, Judy notes that dealing with different value systems presents challenges. Judy writes, "Our daughter has adapted to college life. It did take some time to find friends who shared her more conservative values—not drinking, not sleeping around, and not pirating software, for example. She works, takes ballroom dance and juggling, has made friends, and enjoys her classes and her roommate."

Once admitted, homeschoolers can often negotiate for programs that fit their situation. "Because of her strong background, our daughter talked the head of the English department into excusing her from the mandatory freshman English course," Judy explains. "Our daughter also began with upper-division (junior- and senior-level) courses in French and math. Last fall, she audited a Shakespearean literature course and attended a weekend of Shakespeare at the Shakespearean festival in Stratford, Ontario. Many of her fellow

> "It did take some time to find friends who shared our daughter's more conservative values—not drinking, not sleeping around, and not pirating software, for example," writes Judy.

HOMESCHOOL GRADS SAY

Many of my fellow students have a totally different view toward learning than I do. I see education as a privilege I must work for and earn. On the other hand, many of my peers believe they can put assignments off until the last minute. I know many people here who struggle to adjust to college. The difference in degree of difficulty between high school work and college work, for many traditionally educated students, is very high.

—MARIE, NOW AT FRANCISCAN UNIVERSITY (OH)

students found it strange that anyone would take a class without the reward of a grade or credit toward graduation."

An impressive proportion of homeschool graduates value learning for its own sake. They agree with writer Norman Cousins, who says, "The growth of the human mind is still high adventure, in many ways the highest adventure on earth."

DEALING WITH CHALLENGES

HOMESCHOOLERS, LIKE ALL other college freshmen, have to adjust to their new surroundings. "Our son loves his college experience," reports Daria, whose oldest child attends Bryan College (TN). "He works hard. He probably got involved in too many extracurricular activities his first semester. As a result, he figured out he needed to cut back his second semester. He is stressed (as is every student trying to make good grades) but seems to be handling it well. I now wish I had let him take a local community college course during his senior year, for the experience of independent study, working under deadlines, meeting teachers' requirements, and so on."

Daria adds a cautionary note: "Our son did not understand the relationship between college GPA and keeping his scholarships. I failed to emphasize that to him, probably because we had never focused on grades. I recommend parents have that talk with their children about this before they arrive on campus, not midway through the first semester, like we did!"

Julie's homeschooled son, Steve, is an accomplished violinist who describes his musical background as "an unconventional aesthetic of mixing the folk fiddle with classical and throwing in a little jazz for good measure." During his

> An impressive proportion of homeschool graduates value learning for its own sake. They agree with writer Norman Cousins, who says, "The growth of the human mind is still high adventure, in many ways the highest adventure on earth."

high school years, he combined classical music lessons with bluegrass jamming. With excellent SAT scores and an equally good audition, he was admitted to his first-choice college, Vanderbilt University (TN).

"Vanderbilt was a world of extremes for our son, Steve," Julie writes. "Most of the other students were on a different wavelength, although the more like-minded were easy to identify. He made some close friends there, and some of his teachers were wonderful. However, the overall atmosphere was unhealthy. On the downside were sneering students, horrible food (vegetarians were unheard of), many requirements, and not enough time to practice."

Steve solved his problems—with his feet. He transferred to another college. "This year he is a sophomore music major at Macalester (MN), a liberal arts school, and finds it much more to his liking," Judy continues. "Requirements are less restrictive, they provide sufficient practice time, students are more down-to-earth, and the food seems fairly healthful. Steve's biggest difficulty has been getting used to the drunken dorm parties that seem to be universal. He does not have the same need to cut loose as most other students."

Julie comments, "Steve was disappointed to find out how many students don't care about their studies. We have to remember that former high schoolers make up the student bodies at colleges, and these students have not changed that much since graduation. Also, many teenagers who attended traditional schools put forward a false front, which can limit socializing to role-playing. Our son finds that frustrating and lonely, because he is used to real relationships and sharing, but I think he is making inroads."

Julie says that gradually Steve has found his niche. She writes, "It has taken Steve time to find others interested in serious relationships and mind-expanding activities. Our son and some new friends found a cave by the Mississippi River for gatherings and have organized a 'dead poets' society. He is interested in working in the radio station, and he participates in several musical groups."

All homeschool graduates will encounter challenges when they begin college. As they make the transition, they move from

HOMESCHOOL GRADS SAY

I went to college for music training and a general liberal arts background. I also wanted to see a different part of the country and meet interesting people my own age. Finally, because I may want to teach at a college someday, I knew I would need a college degree.

There have been many adjustments. First, I had to get used to taking orders so much of the time and being talked at. That is what it feels like to me—professors talk at you and not to you. Unfortunately, learning in college is often constrained to studying the way academicians see things and seldom about the real guts of the way things work.

One of the biggest things missing from college is the lack of concern for my well-being. At home, my family was willing to help if I had problems or was upset emotionally. Although people do care about you at college, it's not in the same way.

As a musician, I feel that my music springs from this sort of heartfelt communication between people, so I think that my music has suffered somewhat. I also had to get used to being in an environment with people my age and few older adults. This has been strange and has contributed to my feeling that college is a socially unhealthy atmosphere.

To my distress, many fellow students are just acquaintances and not deep friends. In college, people get used to not knowing others on a deep level. I try to enjoy as much of life's experiences as I can, an attitude lacking in many tradition-ally schooled students, who seem to be forever postponing their happiness.

cooperative, individualized, family-oriented programs to competi-tive, group-based, peer-group-oriented situations. Many also move from environments that take education seriously to those where dis-playing "goal-oriented behavior" takes precedence.

Academically, I have maintained around a 3.33 grade average, which is just short of the dean's list in most schools. I have adjusted to having a lot of assignments, some of which are useless. In contrast, at home I considered the majority of the studying I did to be useful.

Musically, I have a lot more experience in the real world, especially in the area of bluegrass. This helps me, for example, in a class like ear training, where I hear chord progressions more readily than others.

Has college lived up to my expectations? I have to answer an emphatic "No." I started out at Vanderbilt University (TN) last year. It was a big disappointment. Besides the fact that a specific musician I wanted to study with moved away, I also could not relate to the majority of the other students, who seemed most interested in partying.

I finally found a few people I could relate to, but in general it has been disappointing. I thought students would be interested in learning and that they would do the work assigned. I never suspected the reality—what people seem to learn in college is how to get by with the least amount of work, how to fake it and look good anyway.

I was unhappy enough to transfer to Macalester College (MN) this year, a school with a more liberal outlook and an emphasis on multiculturalism. I moved away from the serious music school at Vanderbilt for the sake of the environment. Although things are significantly improved here, the unhealthy social scene remains, with drinking and carrying on.

—STEVE, NOW AT MACALESTER COLLEGE (MN)

Whatever the challenges, homeschoolers seem well equipped to meet them. Perhaps the day will soon come when all colleges aggressively seek the fresh viewpoints that young people educated in home-based settings bring to any campus. Let's hope.

INDEX

A

Academics. *See also* Credits
  college experiences, 294–299, 300,
    301–302
  educationese for, 120–121
Accessibility of college to homeschoolers,
  70–71
ACT Assessment
  dates for, 220
  homeschoolers' averages for, 216
  overview, 219–220
  preparing for, 223–225
  purposes of, 210, 219, 220
  registering for, 220
  requirements for, 216, 218
  resources, 227, 228
  SAT vs., 219–220
Activities. *See also* Credits
  educationese for, 120–121
Admissions departments. *See also* College
    planning checklist
  applying early, 274
  contacting, 8
  deadlines from, 274–275
  discriminatory policies in, 12–14
  follow-up calls, 276
  homeschooling specialists in, 9, 17
  negotiating with, 12, 13–17
  questions to ask, 16, 274–275
  resources, 19–20
Admissions interviews. *See* Interviews
Admissions issues. *See also* College planning
    checklist
  back-door admissions, 17–18
  college admissions tests, 210,
    216–225, 228
  competitiveness, 77–78
  discriminatory policies, 12–14
  instrumental goal-oriented behavior,
    43, 44

  involving teens in decision making,
    18–19
  parental involvement needed, 274–275
  part-time college transcripts, 17–18
  resources, 19–20
  simple starting points, 18–19
Advanced Placement (AP) tests, 210,
    221–222, 228, 266–267
Agnes Scott College, 73, 190
Albright, John, 210
Allen University, 216
Alternatives to college, 28–35
  internships and apprenticeships, 32–35
  military, 31–32
  self-directed learning, 25–26, 30–31
  table of, 27
  volunteering, 31, 32
  work, 28–30
American School in Illinois, 46
"America's Best Colleges," 79
America's Top Internships, 34
AmeriCorps, 32
Amherst College, 102
Annapolis (United States Naval Academy),
    81, 241, 265
Antioch College, 73, 85–86
AP (Advanced Placement) tests, 210,
    221–222, 228, 266–267
Application essays, 188–206
  answering the question, 192
  avoiding generic topics in, 193
  concreteness in, 194
  editing and revising, 196
  emotional impression in, 192–193
  example essays, 196–205
  example questions, 190, 192, 195, 202
  explaining homeschooling, 191
  importance of, 189, 190–191
  lessons learned example, 203–205
  music student's example, 201, 203

Application essays, *cont.*
    outside opinions for, 196
    religious homeschooling example,
        200–201
    requirements for, 190–191
    resources, 206
    rhetoric for, 194
    Samford University example, 200–201
    self-directed learning example, 196–198
    Shakespeare's influence example, 201, 203
    simple starting points, 205
    tips, 192–194, 196
    West Point example, 198–199
Apprenticeships
    as alternatives to college, 32, 33–35
    internships vs., 33
    resources, 35
Army University Access Online, 268
Athletic scholarships, 263–264, 270
Attending college, or not. *See* Deciding
        about college

B

Back-door college admissions, 17–18
Bard College, 86
Bates College, 216
Belhaven College, 6
Bell, Debra, 159
Berea College, 81, 265
Bluefield State College, 77
Bob Jones University Press, 110
Bob Jones University Video School, 47
Body language in interviews, 245–246
Books (curricula) as documentation,
        102–104, 113
Books (resources)
    on admissions information, 19
    for admissions interview information, 249
    on application essays, 206
    for campus visit information, 249
    college view books, 232
    for deciding about college, 36, 38–39
    on diplomas and credits, 135
    on distance learning, 91
    for documentation information, 114
    for financial aid information, 269
    on GED preparation, 19
    on homeschooling college, 91
    on internships and apprenticeships, 33,
        34, 35
    on planing high school at home, 61
    on planning for college, 290
    on portfolios, 114, 155
    for researching colleges, 90
    for test preparation, 19, 227
Bryan College, 6
Bunday, Karl, 5

C

California admissions requirements, 15–16
California High School Proficiency
        Examination (CHSPE), 132, 133
California State University, San Marcos,
        15–16
Callaway, Sean, 68
Cambridge Academy, 47
Campus Crusade, 299
Campus visits, 232–240. *See also* Interviews
    age for, 73, 232, 233, 236
    carpooling, 235
    class attendance, 235
    during vacations, 73
    evaluation and follow-up, 239–240
    group tours, 235
    informal walks, 234–235
    itinerary for, 239
    need for, 232–233
    overnights or weekends, 235, 239
    preparing for, 238
    questions to ask, 240
    resources, 249
    serious planning stage, 234–235, 237
    simple starting points, 248
    summer programs and sports "camps,"
        235–237
    tips, 237–240
    video visits, 242
    view books vs., 232
    when to visit, 233–235, 237, 238
    window-shopping stage, 233–234
Careers. *See* Work
CD-ROMs for test preparation, 227
Checklists. *See also* College planning
        checklist
    college planning, 276–289
    shopping for colleges, 69–70

Christian Home Educator's Curriculum Manual, The, 54
CHSPE (California High School Proficiency Examination), 132, 133
City University of New York Medical School, 266
Class rank in transcripts, 176–177
CLEP (College Level Examination Program) test, 210, 221–222, 228, 266–267
COA (cost of attendance), 255–256
Colfax, David, 43, 44, 173
College Board Web site, 95, 105, 147, 219
College experiences of homeschoolers, 292–307
  academics, 294–299, 300, 301–302
  dealing with challenges, 296–297, 304–307
  enthusiasm, 299–302
  value systems, 301, 302–304
College Level Examination Program (CLEP) test, 210, 221–222, 228, 266–267
College of the Ozarks, 81, 265
College of William and Mary, 9
College planning checklist, 276–289
  grade 7 and 8, 278–280
  grade 9, 280–282
  grade 10, 282–283
  grade 11, 284–286
  grade 12, 286–289
  personalizing, 276–278
  resources, 290–291
  simple starting points, 289–290
College preparatory programs, 55
Colleges. *See also* Alternatives to college; Campus visits; Deciding about college; Shopping for colleges
  campus visits, 73, 232–240, 242
  discriminating against homeschoolers, 12–14
  homeschool-friendliness of, 5, 6–11, 70–71
  homeschooling, 83–84, 91
  narratives and, 101–102
  planning checklist, 276–289
  recommended by home educators, 7
  researching, 85, 90–91
  retention rates, 79–80
  of special interest to homeschoolers, 85–90

  types of, 69
  view books, 232
Colleges That Admit Homeschoolers Web site, 5
"Colleges without Walls," 251
Colorado College, 74, 86
Community organizations
  classes from, 56
  scholarships from, 260
Competitiveness for admissions, 77–78
Completion criterion for credits, 123–124
Concordia University, 8
Cooper Union for the Advancement of Science and Art, 81
Cornell University, 71
Cost of attendance (COA), 255–256
Costs. *See* Financial aid; Financial issues; Scholarships
Courses. *See also* Credits
  AP courses, 228
  college courses and admissions, 17–18, 146, 210–211, 226
  deciding about college, 39–40
  descriptions for documentation, 112
  descriptions in transcripts, 172
  for SAT and ACT preparation, 225
  titles in transcripts, 165–166
Covey, Stephen, 50
Cracking the SAT, 224
Credits. *See also* Diplomas; Transcripts
  awarding, 122–125
  college credits and admissions, 17–18, 146, 210–211, 226
  college-credit tests, 210, 222–223, 228, 266–267
  completion criterion for, 123–124
  dilemma about, 118
  educationese for, 120–121
  from ISPs or umbrella schools, 125
  record keeping for, 125–128
  resources, 135–136
  seat time criterion for, 123
  simple starting points, 134
  subjective assessment for, 124
  testing or discussion as assessment, 123, 124
  in transcripts, 168–169, 172
  what counts, 120, 122

Cronkite, Walter, 24
Culbreath, Alice, 33

D

Dates. *See also* College planning checklist;
    Timing
    for ACT Assessment, 220
    applying early, 274
    for PSAT, 218
    for SAT, 219
    transcript date issued, 164
    n transcripts, 172–173
Deciding about college, 24–36. *See also*
    Alternatives to college; College
    experiences of homeschoolers;
    Shopping for colleges
    alternatives to college, 25–26, 27, 28–35
    career-counseling programs, 36
    college experiences of homeschoolers,
        292–307
    cost issues, 24, 26
    delaying college, 27–28, 29
    extracurricular benefits of college, 26–27
    graduate school admission and, 28
    knowing what you want, 26, 35–36, 300
    resources, 38–40
    simple starting points, 37
    work requiring college education, 24, 25,
        26, 35–36
Deep Springs College, 81, 265
Delaying college, 27–28, 29
Departmental scholarships, 258
DigiPen Institute of Technology, 86
Diplomas. *See also* Credits; Documentation
    criteria for granting, 131–132
    graduation ceremonies, 130
    from ISPs, 46, 128, 130
    lack of, 117, 128–129
    making your own, 118, 129, 130
    questions on forms about, 129–130
    resources, 135–136
    simple starting points, 134–135
    testing for, 132–134
Disabilities and college choices, 83
Discriminatory policies
    dealing with, 13–14
    SAT II requirements, 12–13
Discussion as credit assessment, 123

Distance learning resources, 91
Distance of college from home, 72–73, 265
Dobson, Linda, 293
Documentation, 94–114. *See also* Credits;
    Diplomas; Portfolios; Record keeping;
    Transcripts
    combination formats, 99, 101
    course descriptions, 112
    deciding which to use, 96–97,
        112–113
    formats, 98
    high school profile, 112
    for interviews, 244
    from ISPs and umbrella schools, 49, 51
    labeling as transcript, 99
    logbooks, 105, 106
    narratives, 100, 101–103, 113
    parents as guidance counselors and,
        97–98
    portfolios, 107, 110, 114, 138–156
    reading lists, 102–104, 113, 152
    record keeping, 11, 106–108, 125–128
    resources, 114
    résumés, 106–107, 108–109, 113,
        143–144
    simple starting points, 113–114
    tables of contents, 104
Draves, William A., 84
Dressing for interviews, 246
Drury College, 86, 266
Duffy, Cathy, 54
Duke University, 244

E

Eastman School of Music (University of
    Rochester), 236
Eclectic approach to homeschooling,
    44, 104
Educational philosophy
    of colleges, 74–76, 160
    of homeschools, 149, 155, 162
    transcripts and, 162
Educationese, 120–121
EFC (expected family contribution),
    255–256
Emporia State University, 77
Enthusiasm, college experiences and,
    299–302

Entrepreneurship, combining with college, 29–30

Essays, application. *See* Application essays

Evaluations. *See* Credits; Outside evaluations; Tests and testing

Evergreen State College, 86–87

Expected family contribution (EFC), 255–256

Expenses. *See* Financial aid; Financial issues; Scholarships

Experiences. *See* College experiences of homeschoolers

Expertise from ISPs and umbrella schools, 51

F

FAFSA (Free Application for Federal Student Aid), 255, 256–257, 258, 268

FairTest, 216

Faulkner University, 6, 8

Ferguson's Guide to Apprenticeship Programs, 35

Financial aid. *See also* Scholarships
  aiming low, 267
  athletic scholarships, 263–264, 270
  calculating need for, 255–256
  college financial aid offices, 254–259

Free Application for Federal Student Aid (FAFSA), 255, 256–257, 258, 268
  gift aid, 253
  grants, 253
  increase in need-based aid, 253
  loans, 253–254, 256, 257
  negotiating for, 258–259
  at private schools, 252–253
  from private sources, 259–261
  resources, 269–270
  ROTC scholarships, 262–263
  self-help aid, 253–254
  simple starting points, 268–269
  state-approved home education programs and, 259
  student employment, 81, 254, 267
  three-year degrees, 266–267
  timing for applications and inquiries, 255, 259, 260
  Web sites, 261

Financial issues. *See also* Financial aid; Scholarships
  carpooling campus visits, 235
  college-credit tests, 222, 266–267
  costs of college education, 24, 72, 80–82, 251–253
  distance of college from home, 72, 265
  enlistment, 268
  free classes, 56
  free tuition or all expenses paid, 81, 265–266
  GED costs, 133
  ISPs and educational expenses, 47
  overlooked budget alternatives, 265–268
  tax breaks, 268

Florida Bright Futures Scholarship, 259

Florida Gulf Coast University, 8

Flynn-Keith, Diane, 224

Free Application for Federal Student Aid (FAFSA), 255, 256–257, 258, 268

From Homeschool to College and Work, 99, 144

G

Games, educationese for, 120

Gates, Bill, 24

General Educational Development (GED) test
  age limits for, 133
  challenging the requirement for, 12, 132, 133
  costs of, 133
  percentage of colleges requiring, 5, 11
  preparing for, 11–12
  resources, 19, 20, 133

George Wythe College, 87

Georgia State University, 13

Gift aid, 253. *See also* Financial aid; Scholarships

Goddard College, 87

Governmental regulations, ISPs and, 46

Grade point average (GPA)
  keeping scholarships and, 304
  in transcripts, 174–176

Grades
  in college classes, 210–211, 226
  in transcripts, 173–174

Graduation ceremonies, 130

Grants, 253. *See also* Financial aid;
      Scholarships
Group activities, 47
Grove City College, 6, 87

H

Hammond, Bruce, 209
Hampshire College, 87, 102
Harp camp, 236
Hartle, Terry, 252
Harvard University, 77, 221, 252, 256
Hawaii Pacific University, 216
"Helping Homeschoolers go to College," 67
Henry, Barbara, 67
High school at home, 42–64. *See also*
      College planning checklist
   college planning checklist, 276–289
   college preparatory programs, 55
   do-it-yourself approach, 51–57
   ISPs and umbrella schools, 45–51
   non-academic activities, 57–59
   resources, 60–64
   simple starting points, 59–60
   terminology, 44
High school profile, 112
High school, public. *See* Public
      high school
Hillsdale College, 76
Hobbies, educationese for, 121
Holt, John, 23
Home, distance of college from, 72–73, 265
HomeFires, 224
Homeschooler Narrative example,
      102–103
Homeschoolers' Success Stories, 293
Homeschooling: The Teen Years, 54, 105
Homeschooling. *See also* College experiences
      of homeschoolers; High school at
      home
   college, 83–84, 91
   growth of, 4
   high school, 42–64
"Homeschooling and the admission
      evaluation process," 3
Homeschooling for Excellence, 43, 173
Home School Legal Defense Association
      (HSLDA), 263, 264
Homeschool Source Book, The, 37

Homeschool-Teens-College Web site, 45
Honesty in interviews, 246–247
Hope College, 102
Hope Scholarship, 268
Household tasks, educationese for, 120
HSLDA (Home School Legal Defense
      Association), 263, 264
Humboldt State University, 73
Hunter College, 298–299
Huntington College, 191

I

Independent study programs, 46–51
   accredited, 44, 46
   credits from, 125
   diplomas from, 46, 128, 130
   growth of, 45
   homeschoolers on, 50
   questions to ask, 48–49
   resources, 60–64
   services provided by, 46–49, 51
Indiana University, 8–9, 10, 14
Internal Revenue Service Web site, 268
Internships
   as alternatives to college, 32–33
   apprenticeships vs., 33
   college programs, 80
   examples of, 33
   resources, 34
Interviews, 240–248
   alumni interviews, 242
   colleges requiring, 241
   follow-up, 248
   group interviews, 242
   homeschoolers who should avoid, 242
   importance of, 241
   informal vs. evaluative, 242–243
   personal interviews, 242–243
   preparing for, 243–245
   presenting homeschooling at, 240,
      241–242, 244
   resources, 249
   sample questions, 245
   simple starting points, 249
   tips, 243–248
Iowa Test of Basic Skills, 140
ISPs. *See* Independent study programs
"Is That the Real Price?," 257

J

Jobs. *See* Work

K

Kettering University, 88, 267
Kohl, Herbert, 36, 37

L

Lake Superior State University, 266
Landmark College, 88
Learning Resources Network, 84
Letters of recommendation. *See*
    Recommendation letters
Llewellyn, Grace, 28, 34
Loans, 253–254, 256, 257
Logbooks, 105, 106
Long Beach City College, 82
Lundquist, Dan, 231

M

Macalester College, 305
Majors offered by colleges, 78–80
Matching college to your student, 68–83
    accessibility to homeschoolers, 70–71
    checklist items, 69–70
    competitiveness for admissions, 77–78
    cost, 80–82
    distance from home, 72–73, 265
    educational philosophy, 74–76
    majors and programs of study, 78–80
    retention rates, 79–80
    setting, 73–74
    size, 71–72
    special needs, 83
    special programs, 80
    types of colleges, 69
McKee, Alison, 99, 144–145, 153
McKee, Christian, 139
Merit scholarships, 258
Michigan Technological University, 236
Military educational opportunities, 268
Military occupations as alternatives to
    college, 31–32
Mississippi College, 72
MIT, 77
Money. *See* Financial aid; Financial issues;
    Scholarships
Moskowitz, Gayle, 189

N

NAIA (National Association of
    Intercollegiate Athletics), 263, 264
Narratives, 100, 101–103, 113
National Association of College Admissions
    Counselors, 68
National Association of Intercollegiate
    Athletics (NAIA), 263, 264
National Center for Home Education
    (NCHE)
    "1999 College Survey," 4–5, 19
    admissions policy recommenda-tions, 17
National Civilian Community Corps
    (NCCC), 32
National Collegiate Athletic Association
    (NCAA), 263–264, 270
National Merit Scholarship Qualifying Test
    (NMSQT). *See* Preliminary Scholastic
    Assessment Test (PSAT)
NCAA (National Collegiate Athletic
    Association), 263–264, 270
NCCC (National Civilian Community
    Corps), 32
NCHE. *See* National Center for Home
    Education (NCHE)
Neal, Sandra K., 33
Negotiating admissions requirements,
    14–17
    explaining home education, 14–15
    GED requirement, 12
    persisting, 17
    questions to ask, 16
    SAT II Subject Test requirement, 13–14
    talking to the right people, 15, 16–17
    understanding the policies, 15–16, 17
Negotiating for financial aid, 258–259
New College of the University of South
    Florida, 88
NMSQT (National Merit Scholarship
    Qualifying Test). *See* Preliminary
    Scholastic Assessment Test (PSAT)
Non-academic activities, 57–59
Northwestern University, 10
Nyack College, 6

Music

Music
    college experiences, 306–307
    educationese for, 121

O

Occupations. *See* Work

Office of Admissions. *See* Admissions departments

Oglethorpe University, 88, 144

Ohio State, 8–9

Outside evaluations, 208–228. *See also* Tests and testing
  college admissions tests, 210, 216–225, 228
  college courses, 17–18, 146, 210–211, 226
  college-credit tests, 210, 222–223, 228
  need for, 210–211
  in portfolios, 151
  preparing for tests, 223–225
  recommendation letters, 210, 211–215
  resources, 227–228
SAT II Subject Tests, 12–14, 221–222, 227, 228
  simple starting points, 226–227

P

Parent Loan for Undergraduate Students (PLUS), 256

Parent Narrative example, 100

Part-time college transcripts, 17–18

Patrick Henry College, 88

Pennsylvania portfolio require-ments, 147

Peterson's Internships, 34

Planning for college. *See also* College plan-ning checklist; Timing; *specific topics*
  campus visits, 73, 232–240
  checklist, 276–289
  deciding about college, 24–36
  interviews, 240–248
  need for, 274
  resources, 290–291
  shopping for colleges, 66–91
  simple starting points, 289–290

PLUS (Parent Loan for Undergraduate Students), 256

Portfolios, 138–156
  adoption by homeschoolers, 140
  advantages of, 107, 140–141
  audience for, 153
  brevity and conciseness in, 153
  colleges suitable for, 141, 145

contents suggestions, 144, 147–153
educational philosophy in, 149, 155
end-of-year summaries in, 152
examples, 142, 148, 151, 152
for general college credits, 146
identifying information in, 147–148
items to include, 107, 110
mini-portfolios, 143, 155
organization of, 142–143, 152, 153–154
outside evaluations in, 151
in public schools, 140
reading lists in, 152
as record-keeping aids, 142–143
resources, 114, 155–156
for scholarship applications, 145–146
simple starting points, 155
subjects and activities in, 149, 150
as supplements to transcripts and résumés, 143–144
test scores in, 148–149
transcripts vs., 141, 145, 154, 161
for unschooling or interest-initiated learning, 144–145
for work applications, 146
work samples in, 150

Portland State College, 13

Preliminary Scholastic Assessment Test (PSAT)
  dates for, 218
  as National Merit Scholarship Qualifying Test, 210, 217–218
  overview, 217–218
  purposes for, 210, 217
  registering for, 218
  resources, 227, 228

Pride, Mary, 242

Private school costs, 252–253

Private sources for financial aid, 259–261

Profiles of American Colleges, 79

Programs of study at colleges, 78–80
  special programs, 80

PSAT. *See* Preliminary Scholastic Assessment Test (PSAT)

Public high school
  senior year attendance at, 14
  transcripts from, 96

Purdue University, 13, 14, 298

Q

Quail Haven's High School homeschool Links, 112
Question Is College, The, 36, 37

R

Randy Potter School of Piano Technology, 30
Reading
 college experiences, 300
 educationese for, 120–121
Reading lists (documentation), 102–104, 113, 152
Recommendation letters, 211–215
 asking for, 212–214
 contents of, 214
 examples, 214, 215
 items to give recommenders, 212–213
 purposes of, 210, 211
 when to ask for, 212–213
 who to ask for, 211–212, 213
 writing for recommenders, 214
Record keeping. *See also* Credits; Diplomas; Documentation; Transcripts
 for credit assessment, 125–128
 educationese for, 120–121
 need for, 11, 106–108, 127–128
 portfolios for, 142–143
 resources, 135–136
 starting early, 127, 128
 types of records, 126
Recreation, educationese for, 120, 121
Reed, Donn, 37
Reporting requirements, ISPs and, 46
Researching colleges. *See* Campus visits; Shopping for colleges
Reserve Officer Training Corps (ROTC) programs, 80, 262–263
Resources. *See also* Books (resources); Web sites
 admissions information, 19–20
 admissions interviews, 249
 AP courses, 228
 application essays, 206
 campus visits, 249
 college admissions testing, 228
 deciding about college, 36, 38–40
 diplomas and credits, 135

distance learning, 91
documentation information, 114
educational resources and curriculum suppliers, 60–64
financial aid, 269–270
GED preparation, 19, 20, 133
high school scope and sequence, 60
homeschooling college, 91
independent study programs, 60–64
internships and apprenticeships, 33, 34, 35
portfolios, 114, 155–156
record-keeping systems, 135–136
researching colleges, 79, 90–91
test preparation, 19, 20, 133, 227
transcript forms, 110, 112, 179
transcript information, 179
Résumés, 106–107, 108–109, 113, 143–144
Rhodes College, 13, 74
Rice University, 11, 13, 77, 257
Richman, Howard, 251
Rose-Hulman Institute of Technology, 11, 76, 89, 256–257
ROTC (Reserve Officer Training Corps) programs, 80, 262–263

S

St. John's College, 89, 102
Samford University, 72, 200–201
SAT I. *See* Scholastic Assessment Test I (SAT)
SAT II Subject Tests
 challenging requirements for, 13–14
 colleges requiring, 12–13, 221
 overview, 221–222
 resources, 227, 228
 uses for, 222
SAT (Stanford Achievement Test), SAT I vs., 218–219
Scholarships. *See also* Financial aid
 aiming low, 267
 athletic, 263–264, 270
 from college financial aid offices, 254–259
 departmental, 258
 discriminatory policies and, 13–14
 GPA and retention of, 304
 for homeschooled graduates, 6
 Hope Scholarship, 268

Scholarships, *cont.*
merit, 258
negotiating for, 258–259
portfolios for applications, 145–146
from private sources, 259–261
refusing federal aid and, 257–258
Reserve Officer Training Corps (ROTC), 262–263
resources, 269–270
scholarship search services, 262
simple starting points, 268–269
special-category, 258
state-approved home education programs and, 259
for summer programs, 237
timing for applications and inquiries, 255, 259, 260
Web sites, 261
Scholastic Assessment Test I (SAT)
ACT vs., 219–220
dates for, 219
homeschoolers' averages for, 216
overview, 218–219
preparing for, 219, 223–225
PSAT and, 210, 217, 220
purposes of, 210
registering for, 219
requirements for, 216, 218
resources, 227, 228
Stanford Achievement Test (SAT) vs., 218–219
Scholastic Assessment Test II. *See* SAT II Subject Tests
School Is Dead, Learn In Freedom Web site, 5
School name for transcripts, 165
Seat time criterion for credits, 123
Self-directed learning
as alternative to college, 30–31
application essay example, 196–198
Self-help aid. *See* Financial aid
Setting of colleges, 73–74
Seven Habits of Highly Effective People, The, 50
Shopping for colleges, 66–91. *See also* Campus visits
accessibility to homeschoolers, 70–71
best college vs. best fit, 68
campus visits, 73, 232–240, 242

checklist items, 69–70
colleges of special interest to home-schoolers, 85–90
competitiveness for admissions, 77–78
cost, 80–82
distance from home, 72–73, 265
educational philosophy, 74–76
homeschooling college, 83–84, 91
majors and programs of study, 78–80
matching college to your student, 68–83
researching colleges, 85, 90–91
resources, 90–91
retention rates, 79–80
setting, 73–74
simple starting points, 90
size, 71–72
special needs, 83
special programs, 80
types of colleges, 69
Simon's Rock College, 89
Size of colleges, 71–72, 141, 160
Sophie-Davis School of Biomedical Education, 266
South Dakota State University, 15
Southern Methodist University, 13
Special-category scholarships, 258
Special needs and college choices, 83
Special programs at colleges, 80
Sports programs, 80
Spring Arbor College, 261
Stanford Achievement Test (SAT), SAT I vs., 218–219
Stanford University, 6, 77, 221, 241, 256
Student Advantage Guide: The Internship Bible, 34
Student employment, 81, 254, 267
Sullivan, Sean, 70
Summer programs at colleges, 235–237

T

Tables of contents (documentation), 104
Tax breaks, 268
Teach Your Own, 23
Teenage Liberation Handbook, The, 28
Television, educationese for, 120
Terminology
educationese, 120–121
homeschooling, 44

Testing the Waters: A Teen's Guide to Career Exploration, 33
Tests and testing. *See also specific tests*
  ACT Assessment, 210, 216, 219–220, 227, 228
  Advanced Placement (AP) tests, 210, 221–222, 228, 266–267
  college admissions tests, 210, 216–225, 228
  college-credit tests, 210, 222–223, 228, 266–267
  College Level Examination Program (CLEP) test, 210, 221–222, 228, 266–267
  for credit assessment, 123, 124, 210
  for diplomas, 132–134
  general Educational Development (GED), 5, 11–12, 19, 20, 132–133
  including scores in portfolios, 148–149
  including scores in transcripts, 177
  Iowa Test of Basic Skills, 140
  ISPs and admissions requirements, 46
  National Merit Scholarship Qualifying Test (NMSQT), 217–218
  Preliminary Scholastic Assessment Test (PSAT), 210, 217–218, 227, 228
  preparing for tests, 11–12, 223–225
  purposes of, 210
  resources, 19, 20, 133, 227–228
  SAT II Subject Tests, 12–14, 221–222, 227, 228
  Scholastic Assessment Test I (SAT), 210, 216, 218–219, 227, 228
  Stanford Achievement Test (SAT), 218–219
Thomas Aquinas College, 6, 78, 89
Thomas, Charlotte, 232, 273
Thomas Edison State College, 89–90
Three-year degrees, 266–267
Timing. *See also* College planning checklist
  ACT Assessment dates, 220
  applying early, 274
  calendar for, 276
  campus visits, age for, 73, 232, 233, 236
  college planning checklist, 276–289
  deadlines, asking about, 274–275
  for financial aid applications and inquiries, 255, 259, 260

GED test age limits, 133
parental involvement needed, 274–275
PSAT test dates, 218
for recommendation letter requests, 212–213
SAT test dates, 219
Titles for transcripts, 164
Traditional approach to home-schooling, 44
Transcripts, 110–111, 158–186. *See also* Credits
  blank forms for, 110, 112, 179
  class rank in, 176–177
  college size and, 141, 160
  course descriptions in, 172
  course titles in, 165–166
  credibility concerns, 162–163
  credits in, 168–169, 172
  date issued, 164
  dates in, 172–173
  examples, 167, 168, 170–171, 176, 179–186
  grade point average in, 174–176
  grades in, 173–174
  homeschooling philosophy and, 162
  identifying information in, 165
  from ISPs and umbrella schools, 49, 51
  as label for all documentation, 99
  mandatory information in, 163, 164–166
  mini-portfolios with, 143
  need for, 96, 160–161
  official, 17–18, 49, 51, 96, 177–178
  optional data in, 163, 166, 168–169, 172–177
  outline for, 113
  outside courses in, 177
  for part-time college attendance, 17–18
  portfolios vs., 141, 145, 154, 161
  from public schools, 17–18
  resources, 179
  school name in, 165
  simple starting points, 178–179
  three-tiered format, 99, 101
  titles for, 164
  uses for, 160–162
  writing your own, 110–111
Travel, educationese for, 120
Trinity Christian College, 146

U

Ultimate Guide to Homeschooling, The, 159
Umbrella schools. *See also* Independent
    study programs
  credits from, 125
  defined, 46
  homeschoolers on, 50
  questions to ask, 48–49
  services provided by, 46–49, 51
Uncollege Alternative, The, 31, 32, 36, 37
Union College, 231
United States Air Force Academy, 17, 81,
    241, 265
United States Coast Guard Academy, 81, 265
United States Merchant Marine Academy, 81
United States Military Academy, 77, 81,
    198–199, 265
United States Naval Academy, 81, 241, 265
U.S. News and World Report, 79
Unit study approach to home-schooling, 44
University of California, Berkeley,
    70–71, 221
University of California, Los Angeles, 46
University of Chicago, 195
University of Colorado (CO), 10
University of Georgia (GA), 210
University of Houston, 216
University of Mobile, 72
University of North Carolina, Wilmington,
    12–13
University of Notre Dame, 13
University of Rochester, 236
University of South Carolina,
    Spartanburg, 266
University of Toledo, 8–9
University of Virginia, 9, 75, 202, 241
Unschooling approach to home-schooling
  application essay example, 196–198
  applications process and, 45
  defined, 44
  portfolios for, 144–145, 150
  tables of contents documentation and, 104

V

Vacations, visiting colleges during, 73
Value systems, college experiences and, 301,
    302–304
Vanderbilt University, 10, 201, 305

Videos
  of campus visits, 242
  educationese for, 120
VISTA (Volunteers in Service To
    America), 32
Vocations. *See* Work
Volunteering
  as alternative to college, 31, 32
  educationese for, 121
Volunteers in Service To America
    (VISTA), 32

W

Wayne State University, 216
Web sites
  for admissions information, 19–20
  for admissions interview information, 249
  application essay aids, 206
  for campus visit information, 249
  College Board site, 95, 105, 147, 219
  Colleges That Admit Homeschoolers
      site, 5
  for deciding about college, 39–40
  for diplomas and credit informa-tion, 135
  for distance learning information, 91
  for documentation information, 114
  ducational resources and curriculum
      suppliers, 60–61
  FAFSA site, 255
  for financial aid information, 269–270
  for GED preparation, 20
  for high school scope and sequence
      information, 60
  for homeschooling college
      information, 91
  Homeschool-Teens-College site, 45
  for independent study programs, 60–64
  Internal Revenue Service site, 268
  for planning for college, 290
  for portfolio information, 156
  for private scholarship commit-tees, 261
  for record-keeping systems, 135–136
  for researching colleges, 91
  for transcript forms, 112
  for transcript information, 179
West Point (United States Military
    Academy, NY), 77, 81, 198–199
What Color Is Your Parachute?, 36

Wheaton College, 74–75, 191, 192

Wildavsky, Ben, 257

"Will Homeschooling Hurt Your Child Later On?," 209

Wilmington College, 77

Wood, Danielle, 31, 32, 36, 37

Work

    as adjunct to college, 29–30, 267

    as alternative to college, 28–29, 32–35

    career-counseling programs, 36

    career vs. variety, 37

    college education and, 24, 25, 26, 35–36

    educationese for, 120, 121

    internships and apprenticeships, 32–35

    job growth outlook, 25

    military occupations, 31–32

    portfolios for applications, 146

    resources, 38–40

    student employment, 81, 254, 267

    volunteering, 31, 32

Wright, Frank Lloyd, 24

Writing, educationese for, 121

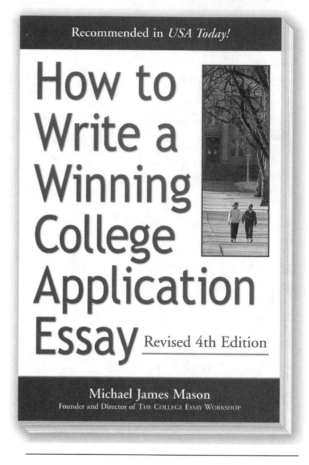

In a Class of Their Own

Pro football player, bestselling author, entrepreneurial millionaire . . . these successful people all have one thing in common: They were all homeschooled as children. In *Homeschoolers' Success Stories,* you'll discover their inspiring stories, along with those of a dozen other homeschooling "graduates" who have achieved success on many levels. In addition, you'll meet 12 younger people already well on their way to personal success.

"This beautiful book resonates with a feeling for how things really happen. It will make you smile, stimulate your spirit, chase away your fears. Read it today!"

—JOHN TAYLOR GATTO, author of *The Underground History of American Education*

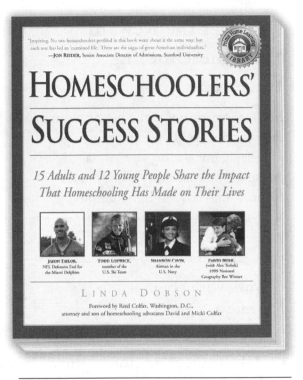

ISBN 0-7615-2255-7 / Paperback / 304 pages
U.S. $16.95 / Can. $25.95

PRIMA

To order, call (800) 632-8676 ext. 4444 or visit us online at www.primalifestyles.com

To Order Books

Please send me the following items:

Quantity	Title	Unit Price	Total
_____	How to Write a Winning College Application Essay	$ _____	$ _____
_____	Homeschoolers' Success Stories	$ _____	$ _____
_____	Homeschooling: The Teen Years	$ _____	$ _____
_____	Homeschooling Almanac, 2000–2001	$ _____	$ _____
_____	_____	$ _____	$ _____
_____	_____	$ _____	$ _____
			$

Subtotal	$ _____
7.25% Sales Tax (CA only)	$ _____
7% Sales Tax (PA only)	$ _____
5% Sales Tax (IN only)	$ _____
7% G.S.T. Tax (Canada only)	$ _____
Priority Shipping	$ _____
Total Order	$

FREE
Ground Freight in U.S. and Canada

Foreign and all Priority Request orders:
Call Customer Service
for price quote at 916-787-7000

By Telephone: With American Express, MC, or Visa,
call 800-632-8676, Monday–Friday, 8:30–4:30
www.primapublishing.com

By E-mail: sales@primapub.com

By Mail: Just fill out the information below and send with your remittance to:
Prima Publishing ▪ P.O. Box 1260BK ▪ Rocklin, CA 95677

Name _____

Address _____

City _____ State _____ ZIP_____

MC/Visa/American Express# _____ Exp. _____

Check/money order enclosed for $ _____ Payable to Prima Publishing

Daytime telephone _____

Signature _____